T0295523

# CEOs on a Mission

# Communicating Responsible Diversity, Equity, and Inclusion

**Series Editor: Donnalyn Pompper**

This Communicating Responsible Diversity, Equity, and Inclusion series brings together leading scholars of public relations, communication management, (corporate) social responsibility, sustainability, and diversity, equity, and inclusion (DEI). Together, we offer critique and map new arenas for discovery in an effort to advance a collective goal of eliminating bias/discrimination from organizations and other public spaces. Simultaneously, we amplify the virtues of equality and respect among humans and for all species.

Despite nearly two decades of public relations theory building and formal study about the importance of DEI, numbers of public relations practitioners who are not male or Caucasian/White have not grown in meaningful ways and research directions seem to have hit a wall. Examining public relations as a "responsibility" provides new avenues for critiquing ways power operates in and through public relations work. This proposed series will add a much-needed contribution to global understanding of intersections among DEI with social responsibility to enable public relations practitioners and organizations (corporations and non-profits) to take lip service to the next level. To be authentic, DEI must be a component of social responsibility and sustainability. And the public relations practitioner, as insider-activist and ethics guardian, is the logical point person to infuse DEI-thinking in policies, decision-making, and everyday life throughout organizations.

**Volumes in this series:**
Public Relations for Social Responsibility – Edited by Donnalyn Pompper

# Praise for *CEOs on a Mission*

Eric's approach to understanding activism is to build what social scientists call a "process model." This means that he approaches CEO activism not as a static role or a category, but as a process that unfolds over time and evolves as external stakeholders react to a CEO's words and actions. Eric digs into his interviews to smoke out the motives that drive some CEOs to activism, to explain how they chose the issues and causes for their advocacy, to spell out the tactics and safeguards they employed, and to reflect on activism's consequences for society, companies, and CEOs themselves.

In an era roiled by acronyms that include CSR (corporate social responsibility), DEI (diversity, equity, and inclusion), and ESG (environmental, social, and governance factors), this book is an eye-opener. For executives, it presents a model for those who want to undertake activism or understand colleagues that do. For academics, it affords insights into the antecedents, dynamics, and consequences of CEO activism, informed by Eric's postmodern perspective. For everyone, *CEOs on a Mission* provides a good read.

**Alan Meyer, PhD**
Professor Emeritus of Management
Lundquist College of Business
University of Oregon
Eugene, Oregon
USA

# CEOs on a Mission: Reimagining CEO Activism, Development, and Difference

BY

**ERIC KWAME ADAE**

*Drake University School of Journalism and Mass Communication, USA*

United Kingdom – North America – Japan – India – Malaysia – China

Emerald Publishing Limited
Howard House, Wagon Lane, Bingley BD16 1WA, UK

First edition 2023

**British Library Cataloguing in Publication Data**
A catalogue record for this book is available from the British Library

ISBN: 978-1-80382-216-7 (Print)
ISBN: 978-1-80382-215-0 (Online)
ISBN: 978-1-80382-217-4 (Epub)

INVESTOR IN PEOPLE

*This book is dedicated to God Almighty; It is in loving memory of my father Victor Kwaku Adae; to my children, and to yours.*

# Table of Contents

# List of Figures

# List of Abbreviations

| | |
|---|---|
| 1D1F | One District, One Factory (Program of Ghana) |
| AGITPROP | Agitation and Propaganda (tactics) |
| AIDS | Acquired Immunodeficiency Syndrome |
| BA | Brand Activism |
| BR | Brand Responsibility |
| CEO | Chief Executive Officer |
| CIA | Central Intelligence Agency |
| CPA | Corporate Political Activity |
| CPP | Convention People's Party |
| CSA | Corporate Social Advocacy |
| CSE | Comprehensive Sexuality Education |
| CSR | Corporate Social Responsibility |
| DEI | Diversity, Equity, and Inclusivity |
| ECOWAS | Economic Community of West African States |
| EI | Executive Instrument |
| ESG | Environmental, Social, and Governance |
| EWN | Executive Women Network |
| GAB | Ghana Association of Bankers |
| GCBOD | Ghana Chamber of Bulk Oil Distributors |
| HIV | Human Immunodeficiency Virus |
| IEA | Institute of Economic Affairs |
| IFC | International Finance Corporation |
| MoGCSP | Ministry of Gender, Children, and Social Protection |
| NCA | National Communication Authority |
| NDC | National Democratic Congress |
| NGP | National Gender Policy |
| NPP | New Patriotic Party |
| NRC | National Redemption Party |
| PCSR | Political Corporate Social Responsibility |

| | |
|---|---|
| PRSA | Public Relations Society of America |
| SYPALA | Students and Young Professionals African Liberty Academy |
| TBL | Triple Bottom Line |
| TEF | Tony Elumelu Foundation |
| TIN | Tax Identification Number |
| UBA | United Bank for Africa |

# About the Author

**Eric Kwame Adae**, PhD, is an Assistant Professor of Public Relations at Drake University School of Journalism and Mass Communication. He earned his doctorate degree in Media and Communication Studies from the University of Oregon School of Journalism and Communication. He is from Ghana in West Africa, where he earned undergraduate and master's degrees from the University of Ghana. He is an accredited public relations practitioner and was a communications consultant for over 15 years in Ghana. He has presented at various academic and professional conferences, including the National Communication Association (NCA), the International Communication Association (ICA), the Association for Education in Journalism and Mass Communication (AEJMC), and the Public Relations Society of America (PRSA). He was named the Public Relations Professional of the Year (2021) by the Public Relations Society of America Iowa Chapter. In 2021, he and Professor Donnalyn Pompper won the Doug Newsom Award of the AEJMC PR Division with their paper, "PR & Sustainability across the African Continent: Using Afro-Centric Philosophies to Remember What's Been 'Forgotten or Lost'." His research interests include responsible management, corporate social advocacy, corporate social responsibility, sustainability, critical public relations, and Afrocentricity.

**Eric Kwame Adae, PhD, APR**
Drake University School of Journalism and Mass Communication
Des Moines, Iowa USA
Email: eric.adae@drake.edu

# Foreword

In 2020, a study by the Zeno Group (a division of the Public Relations firm Daniel J. Edelman) published a global research report regarding the role of business in society. This study was influenced by the notion that in today's society, many people have lost trust in the traditional institutions that they regularly rely on, including government, the media, and educational institutions. The global pandemic of 2020 and 2021 did little to change these perceptions. As a result, many people now choose to look to business and to the brands produced by companies to address problems that traditional institutions no longer seem capable of addressing. The Zeno Group's study found that people definitely believe that corporations can be *responsible*, with the term *responsible* defined as caring as much about society as they do about profits. When people think a business is responsible, they are four times more likely to purchase the brand and recommend the company. These consumers are also six times more likely to protect the company from public criticism, if any criticism is to be had.

Corporate leaders themselves are aware of the power that business has to address key problems in society. WPP is a British-based international communications holding company, focused on "building better futures for our people, planet, clients, and communities" (WPP.org, 2023). As one of the first companies to publish its own sustainability report, the company is highly invested in addressing their "work, marketing standards, employment, supply chain, and social investment." WPP's CEO Sir Martin Sorrell offered a strong endorsement for the industry and his company tackling key societal problems, saying:

> Yet the big problems that our society faces – those of inequality, unemployment, health crises, water scarcity and climate change – remain far from being resolved. While technology holds the key to tackling some of these problems, it is also exacerbating others. Demographic shifts and the exponential growth of the global middle class look set to further strain our planet's limited resources. I am often asked what the role of business should be in tackling such complex issues. My view is that it has a critical role to play. Indeed, these challenges cannot be addressed without the participation of global business, as a driver of growth and creator of jobs and a force for innovation. In partnership with governments and civil society, business will create many of the solutions we will need over the coming decades. It is in the interests

of business to play its full part. It must do so if it wants to secure future supplies of natural resources, to build skills and to help create strong communities that enable business to prosper. (WPP Group, 2014, p. 2)

Sorrell highlighted the need and opportunity for businesses around the world to create social justice solutions to societal problems, and used his corporate sustainability report to begin to document efforts that his own company had undertaken. He ended by proposing that WPP will help brands embed sustainability into their life cycles, as his firm could provide the specialist knowledge and skills to do so. The firm went on to develop activist work on several brands owned by global giant Unilever, addressing education (with the cleaning brand Persil), beauty standards (for the beauty brand Dove), rural sanitation (for a disinfectant brand called *Domestos*), and rainwater harvesting (for telecommunications company Vodafone) (Sheehan & Morrison, 2018). While no longer leading the company, Sorrell's influence on activist communication is undeniable.

Every company, though, does not have the resources to create global communication campaigns to address social issues. And when companies want to engage, many do not know where to start. In today's chaotic society, the opportunity for corporate and brand activism is great: Pimentel and Didonet (2021) developed a typology that identified a range of areas that companies could address with various types of activism. The first area defined is social activism, where the firm addresses issues such as gender, equality, race, and education. The next area is legal activism, where firms are involved in workplace issues, employment laws, and issues regarding taxation. A third area, business activism, includes addressing CEO pay and worker compensation. The fourth area, economic activism, involves inequality and the redistribution of wealth, while political activism addresses lobbying and voting rights. Finally, environment activism addresses key issues facing the planet, such as global warming, conservation, land use, and pollution.

Corporate activism and society's call to action to address key social issues must be answered by someone in a place of responsibility in a firm. This individual must be capable of embracing and modeling notions of brand activism. As this book will discuss, the CEO occupies a natural position to create a level of activism in the company.

Penn State Smeal Business School professor Donald Hambrick, interviewed for the school's alumni magazine, defined CEO activism as when CEOs speak out on societal debates that have little direct bearing on near-term company performance. Hambrick characterized CEO activism as "a relatively recent, rapidly mounting, and controversial phenomenon. Many observers assume that CEO activism accomplishes very little, while some believe that it's downright risky" (Manno, 2022).

As this book will show, CEOs have a range of responsibilities to shareholders, employees, consumers, and more. Driving these responsibilities of an activist CEO are several key responsibilities to an activist agenda, as outlined by Pimentel and Didonet (2021). These include:

- Environmental responsibilities: making sure the planet exists so the brand can thrive
- Economic responsibilities: strengthening economies by providing jobs
- Public health responsibilities: determining how brands affect people on the physical, emotional, and psychological levels, potentially influencing deep cultural change

Balancing the range of responsibilities and shareholders is at the heart of creating a strong and activist company, and this book will highlight how activist CEOs create and maintain this balance.

Importantly, an activist CEO must have a long-term perspective toward the business. Short-term corporate profits can sometimes grow through unethical and irresponsible means (Carruci, 2016). An activist agenda, though, must be in place for the long term, as doing the right thing may cost a bit more than purely serving the bottom line. However, a commitment to being an activist brand has the potential to build equity in a company that will withstand the test of time.

In this book, Eric Kwame Adae has identified key CEOs that have built strong businesses by being activist CEOs and has probed their perspectives, strategies, and challenges of choosing this method of corporate leadership. He identifies how they create long-term customer loyalty, legal compliance, and strong brand reputations that have led their companies to success. He also articulates the key challenges that CEOs face in this mission. Most importantly, the book shows the role that national and global culture plays in brand activism. Grounded in key theories and enlivened by CEO insights, this book provides a critical and cultural roadmap for any CEO seeking to adopt an activist agenda.

**Kim Bartel Sheehan, PhD**
Professor Emerita
University of Oregon
School of Journalism and Communication
Eugene, Oregon
USA

# References

Carruci, R. (2016). Why ethical people make unethical choices. https://hbr.org/2016/12/why-ethical-people-make-unethical-choices

Manno, M. (2022). CEO activism can benefit companies—But only if employees agree. *Smeal Magazine*. http://magazine.smeal.psu.edu/ceo activism-can-benefit-companies-but-only-if-employees-agree/#:~:text=Their%20findings%20show%20that%20when,ideas%20promoted%20by%20the%20CEO

Pimentel, P. C., & Didonet, S. R. (2021). Brand activism as a marketing strategy: Proposing a typology. *Ix Encontro De Marketing Da Anpad-EMA 2021*, 25–26.

Sheehan, K., & Morrison, D. (2018). Advertising leadership and climate change: The efficacy of industry professionals to address climate issues, *Advertising & Society Review*. https://muse.jhu.edu/article/689165/summary

WPP Group. (2014). *WPP sustainability report 2013/2014.* https://reports.wpp.com/sustainabilityreports/2013/assets/files/pdf/WPP_SR_2013_2014.pdf

WPP.org. (2023). We are the creative transformation company. https://www.wpp.com/about

Zeno Group. (2020). Unveiling the Zeno 2020 strength of purpose study. https://www.zenogroup.com/insights/2020-zeno-strength-purpose

# Acknowledgments

Related to my doctoral dissertation and my general wider research interest in corporate activism, this book project has been a journey of self-discovery. I am exceedingly grateful to a whole village of supporters and helpers. I owe a huge debt of gratitude to Prof Leslie Steeves, Prof Kim Sheehan, Prof Alan Meyer, and Prof Michael Russo. The bells in the chambers of my heart ring in gratitude to Prof Christopher Chavez and Prof S. Senyo Ofori-Parku.

This research project profited from a generous fellowship from the University of Oregon Graduate School. I am very grateful to all the socially minded and forward-leading activist CEOs on a positive social mission in Ghana who collaborated with me. Please accept my heartfelt appreciation: Prof Donnalyn Pompper, Prof Molefi Kete Asante, Prof Kenneth Amaeshi, Prof Robert Hinson, Prof Audrey Gadzekpo, Prof Derina Holtzhausen, and Prof Melissa Dodd. Many thanks to Prof A. B. Assensoh, Prof Yvette Alex-Assensoh, Dr Allen P. Heaman, Dr Emmanuel Adu-Sarkodee, Karen Jean Brown, Nana Akua Mensa-Bonsu, and Ebenezer Nana Hammond of CallPrint Ghana Limited.

I am grateful to my wife, Mrs Brenda Adae for being my best friend, my rock, and my anchor. I love you completely. To my children, Marie-Ann Adae, Marian-Rose Adae, and Eric Adae (II), thank you for giving me a reason to keep going. I am grateful to the Adae, Abbrey, Boni, Asare, and Sampah families for being my unfailing backbone. Thank you, Prophet Gideon Danso, Bishop Oko Bortey-Doku, Rev Dr Paul Lartey, and Rev Ben Johnson.

Abba Father, You are faithful! Thank you for all the blessings. Holy Spirit, thank You for being my ever-present help in times of need. Thank You, dear Lord Jesus Christ. May Your name be praised forevermore. *Selah!*

# Chapter 1

# Introduction: Reimagining CEO Activism, Development, and Difference

## 1.1 Introduction

The terrains of business and politics continue to merge in stronger ways than previously thought (Global Strategy Group, 2016). Although corporations have not always been concerned about wider social, political, and environmental issues that are not directly related to their financial bottom line, some scholars have observed that significant shifts are in the offing (Nalick et al., 2016).

Globally, there are rising calls and activism for changes to perceived injustices in the social order (Dodd & Supa, 2014), and social movements have become a pervasive part of the general pattern of contemporary society (Valencia & Jones, 2018). As activists are increasingly targeting companies and nonprofits, indications are that we are witnessing a growing trend of corporations becoming involved in sociopolitical issues (Wettstein & Baur, 2016).

In 2019, the Business Roundtable, an association of the Chief Executive Officers (CEOs) of some of the most influential companies in America, shook the foundations of the business world by issuing a statement that reimagined the purpose of business and companies in terms of creating long-term shared value for multiple stakeholders, rather than solely for its shareholders (Ludema & Johnson, 2019). This new position that was signed by some 181 CEOs in America is a marked departure from positions taken by both Milton Friedman's (1970, 2007) profit-maximizing corporate role, and the previous shareholder primacy postures of the Business Roundtable. The new position makes an open commitment for companies to be accountable to five strategic constituencies, namely, customers, employees, suppliers, communities, and shareholders (Business Roundtable, 2019; Gartenberg & Serafeim, 2019).

Corporations, their brands, and corporate leaders are taking public stances on diverse social matters through various activist and advocacy campaigns (Weber Shandwick, 2016, 2017). Particularly, CEOs now weigh in on issues that were once the preserve of politicians, nongovernmental organizations (NGOs), civil society organizations, and other advocacy groups (Chatterji & Toffel, 2015; Weber Shandwick, 2016). This may well be a vanguard of a significant movement in public relations, management, and cognate fields (Chatterji & Toffel, 2018).

CEOs on a Mission, 1–36
Copyright © 2023 Eric Kwame Adae
Published under exclusive licence by Emerald Publishing Limited
doi:10.1108/978-1-80382-215-020231001

## 1.2 CEOs on a Mission to Fight for the Greater Good

Although there have been increasing publications about corporate involvement in sociopolitical matters, scholars are yet to agree on various aspects of the phenomenon (Livonen, 2018). There is a palpable disagreement regarding what label to assign to this observable atypical corporate behavior. While some use the label "Corporate Political Advocacy" (see Baur & Wettstein, 2016; Wettstein & Baur, 2016), others prefer the label "CEO activism" (see Chatterji & Toffel, 2015), some have proposed "CEO Sociopolitical Activism" (see Hambrick & Wowak, 2021), and still, others opt for "Corporate Social Advocacy" (see Dodd & Supa, 2014).

Dodd and Supa (2014) conceptualized "Corporate Social Advocacy" as a legitimate field of inquiry within the field of public relations, which spans the boundaries of two vital areas of scholarship and practice, namely Strategic Issues Management (SIM) and Corporate Social Responsibility (CSR). These scholars describe Corporate Social Advocacy (CSA) as instances of organizations making public statements or taking public stances on sociopolitical issues. CEO activism involves heads of profit-oriented corporations making public statements and taking open stances on social and environmental issues that may not directly relate to the economic bottom line of their corporations (Chatterji, 2016; Hambrick & Wowak, 2021). It has been suggested that whether these organizational stances are planned as part of formal corporate communications, or not, the result is the public's perception that the organization is connected to the issue (Park & Berger, 2004).

Nowadays, big business and big-name CEOs carry protest signs, admonish politicians, and sometimes threaten economic reprisals against politicians and federal governments (Laband, 2016). Some scholars argue that the increasingly polarized political environment has created opportunities for others – other than politicians, NGOs, and civil society organizations – to step up and lead from the front on issues of wider social importance (Cronin, 2018). Thus, within the shifting organizational contexts, it is now more difficult for companies to leave politics to politicians (Weber Shandwick, 2017).

Examples of instances of such comingling of business and politics appear to be proliferating (Weber Shandwick, 2016). Chatterji and Toffel (2016) observe that these CEOs and other high-profile corporate executives have been publicly weighing in on hot-button and controversial issues like race relations and gender equality that may be directly unrelated to their core businesses. Some commentators suggest that following public pressure from the CEOs Intel, Salesforce, and Unilever, Governor Nathan Deal of Georgia, a Republican, decided to veto a "religious liberty" bill that would make it possible for faith-based businesses and charities to discriminate against same-sex couples (Chatterji & Toffel, 2016). Similarly, in 2015, Apple CEO Timothy Cook openly resisted a similar bill in Indiana, publicly opposing Governor Mike Pence, a Republican, to sign a revised version of the law that proscribed sexual orientation-based and gender-based discrimination (Chatterji & Toffel, 2016).

These CEOs and several others have become exemplars of corporate chieftains who have taken public stands on an ever-increasing gyre of hot button social and environmental issues, ranging from same-sex marriage, climate change, income fairness, immigration, and racial discrimination to gender equality (Chatterji & Toffel, 2016; Weber Shandwick, 2016). Other examples of CEOs who have recently made public pronouncements on wider sociopolitical issues are Lloyd Blankfein of Goldman Sachs, Jim Rogers of Duke Energy, and Eric Schmidt of Google (Chatterji & Toffel, 2015). Others have included Angie's List's CEO William Oesterle, Howard Schultz of Starbucks, and Dan T. Cathy of Chick-fil-A (Chatterji & Toffel, 2016).

According to trend watchers, the tipping point came early in President Donald J. Trump's administration, following his temporary travel ban to the United States for citizens from seven Muslim countries. This caused many CEOs to speak out publicly against the executive order, particularly on social media, and igniting worldwide protests (Weber Shandwick, 2017). Commenting on the trend and the perceived agency of activist CEOs, Marc Benioff, CEO of Salesforce.com believes: "One thing you're seeing that there is a third [political] party emerging in this country, which is the party of CEOs" (Weber Shandwick, 2016, p. 2). Other CEOs have tersely expressed the need to engage in activism in somewhat moral and ethical terms. For instance, Brian Moynihan has been noted to have remarked that the reimagined role of CEOs now included various political actions that transcended the normal profit-oriented business logic (Chatterji & Toffel, 2018). While recognizing the increasing role of CEOs to pursue causes that appear to be directly unconnected to the operations and financial profitability of their corporations, it is noteworthy that some scholars have argued that the aim of corporate political activity is frequently – some would say always – bottom-line based, with companies traditionally using lobbying and other behind-the-scenes strategies and actors to pursue their interests (Wettstein & Baur, 2016).

Scholars have sought to proffer some reasons for the rising incidence of CEO activism. For instance, some scholars have spoken of a democratic deficit/gap, reflective of an expectation hiatus between what governments promise, relative to their ability to deliver such promises (Cronin, 2018). Thus, employees, customers, and other stakeholders are demanding more from business leaders, even as distrust in governments escalates (Gaines-Ross, 2016, 2017).

Again, there are significant corporate investments in establishing corporate values such as diversity and social inclusion (Gaines-Ross, 2017). For instance, technology giant Google is reported to have invested some $265 m on diversity programs between 2014 and 2016. Government attacks against such values have been noted to cause corporations, their brands, and leaders to speak out (Gaines-Ross, 2017). Not speaking out negatively affects the ability of corporations to attract and retain top talent, particularly Millennials (people born between 1980 and 1994) and Gen-Z (people born between 1995 and 2015).

Lately, most societies are increasingly caught up in an era of political polarization, where people are significantly cloistered in neighborhoods, social networks, and workspaces that serve as echo chambers of ideological beliefs (Chatterji & Toffel, 2016). Thus, corporate neutrality is becoming anachronistic, and may even be a risky corporate strategy (Chatterji & Toffel, 2016). Besides, as brands seek to tell more compelling stories by personalizing their relationships with customers and brand cults, the adoption of a sociopolitical orientation is increasingly becoming a core part of corporate strategy. More corporations are finding it better to be much loved by a few than remain inoffensive to many (Chatterji & Toffel, 2016).

## 1.3 Dangerous Opportunities in the Field

CEO activism is fast emerging as a theoretical concept in scholarly circles (Chatterji & Toffel, 2017), due in part to the significant media spotlight on the phenomenon (Dodd, 2016). However, the concept has undergone some ambivalence, as seen in the few scholars who have sought to research it applying diverse labels to the self-same phenomenon. This lack of unanimity among scholars reflects the newness of the growing trend of a unique sort of engagement where corporations, brands, and executives take an overt and public stance on sociopolitical issues, with the avowed goal of getting others to also rally to the same cause (Wettstein & Baur, 2016).

Buoyed by notions of brand responsibility, the triple bottom line, and sustainability, corporate efforts branded as CSR have tended to serve the dual objectives of creating economic and social value simultaneously, such as initiatives to spark clean technology innovation (Chatterji & Toffel, 2015). However, CEO activism is deemed to be a unique expression of corporate sociopolitical involvement, as some CEOs may even intentionally court some controversy by weighing in on controversial issues without any obvious pretense of raising corporate profits (Chatterji & Toffel, 2015). For instance, Howard Schultz observes that the Race Together campaign "is not some marketing or PR exercise. This is to do one thing: Use our national footprint and scale for good" (Chatterji & Toffel, 2015).

While corporate involvement in sociopolitical issues presents new challenges for organizations, it is also laden with opportunities for corporate executives to change their corporations and society for the better from the inside-out (Holtz-hausen & Voto, 2002). CEO activism may well signal a significant shift in corporate public relations and brand communications, since until relatively recently, most large companies have sought not to alienate large segments of potential customers and other stakeholders, by remaining relatively neutral on controversial issues (Chatterji & Toffel, 2016).

Despite the backlash to the Starbucks "Race Together" campaign, Chatterji and Toffel (2015) noted that CEO activism is a significant step forward for corporate involvement in the public sphere, as reflected by the phenomenon's ability to straddle the intersection between business and public policy. These scholars noticed the significant rise of CEO activism and its increasing influence articulated the need to encourage it and urged relevant stakeholders to help define its limits.

Thus, CEOs are especially using their wealth and the bully pulpit to make their voices lead to major changes in specific states, and nationally in America, with the trend pointing to an increased incidence of CEO activism globally (Chatterji &

Toffel, 2018; Dodd, 2016). It is becoming apparent that men and women CEOs from other parts of the world have been embarking on diverse forms of activism, such as attempts to help address some of the developmental challenges and social injustices in Ghana. Yet, the bulk of current literature on CEO activism has focused on activist CEOs in Western (largely American) contexts.

Related to the Western cultural bias that currently plagues the scholarly field of CEO activism, there is a gender-blind spot. Save for Weber Shandwick's (2016) mention of the pioneering CEO activism of Marilyn Carlson, CEO of the global travel and hospitality firm Carlson Companies, who spoke against human trafficking, arguably all studies on CEO activism have not only focused on Western (United States) contexts but also highlighted the activism of white men who are CEOs.

This is a failure that reflects the general marginalization of the work of women CEOs in general, but especially those of activist women CEOs. Such an elision is regrettable, unfortunate, and problematic since substantial gender inequities still mark major economic sectors, and gender-based differences cut deep. Women workers and executives continue to cope with work environments dominated by men, sexual harassment, and the routinization of discourses of the sexual division of labor, among many other inequities.

Besides the apparent Western domination of the field, studies on CEO activism also display an ideological and paradigmatic bias for modernist perspectives that privilege consensus and the corporate and investor interests, to the exclusion of postmodern perspectives that privilege agonism and the interests of multiple stakeholders (Ciszek & Curtin, 2020; Ciszek & Logan, 2018).

## 1.4 The Current Study

This book offers an inquiry into the nascent phenomenon of CEO activism in Ghana. The mission is to rethink scholarship and the practice of CEO activism in various respects. It seeks to consider some ways in which scholarship and the practice of CEO activism could be advanced by changing some of the current perspectives that have dogged the field. This research study seeks to address the woeful dearth of scholarly work on CEO activism, by investigating how the phenomenon is evolving within the context of a developing society such as Ghana.

## 1.5 The Ghanaian Context

### 1.5.1 The West African Subregion

West Africa is generally described as a part of Africa, south of the Sahara Desert (sub-Saharan continent). Overall, there are some 17 nation-states that call this westernmost section of the African continent home. However, in terms of its geopolitical constitution, there are 16 countries in this subregion, since Mauritania is generally aligned with the North African bloc. Excluding Liberia, all the nation-states in West Africa were once colonies of European states, spanning the early 1600s till the 1980s, when all the colonized nations in the region attained political independence from their European colonial masters.

The people of West Africa share various customs, languages, and traditions, despite the rich diversity of the region's sociocultural formations. While nations in West Africa are resource-rich, they also paint a sad and paradoxical picture of under-development. Generally, some of the developmental challenges of West Africa include high mortality rates, corruption, low education rates, and food insecurity. Founded in 1975, the Economic Community of West African States (ECOWAS) is the regional economic bloc. ECOWAS has the mission of promoting and deepening economic integration and regional prosperity.

### 1.5.2 The Republic of Ghana

The study is set in the present-day English-speaking West African country of Ghana.

Modern-day Ghana shares borders with Togo on its east, Cote d'Ivoire on the west, Burkina Faso on the north, and the Atlantic Ocean on the south. However, the present-day Ghana that is the context of this research study must not be confused with the Old Ghana Empire that thrived in West Africa between the sixth and thirteenth century CE (Cartwright, 2019).

The modern nation-state of the Republic of Ghana which is the context of this research study is named after the medieval Ghana Empire. The geographic coordinates of Ghana are 8 00N, 2 00W and has a total land area of about 239,460 square kilometers, with water resources of 8,520 sq. km. Ghana's land boundaries add up to 2,094 km, comprising Burkina Faso (549 km), Cote d'Ivoire (668 km), Togo (877 km), and a coastline of 539 km. It also lays claim to a maritime territory of 12 nautical miles (CIA World Factbook, 2019). Comparatively, the Republic of Ghana is almost the same size as the United Kingdom (World Population Review, 2019). Interestingly, geographically, Ghana is the country that is closer than any other to the intersection of the equator and the Greenwich Meridian (World Population Review, 2019).

Until its political independence, Ghana was known as the Gold Coast. The early Portuguese adventurers were reported to have found so much gold between the rivers Ankobra and Volta that they nicknamed the place *Da Mina*, meaning "The Mine" when they arrived on its shores in 1482 (CIA World Factbook, 2019). For many years, the Gold Coast attracted various European traders and administrations, including the Dutch (from 1598), the British (seventeenth century), Denmark, and Sweden. However, by the late nineteenth century, only the Dutch and the British remained, with the Dutch leaving in 1874, making the Gold Coast a British protectorate (CIA World Factbook, 2019).

Ghana became the first country south of the Sahara to gain its independence from colonial rule on March 6, 1957. Osagyefo Dr. Kwame Nkrumah is generally regarded as the founder and first president of Ghana. He had the vision of a united Africa and was the first to promote Pan-Africanism, a melding of the views of Marcus Garvey and Dr. W.E.B. Du Bois (CIA World Factbook, 2019).

Notable natural disasters in Ghana include dry and dusty northeastern winds that occur between January and March; recurrent droughts in the northern regions that negatively impact agricultural productivity; deforestation; overgrazing; soil erosion; poaching and habitat destruction, threatening wildlife; water pollution; and inadequate supplies of potable water (CIA World Factbook, 2019).

Ghana's legal system is based on the English Common Law, customary (traditional) law, and the 1992 Constitution. The courts of Ghana are hierarchical. Since mid-1992, Ghana has been a relatively stable democracy, with a multiparty political system. This unbroken run follows about a decade's break from the democratic experiment. The country has made some remarkable advancements in the direction of democracy and a multiparty system, marked by an independent judiciary that has gained some public trust (The World Bank, 2019).

Throughout its fourth republic, Ghana has followed a neoliberal ideology that emphasizes the reduction of the state; deregulation and privatization; free trade; and the promotion of foreign direct investment (Dartey-Baah, 2015). Ghana's 1992 constitution further seeks to deepen a neoliberal context by providing for the creation and deepening of a democratic country based on freedom, regional and gender balance, equality, transparency, accountability, meritocracy, justice, probity, and competence (Dartey-Baah, 2015). The constitution seeks to eliminate the abuse of power and corrupt practices; decentralization and devolution of national administration and financial management to the regions and district levels; renewing, reforming, and building strong institutions; and achieving value-for-money in the provision of public services (Dartey-Baah, 2015).

The main parties in Ghana's Fourth Republic are the National Democratic Congress (NDC) and the New Patriotic Party (NPP) that won the 2016 elections under the leadership of H.E. President *Nana* Addo Dankwa *Akufo-Addo. The NPP is a right-wing party that pursues a* center-right and liberal-conservative party that seeks to energize Ghanaians for the achievement of a property-owning democracy, within the context of the preservation of the right to life, freedom and justice, and the enrichment of the lives, property, and liberty of the people (newpatrioticparty.org).

*The NDC is currently the major opposition party in Ghana. It is* a social-democratic political party, founded by Jerry Rawlings. The party seeks to develop a Ghanaian society that would effectively become a strong force in the West African subregion, and which provides economic and social opportunities for all Ghanaians (officialndc.com).

*The Convention People's Party (CPP) is the successor of Nkrumah's party, bearing the same name (The CIA World Factbook, 2019). This* is a leftist, socialist political party, founded on the ideas of the first President of Ghana, Kwame Nkrumah, including Nkrumahism, African Socialism, and Pan-Africanism. *Other political parties in Ghana's political party ecosystem include the People's National Convention (PNC), the People's Democratic Party (PDP), the Democratic People's Party (DPP), and the Progressive Peoples Party (PPP).*

Ghana has consistently ranked among the top three African countries in terms of freedom of speech and press freedom, with strong broadcast media (especially radio) having the widest reach (UNESCO, 2012), factors that Ghana could leverage as solid social capital (The World Bank, 2019).

### 1.5.3 Ghana's Development Paradox

Some commentators have observed that Ghana's experience with neoliberalism over the past 30 years has been a mixed bag of fortune, comprising some sustained economic growth and reduced rates of poverty, but also marked by uneven regional distribution (Awanyo & Attua, 2016). This unequal distribution of development has tended to focus socioeconomic development in the historically favored parts of the country, located in the southern and the middle regions while leaving other parts of the country (located in the northern regions) in abject poverty.

Some scholars find this uneven pattern of development a paradox indicated in capitalism's tendency to focus development in the Greater Accra and the Ashanti Regions, while at the same time concentrating poverty in the northern regions of Ghana through the dispersal of capital investments and socioeconomic benefits, expressed in ways that deepen the existing unbalanced regional developments in Ghana (Awanyo & Attua, 2016).

The African Development Bank (AfDB, 2019) notes that although consistent bolstering of external demand for Ghana's primary products such as oil and cocoa could has some beneficial effects of boosting growth in the medium term. However, Ghana's history indicates that economic growth, based on revenues from the extractive industry, has failed to address growing inequality and job creation (AfDB, 2019). To help achieve a more balanced allocation of the nation's resources, six new administrative regions were added in February 2019, bringing the total number of regions in Ghana to 16.

### 1.5.4 Gender Diversity in Corporate Ghana

One of the development paradoxes in Ghana is the unequal representation and participation of women in management and the corporate sector in the country. This imbalance has been one of the contentions and advocations of the Executive Women Network (EWN), a coalition of some of the influential women corporate executives in the country.

The presence and participation of women in corporate and private leadership across Africa are rather limited, despite the men-to-women ratio across the Continent being 1:1 (The World Bank, 2016). Comprising over one-half of the nation's population, women play a significant role in economic activity in Ghana (IFC, 2018). Despite their significant demographic composition, most organizations in Ghana's formal sector and the boards of directors in the country lack gender balance, when it comes to women representation (Deloitte, 2015).

Since the Fourth United Nations World Conference on Women in Beijing in 1995, the centrality of gender diversity in the socioeconomic transformation of Ghana has been in sharper focus. Attempts have been made in Ghana to mainstream gender equality in virtually all facets of national life. There have also been moves to better incorporate such notions into the country's legal framework, to guide attempts to address the perceived deeply rooted gender inequalities. For instance, Article 17 of Ghana's 1992 constitution proscribes discrimination based on gender. Accordingly, the Affirmative Action Policy (AAP) of 1998 makes it imperative for a 40% quota of women's representation on all government and public boards.

The Ministry of Gender, Children and Social Protection (MoGCSP) was created by Executive Instrument 1 (E.I. 1) in January 2013 as a successor to the Ministry of Women and Children's Affairs, with the primary responsibility for policy formulation, coordination, and monitoring and evaluation of gender, children, and social protection issues within the context of the national development agenda (mogcsp.gov.gh). Some observers see such a specialized government ministry to be an important step in demonstrating the nation's resolve to promote, address, and achieve gender equity in every aspect of the nation (IFC, 2018).

The International Finance Corporation (IFC, 2018) found that although most corporations in Ghana's private and public sectors have some women representation, the proportion of women to men is still low, due largely to crippling professional challenges that women face, especially stemming directly from family responsibilities.

In 2015, the Government of Ghana launched a National Gender Policy (NGP) to help promote gender equality, and to "move the country towards, women's empowerment and livelihood, women's right and access to justice, women's leadership, and accountable government, among others" (IFC, 2018, p. 4). However, this policy was silent regarding the degree of gender diversity that corporate and private boards and management ought to achieve. At the organizational level, corporations have their policies and benchmarks for the extent of gender representation in executive management and on various boards of directors (IFC, 2018).

Notwithstanding this and other initiatives, the representation of women on the higher rungs of the corporate ladder in Ghana is rather stunted and shallow (Deloitte, 2015). In a recent baseline exploratory study into diversity in Ghanaian boardrooms that considered gender diversity – across sectors, ownership types, legal status, listing status, and several other organizational and board-level characteristics – to serve as empirical evidence to inform the framing of organizational and national policy, the IFC found that women are woefully underrepresented in the boards and C-suites in Ghana (IFC, 2018).

Even though the ideal is for organizations to have gender diversity, a majority (77.85%) of firms surveyed had no policies on gender whatsoever. A minuscule proportion of firms (5.7%) had such policies, with 16.46% not responding to these survey items. It emerged that despite the wide absence of gender policies in organizations in Ghana, some 72.15% of boards had some women representation, although the ratio of women to men was low, with diversity ranging between 20% and 30% (IFC, 2018).

The results indicate that about 86% of organizations in Ghana have no more than two women on their boards. Again, while only 6.33% had established some minimum thresholds for women on their boards, 75.95% did not have such minimum benchmarks, and 17.72% failed to provide valid responses to the survey items relating to such thresholds. It was found that just about 4.43% have a standard for women representation (IFC, 2018).

Gender diversity (operationalized as the proportion of women to the total board members) generally ranged from 7% and 25%. The number of women on boards ranged from one to six among firms sampled, with the highest frequency of the number of women on boards being one. The findings further revealed that 24.05% of the sampled boards are composed of only men (IFC, 2018). It also emerged that most women on boards (49.37%) were nonexecutive directors and that only 6.49% of organizations have women as board chairpersons.

It was also learned that smaller firms were more likely to have higher gender diversity, relative to larger firms. Besides, younger firms were more likely to have high gender diversity than relatively older firms (IFC, 2018). NGOs and micro-finance firms emerged as having higher gender diversity than other types of organizations in Ghana. Further, it appears that organizations in Ghana's financial services sector (banking, insurance, and pensions), except for the microfinance and the asset management industries, have relatively lower gender diversity (IFC, 2018).

Private/unlisted firms (firms not listed/traded on the Ghana Stock Exchange) showed higher gender diversity, compared with listed firms. Parastatal/state-owned enterprises (SOEs) showed higher gender diversity, relative to other ownership types. Foreign firms did not score highly on gender diversity. Family-owned businesses showed higher gender diversity, compared with nonfamily businesses. Additional findings suggest that smaller boards have higher gender diversity than larger boards (IFC, 2018).

The study also indicated that organizations that do not combine CEO and board chair positions tended to have more women on their boards and that a greater proportion of independent boards tended to have less gender diversity. Businesses with women CEOs tended to have more women on their boards than businesses with men CEOs. Businesses with women board chairs also tended to have more women on their boards, compared with businesses with men board chairs (IFC, 2018).

Overall, the IFC's (2018) findings in Ghana suggest that there is a business case for having women on board because the cross-tabulations reveal that companies that perform better tend to have more gender-balanced boards. High-performing firms, based on return on assets (ROA), were associated with higher gender diversity than low-performing firms (IFC, 2018). However, for low-performing firms, based on return on equity (ROE), exhibited higher gender diversity than high-performing firms, but the difference was not significant.

Additionally, most of the high-performing firms exhibited gender diversity (IFC, 2018). In sales growth, high-performing firms were associated with higher gender diversity than low-performing firms. These findings provide support for the value-in-diversity or decision-making perspective that suggests a positive relationship between gender diversity and firm performance, taking into consideration the various factors that enhance decision-making (IFC, 2018).

### 1.5.5 Social Problems in Ghana and the Work of Activist CEOs

Typical of most developing countries, Ghana faces several developmental and systemic challenges, socially, economically, politically, and environmentally. A recent national socioeconomic and governance survey conducted by the public policy institute, the Institute of Economic Affairs (IEA) identified unemployment, poverty, unreliable energy, corruption (especially the political kind), poor education, poor infrastructure, and low income as the most crippling issues facing Ghanaians (ieagh.org). Other contemporary social problems include poor healthcare delivery, the low representation of women in the higher echelons of corporations, political militias and vigilantes, perceived economic mismanagement of the nation's resources, and illegal small-scale mining (popularly termed "Galamsey").

Within this context, a small corps of activist CEOs is emerging. Indications are that, since the dawn of the current democratic dispensation in Ghana in 1992, some CEOs in Ghana have taken public stances on diverse issues, including media freedom, corruption, social injustice, environmental degradation, corruption, and misguided political leadership.

## 1.6 Theoretical Lenses for This Book

The study on CEO activism that is featured in the various chapters of this book draws on diverse theoretical and conceptual lenses. These include notions of *responsible management in emerging markets* (see Adae et al., 2021) and *public relations for social responsibility* (see Pompper, 2021); *Afrocentricity* (see e.g., Asante, 1989) and *Afrocentric philosophies of sustainability* (see Pompper & Adae, 2023) and *Africapitalism* (see e.g., Amaeshi & Idemudia, 2015; Elumelu, 2012); postmodern values in public relations (see Holtzhausen & Voto, 2002); and *CSA* (see Dodd & Supa, 2014) and *CEO activism* (see e.g., Branicki et al., 2021; Chatterji & Toffel, 2018).

### 1.6.1 The African School of Thought in Leadership and Public Relations

Globally, the socioeconomic dysfunctions and negative externalities associated with capitalism and business activities have been investigated (see e.g., Banerjee, 2008). Thus, calls have been made by corporations, especially those operating in developing societies to uphold inclusive management ideologies so as to "be responsible and balance the conflicting interests of diverse stakeholders, including the biosphere and future generations" and "the installation of responsible and sustainable management practices that seek to integrate economic, social and environmental missions into corporate goals and strategies" (Adae et al., 2021, p. v).

In this regard, the field of public relations is positioned to take the commanding heights and lead from the front in helping achieve positive outcomes, principally because of its focus on pursuing multiple stakeholder perspectives. Also, the field of public relations appears to uniquely placed because of its *multidisciplinarity* and *multiperspectival* focus, standing at the crossroads of public relations, CSR, diversity/equity/inclusivity, social development, and the significant role of public relations professionals as insider activists and guardians of corporate and business ethics (see Pompper, 2021).

### 1.6.1.1 Afrocentricity and Afrocentric Philosophies of Sustainability

With the apparent omission of African perspectives and the concurrent Eurocentric colonization of most disciplines, *Afrocentricity* is a pro-African standpoint that is sympathetic to African ethos, genius, and values, and advocates reinvigorating and recentering of the African philosophy, culture, and worldview in all phenomena (see e.g., Asante, 1987, 1989, 2003, 2007). It advocates for the purposeful analysis of human social phenomena from the deliberate perspective of the agency of African people, culture, history, and roles in sociocultural phenomena (Asante, 2017; Asante & Dove, 2021; Mazama, 2003; Rosier & Sekai, 2016).

On the African continent, public relations practice is pivotal in spurring social development, promoting the embracement of social inclusivity, and driving the sustainability logic. A case in point here relates to the agency of public relations professionalism in driving social development and addressing social justice issues (see e.g., Pratt, 1993). Also, it has been found that public relations professionals in the African nation of Nigeria set higher ethical standards and display a stellar commitment to social responsibility than their Western practitioners (Pratt, 1986).

*Afrocentric Philosophies of Sustainability* are conceptualized as traditional African worldviews, beliefs, customs, and usages that not only align with contemporary sustainability transitions but also promote multiple stakeholder interests and perspectives, including such specific concepts as *Bilchiinsi* (see Mohammed, 2022); *Ma'atic philosophy* (see Asante & Dove, 2021); *Caritas, Negritude, Ujamaa, Consciencism, Bantu philosophy, Ubuntu, the spirit of Harambee, Akan philosophy, Yoruba epistemology,* and *Sankofa philosophy* (see Pompper & Adae, 2023), among many other hues and flavors of African holism and human-centered mores. The bedrock of these variants of Afrocentric worldviews are Ma'atic values, including truth, balance, order, harmony, law, morality, and justice (see Asante & Dove, 2021).

### 1.6.1.2 Caritas

In 2011, the Public Relations Society of America (PRSA) adopted what some scholars consider to be a "modern definition of public relations" when the apex association for the practice of public relations in America reimagined the definition of the practice as "a strategic communication process that builds mutually beneficial relationships between organizations and their publics" (Corbett, 2012a,

2012b). According to some scholars, such a view of the discipline of public relations tended to stress the human social aspects and the imperative for an ethical bedrock for the practice of public relations (Tilson, 2009), since it highlights the community-preserving functions of the field for companies and institutions (PRSA, 2003).

The overall goal of public relations involves building and sustaining mutually beneficial relations between organizations and their key publics. While socially responsible corporate behavior had traditionally been driven by strategic corporate self-interest, it is contended that it is essential for companies to "upgrade the quality of life in a community" (Tilson & Vance, 1985, p. 26). Other scholars have further suggested that while CSR had usually been driven by the desire to uphold the social contract (Guth & Marsh, 2005), serving the greater social good does not have to be prompted or encouraged by the expectation of satisfying a corporate goal since good corporate citizenship could be an adequate reward in and of itself (Mescon & Tilson, 1987).

Integral to this paradigm is the notion of Caritas, including such faith-inspired ideas as helpfulness, loving-kindness, charity, and benevolence that form part of the bedrock of many preferable socially responsible corporate social behaviors (Tilson, 2014). Caritas has also been described as including such attributes as "tolerance (respect for others, the practice of justice, reciprocity) and empathy including of its 'fruits' mercy or compassion, which is expressed in various corporal works (e.g., to tend to the sick, and feed the hungry)" (Tilson, 2014, p. 58).

Caritas is also regarded as an essential social commandment (Coe, 2004) and is considered a central element of virtue (Champion & Short, 2003). Thus, some leadership and communication studies have argued that acting according to Caritas (compassion) and nurturing the community and the environment was critical for engendering "trust, credibility and respect" (Oestreicher, 2011, p. 17).

> Caritas argues against notions of reciprocity and represents instead, a genuine commitment to the greater good with no obligation demanded from the recipient in return, contending that compassionate social behavior can simply be its own reward. As such Caritas, in and of itself represents a worldview beyond symmetrical/asymmetrical formulation, with its own set of defining presuppositions.
>
> (Tilson, 2014, p. 59)

Such notions have created some room for a covenantal model of strategic communications as a legitimate theoretical field of inquiry (Tilson, 2014), to serve authentic social ends deemed "desirable in its own right" such as "health, sanitation or justice" (Baker, 2002, pp. 197–199).

Tilson (2014) argues that the notion of Caritas serves as the basis for many efforts at relationship-building in many cultures across the globe, including traditional societies from the Mediterranean Crescent to Asia, the African subcontinent, and the Americas. Evidence abounds that in Africa and the Americas, traditional values of indigenous peoples show how philosophies that emanated from Caritas are employed in relationship and community-building, often with the active participation of ancestors, the environment, and traditional leaders, who are held to possess superhuman knowledge and blessings. Powerful people in such societies are positioned as representatives of the gods and are traditionally expected to attend to the welfare of the wider society.

Thus, Tilson (2014) suggests that such Caritas-inspired roots of social responsibility formed both early and contemporary strategic communication practices, "with forms of communication and relationship building that emphasize collective rather than individual interests, schools of thought that focus on good stewardship, and popular sentiment that defines public relations as essentially 'relating well with people'" (p. 64).

### 1.6.1.3 Ubuntu

Tilson (2014) argues that some early and traditional African cultures had shown strong signs of social responsibility that predated when notions of social responsibility became "... fashionable ... in America and ... Europe" (Buckle, 1999, p. 5). For instance, such highly developed traditional philosophies of social responsibility made for the common situation in Ghana where "there were no orphans or homeless people [and] an elder [was] surrounded and cared for by a big family" (McKissack & McKissack, 1994, p. 37) and the Bantu people of East Africa having no pauper class because of an effective mutual aid scheme (Huxley, 1933, as cited in Gunther, 1955).

Tilson (2014) further contends that similar values form the bedrock of the African philosophy of *Ubuntuism*, as derived from the *isiZulu* term, Ubuntu, that literally means "I am because of others," which underscore notions of community and social collectivism (Blackenberg, 1999, as cited by Worthington, 2011, p. 611). Thus, De Beer and Mersham (2004) argue that such philosophies of Ubuntu pervade every web and tissue of "African forms of communication" that emphasize "community solidarity over individualistic interests" (White, 2009, p. 220) and that in East African country of Uganda where the Bantu people comprise the majority of the population size, "Public Relations ... is mostly understood ... as 'relating well with people' ... [and has] been in existence from time immemorial as a cultural virtue" (Rensburg, as cited in Natifu & Zikusooka, 2011, p. 215).

Other scholars have reported similar findings about several other African societies, including the people of the Kingdom of Melle (present-day Mali), where the kindness and fairness of the thirteenth-century ruler Sundiata Keita in dealing with elites and the poor alike has been on record (McKissack & Mckissack, 1994). Hammer (2006) has equally reported traditional notions of equity, diversity, inclusivity, and justice as some of the values advocated by Islamic societies, as seen in their efforts to promote women's rights and incorporate non-Muslims into largely Islamic societies.

The notion of Caritas and the Ubuntu philosophy serve as important lenses for examining the phenomenon of CEO activism because they comprise worldviews that value community and relationship building that privileges the authentic pursuit of the greater good. As observed by Tilson (2014), "the personal commitment of an individual in a position of authority can foster an organizational and a societal effort in favor of the general welfare regardless of cost or reward to the giver or institution" (Tilson, 2014, p. 69); especially when such motivations derive from spiritually grounded commitments to social justice "toward the common good, pro-social behavior is further encouraged and magnified" (p. 69).

As Haviland (1978) notes, such a compassion-based worldview is diametrically opposed to a self-centered, exclusively profit-oriented, and exploitative view of the world. Tilson (2014) suggests that such worldviews had the proclivity of challenging the traditional basis of defining members of an organization's strategic constituency mainly in terms of individuals and groups of living people only. Such notions favor multiple stakeholder perspectives, with the stretching of the idea of publics to include the welfare of the broader community, the physical as well as the nonmaterial, and the environment, in ways that embraced "diversity in all its forms and effectively advocate for social responsibility around the world" (Tilson, 2014, p. 69).

### 1.6.1.4 Africapitalism

For decades, there have been strident discussions concerning the business–society relationship. Such efforts that have tended to reimagine the critical role of business in Africa's development have spawned the formulation of diverse concepts (Amaeshi & Idemudia, 2015). One such concept is Africapitalism, a notion that was coined by Nigerian businessman and economist Tony O. Elumelu (2012) to undergird the significant role of the private sector to the socioeconomic development of the African continent.

According to Elumelu, Chairman of several corporations, including Heirs Holdings, the United Bank for Africa (UBA), Transcorp, and the Tony Elumelu Foundation, Africapitalism is an economic philosophy that highlights the leading role of Africa's private sector in the socioeconomic development of the continent (Elumelu, 2012; Tony Elumelu Foundation (TEF), 2019). This philosophy is a call for businesses to be innovative in getting involved in the business of social development by partnering governments, donors, and philanthropic organizations in the positive transformation of Africa (TEF, 2019).

Some expected that Africapitalism will "ultimately help businesses become more profitable as the communities they serve become well-off consumers, healthy and better-educated employees, and even entrepreneurs who go on to become suppliers and service providers" (TEF, 2019). Africapitalism is borne out of the enlightened self-interest of businesses since the success of business organizations in Africa is linked up with the progress and well-being of communities in which they operate (Elumelu, 2012).

It has been suggested that the significance of Africapitalism is accentuated by Africa's unfortunately long history of triggers of deep-seated underdevelopment, including colonialism, poor leadership and bad governance, crippling poverty, weak institutions, and distressed civil societies (Amaeshi & Idemudia, 2015). The centrality of Africapitalism is further heightened by Africa's developmental and governance challenges, and the view that the continent needs to employ a unique economic philosophy and business model for its own development.

This call rings truer, especially as efforts to kick-start Africa's development have been compounded by the multinational corporations, foreign governments, aid agencies, international NGOs, and international donors, many of whom have made Africa's development a booming business venture for their own gain (Amaeshi & Idemudia, 2015).

Especially, many multinational corporations in Africa have often found themselves implementing social intervention programs, as part of CSR, most of which have failed to produce the desired currents of social development (see Idemudia, 2014). Thus, within the context of Africa's continued crisis of development in the face of the impotence of governments and the business sector to deliver much-needed social development (Amaeshi & Idemudia, 2015), some scholars have advocated for greater partnership among such actors as the state, business, and civil society (see Idemudia, 2014; Mirvis & Googins, 2018; Richey & Ponte, 2014).

Some have suggested that Africapitalism is reflective of African values of *Ubuntu* that hold that the ultimate purpose of corporations and their management is not to benefit only one group of people, nor is it for the gain of diverse collectivities of people (as posited by stakeholder theory, for instance) (Amaeshi & Idemudia, 2015). Ubuntu philosophy asserts that the ultimate purpose of business is the benefit of the community and the greater good (Lutz, 2009; Norren, 2014).

Generally, Ubuntu values include (i) respect for the dignity of others, (ii) group solidarity, (iii) participation, (iv) sharing, (v) the spirit of harmony, and (vi) interdependency (Mbigi, 2007). Thus, Amaeshi & Idemudia (2015) suggest that Africapitalism is built on at least four Ubuntu values and senses regarding how the world ought to work, namely (i) a sense of progress and prosperity, (ii) a sense of parity, (iii) a sense of peace and harmony, and (iv) a sense of place and belongingness.

In reflecting Ubuntu (African traditional humanism) values, "Africapitalism implies the restoration of African-ness in capitalism, reflecting the economic and social practices implicit in African culture and tradition" (Amaeshi & Idemudia, 2015, p. 215). While not completely against self-prosperity and self-interest, Ubuntu places a burden on the rich to show communal relevance by helping to elevate others and the entire community (Karsten & Illa, 2005; Littrell et al., 2013; Lutz, 2009).

In Ubuntu philosophy, an individual's identity is inexorably linked up with the matrix of his/her society (Amaeshi & Idemudia, 2015), and that one's personal, economic, and social value is directly proportional to one's ability to empower and liberate others (Mbigi, 2007). Thus, just like Caritas, the notion of Ubuntu-derived Africapitalism provides a backdrop for a corporate culture that conditions corporations to pursue sustainability by seeking their profitability, while also advancing social and environmental ideals (Lutz, 2009).

Africapitalism pursues a sense of progress and prosperity by focusing on achieving financial profitability together with social wealth, in ways that transcend material accumulation and includes the psychological and social welfare of all stakeholders (Amaeshi & Idemudia, 2015). This orientation seeks to promote the creation of both financial and social wealth. Thus, progress and prosperity are not conceptualized as the absence of poverty. Rather, they are seen holistically as referring to the creation and maintenance of a matrix of conditions for a fulfilling life for all in society, including good quality and accessible health, education, social capital, and strong and democratic institutions (Brundtland, 1994).

Second, Africapitalism involves a sense of parity, referring to the imperative of seeking social equity, inclusivity, and diversity, and ensuring that wealth accumulation and its distribution are equitable and fair to all parties (Amaeshi & Idemudia, 2015). In Africa, inequity has been described as "the new poverty," the absence of liberalism, and "the entrenchment of crony capitalism and corruption" (Amaeshi & Idemudia, 2015, p. 216). Africapitalism provides a ray of hope in curing these roots of poverty by promoting social inclusivity and equity and in advocating for corporations that seek to adopt a multiple stakeholder orientation.

Third, in seeking a sense of peace and harmony, it has been suggested that Africapitalism can help address the influence of the Schumpeterian drive for creative destruction, self-interest, and the never-ending bouts of struggles, competition, and contestations between places and spaces, generations, regimes, and in other spheres that have marked present-day capitalism (Amaeshi & Idemudia, 2015). This orientation advocates for the negation of contestations, conflicts, and struggles that characterize capitalism (Amaeshi, 2018). Africapitalism is in sync with the pursuit of the values of balance and harmony and drives for holistic human development. Africapitalism advocates for the creation of private wealth, but with due consideration of the production of social capital for all in a harmonious and balanced manner.

Finally, Africapitalism departs from the ideals of global capitalism, by embracing a sense of place and belongingness. Global capitalism takes place for granted, prioritizes cost, and encourages outsourcing and capital flight in the direction of cost minimization (Amaeshi & Idemudia, 2015); thus, "place is consumed" (p. 217). On the contrary, Africapitalism heightens a sense of rootedness and promotes a sense of *topophilia* (Tuan, 1974, 1977) by its linkage of people and place (Duncan & Duncan, 2001). This consciousness may be expressed in economic patriotism (seeking the development of one's community or homeland) (Clift & Woll, 2012) and the pursuit of national development (Audi, 2009).

Africapitalism actively advocates for the eager consideration of the African context in prescribing solutions to the continent's developmental challenges (Amaeshi, 2018). Thus, Africapitalism is also a reflection of corporate patriotism in which corporate behavior is oriented toward contributing to the welfare of citizens and the community while garnering support from stakeholders such as customers, the media, and others (Puncheva-Michelotti et al., 2014).

In tandem with tenets of postmodernism that reject meta-narratives, Amaeshi and Idemudia (2015) argue that Africapitalism is a linguistic project that questions conventional wisdom "and repositions the development of Africa in the world firmly as an indigenous project in which Africans will play significant, active roles" (p. 218); it is "Capitalism by Africa-oriented entrepreneurs for Africa" (p. 219). These scholars see Africapitalism as a force for Africa's sustainable development that stresses the role of the emotions, sentiments, and actions of rational economic actors, including the entrepreneurs and corporate executives of Africa.

By entailing "doing good to do well" (Amaeshi & Idemudia, 2015, p. 218), Africapitalism is consistent with ideas such as CSR, corporate citizenship, the bottom of the pyramid, and the triple bottom line. Amaeshi and Idemudia (2015) however argue that Africapitalism is distinctive in that these cognate concepts seek to tackle some challenges of firm profit maximization but falling short of getting to the very heart of the problem, which other scholars have traced to the issue of individualism (Lutz, 2009).

Africapitalism addresses this issue head-on by casting the corporation as representing a community that evokes a sense of belonging in its members and other stakeholders, an attribute that concepts like Corporate Social Responsibility (CSR) ignore (Amaeshi & Idemudia, 2015). Africapitalism's highlighting of the instrumentality of place and emotion in capitalism also position it as providing a transformative agenda for the role of corporations in Africa's development, and a clarion call for all people who share an emotional attachment with Africa. It is a "deceptively simple notion, but a powerful one that has the potential to remake a continent, and put Africa on an equal economic footing with the rest of the world . . . embodies a private-sector-led approach to solving some of Africa's most intractable development problems" (Amaeshi, 2018).

The phenomenon of CEO activism is an important expression of Africapitalism and post-modernism. CEO activism underlines Africapitalistic calls on Africa's private sector to play active roles in the continent's socioeconomic development. This trend is in keeping with Ubuntu values that enjoin the more powerful and successful people in society to care about and to work to empower the weaker segments of the community.

## 1.7 Postmodern Values in Public Relations

Arguably, postmodernism provides an effective lens for describing, explaining, and predicting aspects of CEO activism. A postmodern view of corporate communications holds that corporate communication practitioners and other high-powered corporate executives will act as organizational and social activists (Holtzhausen & Voto, 2002).

According to this perspective, corporate executives would exhibit some post-modern behavior that translates into one form of organizational activism or the other, including local and situational ethical decision making, a desire for change, the use of biopower to resist dominant power, a concern for the representation of the marginalized sections of society, and the practice of dissensus (Holtzhausen, 2000; Holtzhausen & Voto, 2002).

Holtzhausen (2000) sounded a clarion call for a heightened involvement of public relations practitioners and members of the upper echelons of corporations in wider community activism. She argues that public relations practice – *a field whose luster appears to be growing dim in some circles because of its perceived association with propaganda, manipulation, spin-doctoring, and outright lying* – could become more ethical if practitioners and corporate executives could take activist stances inside and outside their organizations. Particularly, Holtzhausen (2000) equates the role of the postmodern philosopher with that of the public relations practitioner, in stressing the agency of communication practitioners to serve as change agents, articulate and give force to the conscience of their organization, and empower the marginalized in society.

Some scholars have expressed the view that postmodernism has sparked significant social changes in different forms of culture, state, politics, work organization, science, and technology (Boyne & Rottansi, 1990; Crook et al., 1992; Featherstone, 1991; Lyotard, 1989). CEO activism may well be indicative of changes from the modernist view to the postmodern in how CEOs deal with some of the biggest and most contentious issues of the day.

To illustrate such shifts in the internal and external operating contexts of organizations, it would be apt to briefly recapitulate some philosophical differences between the *modern* and the *postmodern*, especially as they relate to corporate sociopolitical involvement. In general, the modernist approach to corporations prioritizes a management discourse by emphasizing corporate goals and objectives as given, legitimate, and the primary driver of every ebb and flow of corporate actions (Deetz, 2001).

Under the modernist view, every organizational action and function is gauged according to economic indices such as profitability, return on investment, contribution to shareholder value, and other "rational economic goals" (Deetz, 2001, p. 19). The mission of the modernist approach is also the creation and establishment of "an orderly, well-integrated world, with compliant members and regulated conflicts, (which) has accepted without examination organizational goals and member positions" (Deetz, 2001, p. 19).

The modernist view stresses the importance of the strategic management function, consensus-building, networks, power, strategic message development, systems approaches, functionalism, and total quality management (Holtzhausen & Voto, 2002). This modernist view is the dominant paradigm in media and communication, strategic management, public relations, and brand management. It is the mainstream approach to organizational studies in North America and most Western countries (Deetz, 2001; Hatch, 1997; Hatch & Cunliffe, 2006; Miller, 2012), and seeks universal explanations, approaching "the status of natural laws" (Hatch, 1997, p. 44).

In response to the modernist focus on single dominant perspectives and metanarratives (Lyotard, 1988), postmodernism emphasizes that there is no central postmodern theory (Holtzhausen & Voto, 2002). Postmodernism thrives in diversity, multiplicity, pastiches, assemblages, and bricolages by even critiquing its very own theoretical perspectives. To Lyotard, "Theories themselves are concealed narratives (and) we should not be taken by their claim to be valid for all times" (Lyotard, 1988, p. 126). Postmodernism is a unique discourse that high-lights such issues as the nexus between knowledge and power, dissensus rather than consensus, and "micropolitical processes and the joined nature of power and resistance" (Deetz, 2001, p. 31).

Postmodern philosophy arose in France, especially from philosophers such as Lyotard, Derrida, Foucault, Baudrillard, Deleuze and Guattari, and Laclau and Mouffe. These philosophers provide an alternative lens through which society in general (Holtzhausen, 2000), and for the purposes of this research study, CEO activism could be analyzed. Such fresh perspectives would not only provide a different interpretation of the experiences of activist CEOs in Ghana but may well serve to contest some of the extant modernist accounts of CEO activism.

One of the areas in which postmodernism is impacting corporate communi-cations is in the area of activism (Holtzhausen & Voto, 2002), and Dozier and Lauzen (2000) believe that the action of corporate activists is generating funda-mental changes in society through "deconstruction and reconstruction of the social order" (p. 14) since corporate activists are loyal to a cause, rather than to a particular organization. Holtzhausen (2000) calls on corporate executives, particularly public relations practitioners to take activist stances within their organizations (but also outside them), and "serve as the conscience of the orga-nization, and give voice to those without power" (Holtzhausen & Voto, 2002, p. 60).

The poor image of some corporations can, in part, be attributable to modernist expectations of corporations and top echelon behavior that runs counter to the realities of the postmodern society (Banerjee, 2008; Holtzhausen & Voto, 2002). To Duggar (1989) (as cited by Banerjee, 2008, p. 51), for instance: "In the corporate economies of the contemporary West, the market is a passive institu-tion. The active institution is the corporation ... and inherently narrow and shortsighted organization .... The corporation has evolved to serve the interests of whoever controls it, at the expense of who[m]ever does not." Thus, by serving the narrow interests of investors/shareholders, corporations, their brands, and executives have been cited for greed, poor ethics, and diverse dubious practices (Banerjee, 2008).

A postmodern lens would likely help to provide a different understanding of the evolving role of CEOs in organizations as activists. Such perspectives would aid the understanding of evolving social roles of organizations, and how CEOs are serving the wider social interests as activists. Influenced by Holtzhausen (2000) and Holtzhausen and Voto (2002), I argue that several postmodernist theoretical threads apply to this research study. These are the notions of (i) organizational politics, (ii) micropolitics and alliances, (iii) postmodern biopower, (iv) dissensus and dissymmetry, and (v) the concepts of local and situational ethics and decision-making. The next sections discuss these postmodern concepts, including their perceived applicability to the phenomenon of CEO activism.

### 1.7.1 Organizational Politics

According to Spicer (1997), when an organization is conceived of as a political system, power then becomes a critical resource. The concept of organizations as political actors focuses on strategic organizational relationships and linkages, strategic constituents, and alliances, as shaped by conflict, power, and resistance to or desire for change (Deetz, 1992; Lyotard, 1992).

Power perspectives in corporate communications highlight the need for corporate executives to seek to become part of the dominant coalition (Dozier et al., 1995). However, postmodern perspectives on corporate communication tend not to necessarily see corporate executives as aligning themselves with the interests of the dominant power centers in the organization (Holtzhausen & Voto, 2002), such as shareholders and boards of directors.

Members of the top echelons of organizations, working as activists, will thus tend to "resist authoritative, organizational power structures even when they themselves are part of the dominant coalition" (Holtzhausen & Voto, 2002, p. 61). They will use other sources of power, such as personal characteristics, expertise, and opportunity to obtain power and drive for positive change (Williams, 1998). While the normal direction of authoritative power in organizations is downwards, postmodern power is multidirectional (Hatch, 1997; Hatch & Cunliffe, 2006), including serving the needs of multiple stakeholders (Ofori-Parku, 2015).

### 1.7.2 Micropolitics and Alliances

Power at the macro level is fed only by power networks at the micro level that work in ways to support micropolitics (Best & Kellner, 1991; Foucault, 1980). Thus, political actors who strive for power for positive change must seek to first build their power bases by forming alliances at the microlevel (Baudrillard, 1975; Holtzhausen & Voto, 2002).

The postmodern view that micropolitics is built on the pillars of micropolitical power bases could be instrumental to our understanding of CEO activism. Modernist power permeates every web and tissue of society and micropolitical power, including the family, educational institutions, religious systems, business, and state organizations (Althusser, 1971; Deleuze & Guattari, 1983; Foucault, 1980). To give some fighting chances for their advocacy campaigns, corporate executives must first seek out and identify zones of micropolitical power within their organizations, form alliances and coalitions with like-minded people and groups who can assist them in their activism campaigns, and thus be influential within their organizations, but also externally (Spicer, 1997).

Chatterji and Toffel (2018) suggest that activist CEOs should consult their executive teams, including chief communication officers. Such a "kitchen cabinet" should help decide on what matters to them and why, reflect on when to weigh in, agree on campaign tactics, perform vulnerability audits, decide on messaging strategy, and debriefing. Forming alliances not only with external coalitions but also internally with other organizational functions such as research and development, finance and accounting, human resources, and strategic planning (Hatch,

1997; Hatch & Cunliffe, 2006) could be a typical postmodern CEO activist behavior.

### 1.7.3 Postmodern Biopower

Organizational power play depends on the inner power, or biopower, of the individual to feel empowered to resist subjugation and social injustice (Holtzhausen & Voto, 2002), based on the conception of the individual as a conscious participant, imbued with the power to oppose micropower (Foucault, 1988a, 1988b; Lyotard, 1993a). In postmodernism, power is innately regarded as being for positive ends, but such power must be biopower that is employed to resist the dominating genres of power (Holtzhausen & Voto, 2002).

The centrality of the purpose of power in organizations to be employed to resist marginalization of sections of society emanates from the postmodern philosophy that domination is perpetuated when people come to accept as routine their subjugation and domination by power (Holtzhausen & Voto, 2002). Resistance to the marginalizing tendencies of society by activist CEOs, I believe, could explain this postmodern behavior of CEOs. Such postmodern CEO activists could well be working to get their organizations and the dominant/modernist power centers within them to become activists by resisting the deleterious exercise of power in society in general.

> Organizations that take on government policies that harm the environment or take a stand on behalf of marginalized social groups will be a typical example of such activism. Perhaps, the best-known example is the international Benetton Group with its outspoken stance on issues such as the death penalty.
> (Holtzhausen & Voto, 2002, p. 63)

### 1.7.4 Dissensus and Dissymmetry

Dissensus and dissymmetry have been cited as significant sources and drivers of change that can generate innovative ideas and creative solutions to social problems (Docherty, 1993; Lyotard, 1992, 1993a). Consensus yields diverse forms of social injustice since it is bourgeoise that determines the outcomes of consensus (Lyotard, 1988). By working for the status quo and consensus, corporate executives who choose not to engage in corporate activism would only be working to reaffirm the position of the powerful (Holtzhausen & Voto, 2002).

Innovativeness and creativity are the fruits of dissensus (Lyotard, 1992), generated through "tensors" (Lyotard, 1993b, p. 54), events that entail dissenting voices. Thus, the postmodern communications and other corporate executives would exercise dissensus by identifying tensors/points of discord or dissonance between their organizations (mission, vision, values, and related world views) and the internal and external strategic stakeholders (Holtzhausen, 2000). This way, corporate executives could engender the creation and promotion of "situations in which new meaning is produced through difference and opposition" (p. 107).

### *1.7.5 Local and Situational Ethics and Decision-Making*

Their modus operandi is for postmodernists to oppose philosophical and theoretical metanarratives (Lyotard, 1992) while pushing for instant action for a new social order (Eribon, 1991; Foucault, 1980; Williams, 1998). Postmodernists oppose metanarratives and "foundations" (Deetz, 2001, p. 34) because it is the ideology and hegemony of dominant power structures that serve to entrench, routinize, and legitimize bourgeoise privileged positions of the that are unjust to those living on the margins of society such as women and ethnic minorities (Holtzhausen & Voto, 2002).

By immediate action, Foucault (1980) and Lyotard (1984) serve to indicate that the local situation determines the best and most humane course of action. Both Foucault and Lyotard advocate for immediate individual antiestablishment action, in favor of ethically responsible moves (Küng, 1992). Postmodernist ethical decision-making is sympathetic to "particularism," based on the complexities and contingencies of specific situations, rather than on the "universalism" and the standard of social norms of right and wrong (Adler, 1997, p. 59). This is because social norms are usually unjust and only privilege the powerful in society.

## 1.8 Concept of Corporate Social Advocacy

Activism entails efforts by social actors and institutions to promote, impede, or direct sociopolitical, economic, and environmental reforms or stasis, to improve society (Kotler & Sarkar, 2017). Activism is essentially the process of exerting political pressure to change policies (Smith, 2013) and campaigning for change regarding sociopolitical issues (Council of Europe, 2017). Activism involves various tactics, including letters to politicians and the media, political campaigns, rallies, marches, strikes, sit-ins, and even economic boycotts (Kotler & Sarkar, 2017).

Wettstein and Baur (2016) note that etymologically, advocacy is based on the past participle of the Latin verb *advocare*, referring to a call on others for help. They further note that it is "also contained in the term is the Latin word for voice (vox)" (p. 200). In effect, *advocacy* involves an act of promoting and voicing support for an individual, organization, or idea, and working to persuade others to embrace such individuals, organizations, or ideas (Edgett, 2002). Thus, by extension, corporate political advocacy entails a corporation voicing and making explicit public support for an individual, organization, or idea to persuade others to do the same (Wettstein & Baur, 2016).

In their effort to capture the evolving nature of corporate activism, Dodd and Supa (2014) took a sociological path, apparently to reflect the sociocultural expressions of present-day corporate activism. Dodd and Supa (2014, 2015) conceptualize CSA as organizational stances on sociopolitical issues. Brands such as Ford, Microsoft, Starbucks, Barilla, and Chick-fil-A have engaged in CSA (Dodd & Supa, 2014). For instance, companies and their leaders have taken public stances on such issues as gay marriage, healthcare reform, and emergency contraception.

CSA may be spearheaded by several corporate actors, including corporations as such (corporate activism), CEOs (CEO activism), shareholders (shareholder/investor activism), brands (brand activism), and other corporate executives (see Fig. 1 below). Thus, the literature on corporate activism/advocacy contains at least these notable labels/classifications.

## 1.9 Business Chieftains in Ghana Fight for the Common Good

In Ghana, both men and women CEO activists engage in various forms of activism. CEOs have taken public stances on an increasing array of contentious issues within contemporary Ghanaian society. Such issues have included the planned introduction of Comprehensive Sexuality Education (CSE) in the elementary, junior high, and senior high schools in 2019, financial and economic crimes, political vigilantism, media freedom, public finance and economic mismanagement, and educational reforms, among other issues.

While some CEOs in the country have engaged in solo activism campaigns, others have done so as a group. Present-day activists in Ghana include Charles Wereko-Brobbey (media freedom and plurality; national economic management); Kenneth Thompson (economic mismanagement of the national resources); David Ampofo (social injustice and political reforms), Emmanuel Awumee (youth empowerment); Dr. Kwesi Nduom (poverty alleviation, wealth creation, and jobs); and Kenneth Ashigbey (environmental protection). Kofi Bentil is CEO of

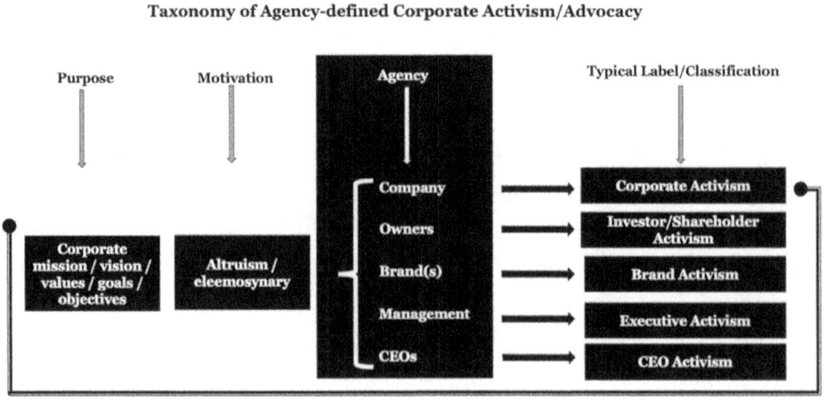

Fig. 1.    Taxonomy of Agency-Defined Corporate Activism/Advocacy.
*Source:* Author (2023).

law and business advisory firm, Lex Praxis. Bentil has been advocating for various civil rights issues, including the Right to Information Bill, better economic management, governmental transparency and accountability, and environmental conservation. Senyo Hosi, CEO of the Ghana Chamber of Bulk Oil Distributors (GCBOD), has been taking public stances on economic and social development matters in Ghana.

Some women have broken the glass ceiling and now serve as CEOs of diverse organizations in Ghana (IFC, 2018) and are playing activist roles as CEOs by mobilizing not only as individuals but also as groups to challenge and change their socioeconomic and political situations (Badri & Tripp, 2017). These have included Juliet Yaa Asantewaa Asante (political party vigilantes and election-related violence).

Others are some leading members of diverse professional women's groupings, including the EWN, Women in Media (Ghana), Women in Broadcasting (WIB), and Women in Public Relations (Ghana). These professional women include Edith Dankwa (Group CEO of the Business & Financial Times Group), Lucy Quist (former CEO of telecommunications company Airtel Ghana, and founder and current CEO of business advisory firm Quist Blue Diamond), Patience Akyianu (former Managing Director of Barclays Bank Ghana, and currently the Group CEO of insurance group Hollard Ghana), and Dzigbordi Dosoo (CEO of beauty and wellness group Allure Ghana).

Others are Yvette Atekpe (Regional Managing Director of Internet Solutions Ghana), Esther Cobbah (CEO of communications advisory firm StratCom Africa), Maidie Arkutu (Chairman & Managing Director, Unilever Francophone Africa), Pearl Esua-Mensah (CEO of the Ghana Deposit Protection Corporation, and President of Ashesi University Ghana), Dr. Joyce Aryee (former CEO of the Ghana Chamber of Mines), Fredua Duplan (former CEO of Nestle Ghana, and current CEO of Nestle Pakistan), and Sheila Minkah-Premo (Managing Consultant at Apex Law consult Ghana).

Oheneyere Gifty Anti, CEO of GDA Concepts, a media production company has been advocating for improved social protection and inclusivity in Ghana. For well over a decade now, she has been producing and transmitting a television program called "The Stand-Point" that has become an advocacy platform for the vulnerable in the Ghanaian society.

These women are driven to empower women in Ghana to increase their influence and participation not only in Ghana but also internationally. They work to influence and drive policy changes that increase the representation of women in senior leadership positions in Ghana while promoting women's rights in support of the United Nation's Sustainable Development Goal Five (5) on gender equality and empowerment for all women and girls.

Generally, these CEOs have seen the need to publicly speak up about diverse sociopolitical matters while seeking to drive change from their high perches atop the C-suite. Even when such activist CEOs in Ghana such as Kenneth Thompson weigh in on economic issues facing the nation, it appears that the objective is not only to help engender a more business-friendly economic system in Ghana but also to see the government pursuing sound economic policies that would spur economic growth and produce better life chances and improved quality of life for the generality of Ghanaians.

These activist CEOs are motivated to seek the greater good. As the incidence of CEO activism may be new in most non-Western parts of the globe (Chatterji & Toffel, 2016), one can argue that the phenomenon may not be so new in Ghana since it may well be a modern reexpression of age-old elements of the Ghanaian/African cultural values. Could an effort to reminisce about such ancient African cultural traits effectively navigate us in the direction of a glorious future for CEO activism?

## 1.10 Collecting and Analyzing Data for This Book

The use of qualitative methods is the logical choice for an exploratory study to gain a better understanding and build a foundation upon which further empirical studies can be conducted (Malhotra & Grover, 1998). Hence, this study employed semistructured interviews because of the nascency of the phenomenon of CEO activism (Wettstein & Baur, 2016) and the researchers' goal to inductively and interpretively examine (Daymon & Holloway, 2002) the CEO activism tactics question.

### 1.10.1 Data Sources and Data Collection

Overall, some 24 purposively selected business executives in Ghana served as our informants (See mini profiles of the study participants in Table 1 below). The interviews were semistructured conversations (Brinkman, 2018) with the selected collaborators, conducted over the course of three separate data collection phases. The pilot study involved seven CEOs in 2018, a main data gathering phase in 2019 featuring 17 CEO collaborators, and a mop up exercise between December 2020 and January 2021 involving 12 informants from the previous two phases. All the participants were Ghanaians. The use of multiple subjects facilitated the identification of common themes and patterns and the triangulation of findings while reducing response bias from any one participant.

The research instruments were supervised and approved by the Human Subjects Board of the University of Oregon, which permitted participants' self-identifying information to be published in research reports so long as participants consented. While all participants agreed (and many demanded) to have their identities disclosed and their sayings attributed to them, I have decided to anonymize all participants in this book. Considering the lack of formal institutional structures and the potential for reprisals against dissenting voices within the African context, this decision is purely out of an abundance of caution to safeguard the identities, safety, and business interests of the participants. The participants were treated as collaborators, coinvestigators, informants, and cocreators of this inquiry (May, 1980), rather than subjects.

### 1.10.2 Inclusion Criteria and Sampling Procedure

The selection/inclusion criteria required that participants be (i) men and women CEOs who are leading/have led companies that operate in Ghana (be they

Ghanaian nationals or not) and (ii) who have embarked on some form of CEO activism in Ghana within between 2014 and 2019. This defined the purposive sampling method in selecting participants who met the study criteria. Although a five-year CEO activism timescale was originally set, it emerged that some of the participants identified had longer activist CEO track records.

The purposive sampling strategy yielded an initial list of participants who met the selection criteria. Snowball sampling supplemented the participants' pool, where informants recommended others who met the inclusion criteria. We kept an open-ended sample size and added participants until data saturation was reached.

The pilot study sought to ascertain the extent to which CEO activism was observable in Ghana. The focus of the pilot study was to gather preliminary data on the phenomenon from an identified group of both men and women activist CEOs and to identify more participants through snowball sampling. The procedure started with an initial search to identify a corps of CEO activists who met the inclusion criteria. This was done through Internet searches focusing on CEOs who have embarked on such campaigns. We also used personal contacts in Ghana to identify some participants.

Purposive sampling produced an initial group of seven CEO activists who were interviewed during the pilot phase. All interviews took place within face-to-face contexts at participants' offices, with the exception of one participant who was interviewed over *Skype*, since they were traveling internationally. The interviews ranged between 30 minutes and 45 minutes in duration and were digitally recorded. The audio recordings were each transcribed, prepared for data analysis, and subsequently analyzed manually in a systematic manner consistent with qualitative research techniques (Huberman & Miles, 1994; Miles & Huberman, 1984).

Lessons learned from the pilot study helped to not only validate the interview question guide but also produced refinements for the subsequent data collection phase. For instance, we learned during the pilot phase that although participants had previously engaged in such actions, participants were unfamiliar with the term "CEO activism" (some described it as their "personal" CSR). Thus, we decided to include a set of formal definitions and examples of CEO activism from America, the African continent, and the nation of Ghana at the start of each interview session during the subsequent phases, in order to establish a common frame of reference for the discussions. It is interesting to note that some of the exemplars involved some of the study participants.

### 1.10.3 Main Data Collection

This phase sought to build on the participant pool from the pilot study and delve deeper into collecting insights from more participants, using a more focused interview protocol, until data saturation was achieved. Once identified, prospective informants were contacted through emails and phone calls to brief them about the study's purpose and gauge their willingness to participate. Some were contacted through their social media accounts.

Prospective participants who expressed the desire to be interviewed were emailed formal invitation letters, issued on official letterheads of the University of Oregon School of Journalism and Communication for added credence and formality. Interview sessions were then scheduled with each participant.

Data collection involved semistructured face-to-face interviews with participants. The qualitative interview is a purpose-driven conversation between the
researcher and the informant (Englander, 2012), to discuss various experiences,
issues, and themes (Denzin & Lincoln, 2018), describe the lived experiences of
interviewees, and illuminate the essence of the phenomenon under investigation
(Brinkman & Kvale, 2015).

During this phase, we collected data from 17 CEO activists, comprising nine
women and eight men. All interviews were conducted in English, based on an
interview guide that covered the major themes, while containing prompts for
follow-up questions and deeper probing. These interviews averaged 60 minutes
and were digitally recorded. Journals were maintained for taking field notes. A
cut-point was reached on December 12, 2020, because data saturation point had
been reached.

### *1.10.4 Data Analysis*

The conversations with informants in this study produced digitally recorded
narratives, which were transcribed verbatim and carefully prepared for data
analysis based on the human science approach of van Manen (2016). Data
analysis sought to systematically interrogate the data and organize the voices of
informants according to the research question. In a qualitative study, data
analysis involves studying, categorizing, tabulating, and otherwise recombining
evidence to ascertain meaning related to the study's initial objectives and research
questions (Eisenhardt, 1989; Yin, 1994).

Data analysis followed the hermeneutic phenomenological thematic method
that organized the voices of the collaborators and rhetorically interrogated their
sayings, based on the research question (van Manen, 2016). An open coding
system was employed to compare the similarities and differences in patterns of
data collected (Corbin & Strauss, 1990).

## 1.11 Mini Profiles of Study Participants

Table 1. Summary of Study Participants.

| Participants | Sex Self-Identification | Age Range | Industry/Sector | Estimated Tenure as CEO |
|---|---|---|---|---|
| Participant #1 | Woman CEO | 45–50 years | Media and Communication | 16 years |
| Participant #2 | Woman CEO | 45–50 years | Banking and Finance; Business Advisory; Telecommunications | 12 years |

Table 1. *(Continued)*

| Participants | Sex Self-Identification | Age Range | Industry/Sector | Estimated Tenure as CEO |
|---|---|---|---|---|
| Participant #3 | Woman CEO | 50–55 years | Television Production | 15 years |
| Participant #4 | Man CEO | 55–60 years | Petroleum; Strategic Communications | 26 years |
| Participant #5 | Man CEO | 60–65 years | Leasing and Finance | 15 years |
| Participant #6 | Man CEO | 45–50 years | Telecommunications Advocacy; Media Management | 10 years |
| Participant #7 | Man CEO | 45–50 years | Car Care Consult; Social Enterprise | 20 years |
| Participant #8 | Man CEO | 50–55 years | Legal and Business Advisory | 15 years |
| Participant #9 | Woman CEO | 50–55 years | Banking and Insurance | 8 years |
| Participant #10 | Man CEO | 50–55 years | Legal Advisory | 26 years |
| Participant #11 | Woman CEO | 45–50 years | Power and Energy | 10 years |
| Participant #12 | Man CEO | 65–70 years | Power and Energy | 30 years |
| Participant #13 | Woman CEO | 45–50 years | Film and Television Production; Streaming Services; Film Festival | 15 years |
| Participant #14 | Man CEO | 40–45 years | Oil and Gas Advocacy | 8 years |
| Participant #15 | Woman CEO | 40–45 years | Media and Communication; Tourism and Leisure Advocacy | 3 years |
| Participant #16 | Man CEO | 50–55 years | Commercial Printing; Self-Help, Motivation, and Business Advisory | 26 years |
| Participant #17 | Woman CEO | 45–50 years | Small Business Advisory; Catering | 23 years |

Table 1. *(Continued)*

| Participants | Sex Self-Identification | Age Range | Industry/Sector | Estimated Tenure as CEO |
|---|---|---|---|---|
| Participant #18 | Man CEO | 50–55 years | Banking Advocacy; Wealth Management; Banking | 6 years |
| Participant #19 | Woman CEO | 35–40 years | Information Technology Services | 4 years |
| Participant #20 | Man CEO | 55–60 years | Accounting, Auditing, and Business Advisory | 11 years |
| Participant #21 | Woman CEO | 40–45 years | Strategic Communication; Chocolate and Confectionary | 14 years |
| Participant #22 | Man CEO | 60–65 years | Petroleum; Banking | 20 years |
| Participant #23 | Woman CEO | 50–55 years | Banking Deposit Protection; Business Advisory | 10 years |
| Participant #24 | Woman CEO | 50–55 years | Agribusiness | 15 years |

## 1.12 Toward a Postmodern Communicology of CEO Activism

Against this theoretical background, this research study is aiming to extend the postmodern organizational activist perspectives of Holtzhausen (2000) and Holtzhausen and Voto (2002) in helping profile the postmodern CEO as a distinctive organizational archetype.

This study examines whether activist CEOs are serving as the conscience of their organizations (as well as of their personal brands) by resisting dominant power structures (especially when such structures are unjust and do not promote diversity and social inclusivity), and preferences employees and external stakeholders' discourses over that of their organizations and investors.

Activist CEOs could be expected to make the most humane decisions regarding their advocacies, given the specifics of the situation, and they would promote new ways of thinking and solving problems through overt dissensus and conflict, while contributing to a culture of free and frank communication, liberation and emancipation inside and outside of their organizations.

## 1.13 Conceptual Framework: Toward a Process Model of CEO Activism

Recently, some scholars called for a deeper consideration of process studies in organization and management, focusing on the importance of "temporality, activity, and flow" in addressing "questions about how managerial and organizational phenomena emerge, change, and unfold over time" (Langley et al., 2013, p. 1). These scholars characterize the uniqueness of "process studies" as concerning the explication of the emergence, development, growth, and termination of issues, phenomena, and questions.

Taking an evolutionary stance, process research intentionally adopts traces of the "temporal progressions of activities as elements of explanation and understanding" (Langley et al., 2013, p. 1). By privileging the importance and ubiquity of time in human and organizational processes, Langley and colleagues argue that process conceptualizations could "offer an essential contribution to organizational and management knowledge that is not available from most variance-based generalizations" (p. 4) which tend to currently dominate the field. Essentially, variance-focused research orientation has the propinquity to completely ignore the influence of time, reduce its effect to one of lagging consequences, melding the influence of time with other variables, or generally fail to assign the right level of significance to time (Langley et al., 2013).

However, process research is based on the philosophy that of significant importance in organizational life is the element of temporality, with process questions having both academic and practical utility (Langley et al., 2013). This book adopts a process ontology in conceptualizing the phenomenon of CEO activism as:

> ...a form of practice continually constituted and adapted through ongoing 'values work' enacted by organization members ... context is not something that is held constant and outside the changes being analyzed but is itself continually reconstructed within and by the process of interaction over time ... generating unexpected and largely uncontrollable chain of activity and events in which actors, environments, and organizations are all in constant and mutually interacting flux.
>
> (Langley et al., 2013, p. 5)

At the heart of this book is a conceptual framework dubbed the "CEO Activism Development Model," which serves as a major organizing principle of the contents of this book (see Fig. 2 on next page for its basic form). A road map for the book, this model lays out the author's conception of the interrelationships among several concepts in the development of CEO activism, based on the process ontology (Langley et al., 2013). In taking this point of departure, this "CEO Activism Development Model" seeks to explain the temporal process of how and why CEOs develop the activist stance.

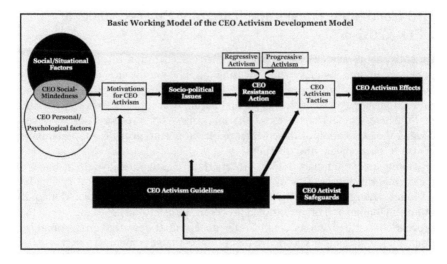

Fig. 2.   A Basic Working Model of the CEO Activism Development Model. *Source:* Author (2023).

This conceptual framework focuses on CEO activism as a distinct form of corporate sociopolitical involvement and highlights the major junctures working together to occasion the development of CEO sociopolitical activism, including factors undergirding the generation of the desire for activism, delimitation of issues and causes, deployment of tactics, and the difference made by the activities of CEO activists.

Based on not only the review of the current literature on CEO activism and cognate fields but also my reflection of the field, it is my considered view that the main epochs in the development of CEO activism include (i) motivations for CEO activism, (ii) selection of issues/causes by activist CEOs, (iii) deployment of tactics of activist campaigns, (iv) production of effects or outcomes of campaigns, and based on the nature of such effects, (v) the adoption of safeguards to insulate CEO activists from undesirable ramifications occasioned by their actions.

Based on this expectation of the flow of factors, this book is designed to focus on the generation of empirical data on five clusters within these complex linkages: motivations for CEO activism (Chapter 3 and Chapter 4), (ii) CEO activism issues (Chapter 5), (iii) CEO activism tactics (Chapter 6), (iv) CEO activism effects (Chapter 7), CEO activism safeguards (Chapter 8), and CEO activism guidelines (Chapter 9).

### *1.13.1 Illuminating the Basic Conceptual Model*

The literature suggests that the genesis of CEO activism occurs within the context of the production of a certain level of social-mindedness within the CEO, as a complex web of social and situational factors interact with some personal and psychological factors within the CEO. While typically, CEOs have not been concerned with wider social issues that do not impact on the profitability of companies, the resultant social mindedness serves to condition some CEOs to start thinking in a wider sociocultural fashion, by considering noncorporate issues and the needs of multiple stakeholders besides investors/shareholders.

When this wider social mindedness is strong enough, it leads to the development of some appetite or motivation for engaging in CEO activism. While some segments of the literature on CEO activism have suggested what some motivations, there is no existing typology of factors that could be regarded as motivating CEO activists generally, but especially within developing countries. Thus, Chapter 3 and Chapter 4 focus on addressing this scholarly lacuna by gathering and presenting data on the motivations of CEOs for becoming/engaging in CEO activism in Ghana.

Once motivated to undertake CEO activism, the literature on CEO activism suggests that the next step would be for CEOs to select a range of sociopolitical issues that would serve as the fulcrum for their activism. Kotler and Sarkar (2017, 2018a) posit that there are six broad classes of such issues that a brand could advocate. In their brand activism typology, these scholars identified political issues, social issues, economic issues, legal issues, environmental issues, and business/workplace issues. Such a typology of the classes of brand activism could be adapted and extended to CEO activism. Thus, the focus of Chapter 5 is to examine the extent to which the range of issues that activist CEOs selected for this study in Ghana could fit these brand activism categories/clusters postulated by Kotler and Sarkar (2017, 2018a).

Once a CEO has identified an issue or a range of issues on which to pivot his/her activism, the main thrust of the CEO's resistance posture/action is generated. As explained earlier in the literature review, brand activism could be regressive or progressive, depending on how such an action is perceived as working to promote the interests of society. Progressive activism entails those actions that are perceived to be contributing to the improvement of society, while regressive activism are those actions deemed to set back society's advancement.

However, the implementation of a CEO resistance action follows some tactics. While Chatterji and Toffel (2018) discussed tactics relating to raising awareness and leveraging economic power, Livonen (2018) isolated the three classes of approaches as persuasive tactics, disruptive/coercive tactics, and support tactics. Thus, the focus of Chapter 6 is to examine the range of tactics employed by activist CEOs in Ghana who were selected for inclusion in this study.

The next web of factors in this model concerns the effects of engaging in CEO activism. What outcomes are produced by the works of CEO activists? What difference is made by activist CEOs? What are the consequences of engaging in CEO activism for society, companies, and the activist CEO? Based on fieldwork, some scholars have identified some outcomes produced by CEO activism. However, these have all been within Western (American) contexts. What are the achievements and consequences of CEO activism in Ghana? The object of

Chapter 7 is to investigate the effects, positive and negative consequences of CEO activism in Ghanaian society, but also on companies and activist CEOs in Ghana.

Within this conceptual framework, CEO activism is conceived as producing two distinct classes of outcomes – toxic/desirable and tonic/undesirable. Negative outcomes are those undesirable consequences, while positive outcomes are relatively desirable results of CEO activism. It is argued that owing to their undesirable impact, CEO activists would employ a range of safeguards to insulate themselves and their companies from the effects of being CEO activists. The focus of Chapter 8 thus is to investigate the various types of safeguards employed by activist CEOs in Ghana.

The final point in this conceptual framework relates to guidelines for engaging in CEO activism. Positive effects for CEO activism are conceived as directly informing guidelines for CEO activism, while negative effects/consequences are first filtered through safeguards, on the way to informing guidelines for future actions, as discussed in Chapter 9. The nature of the guidelines then determines future motivations for engaging in CEO activism, the choice of future issues/ causes, the nature of future actions, and future tactics employed.

## 1.14 Research Questions

Most studies on CEO activism have been focused on activist CEOs in the United States. Thus, the goal of the research is to undertake an interpretive examination of CEO activism in Ghana, focusing on the activism and lived experiences of activist CEOs in the country. The research questions focus on unearthing the meaning and lived experiences of being an activist CEO in Ghana, including characteristics, motivations, activities, and significant differences between men and women activist CEOs in Ghana.

While companies are increasingly serving as advocates on a wide range of issues that may not be directly related to the profitability of companies, it has been noted that CEOs are becoming a popular agent for the expression of such CSA (Dodd & Supa, 2014). Although some reasons have been proffered for CEO activism, most of these supposed motives have been postulations, not backed by empirical sayings or assertions of CEO activists.

Again, the literature is currently nonexistent regarding the motivations for CEO activists in the Global South. Do the same motives that have been suggested for CEO activists in America serve as the drivers for CEO activists in a developing country such as Ghana? Are there some deeper philosophical, personal, and values-based drivers for engaging in CEO activism in Ghana? What new perspectives could the explication for the motivations for CEO activism inform our understanding of CEO activism generally? To what extent could such notions as Caritas, postmodernism, Ubuntu philosophy, and Africapitalism be regarded as serving as motivations for CEO activism in Ghana? These considerations inform the first research question:

### *1.14.1 What Are the Motivations of CEOs in Ghana for Engaging in CEO Activism?*

While some current studies on the emerging phenomenon of corporate sociopolitical involvement have somewhat deepened our understanding of aspects of the issue, there is still a whole lot more to learn about CEO activism (Chatterji & Toffel, 2018). There is no clear typology for talking about the classes of issues that CEO activists generally concern themselves with. To what extent can the brand activism typology of Kotler and Sarkar (2018a) apply to CEO activism? Do activist CEOs in Africa advocate for the same issues/causes as CEOs in Western societies? The focus of second research question is to address some perceived gaps in knowledge regarding the range or nature of issues for CEO activists in Ghana: *What range of sociopolitical issues do CEO activists in Ghana focus on?*

Livonen (2018) and Chatterji and Toffel (2018) have suggested some approaches (strategies and tactics) employed by CEO activists in their social resistance actions, based mainly on their observations of the works of CEO activists. The next research question concentrates on providing an empirical outlining of the tactics employed by CEO activists, presented from the "inside-out" perspective of activist CEOs in Ghana. To what extent do the CEO activism tactics fit into the extant postulations, such as those of Chatterj and Toffel (2018) and Livonen (2018)? Given that these postulations were derived from the Western sociocultural context, I strongly believe that they would not exactly describe the tactical repertoire of a non-Western society such as Ghana. What tactics are adopted by the informants in this study? Such concerns inform the third research question: *What tactics do CEO activists in Ghana employ in their resistance actions?*

The current literature on CEO activism reports on some effects of the phenomenon. Taking a principally modernist view that privileges investors and corporate interests, the focus has been on the effects of CEO activism on some organizational outcomes, including customers' purchase intents (Dodd & Supa, 2014; Weber Shandwick, 2017), public opinion, and employee loyalty and employee resonance (Chatterji & Toffel, 2017).

Currently, there has been no clear research findings on the role of social or community-wide effects of CEO activism generally, especially within emerging market contexts of Africa. Applying a postmodern perspective that stands open to dissensus and multiple stakeholder perspectives, this book explores the views of CEO activists regarding the perceived effects of their social resistance actions on diverse stakeholders. From the perspective of CEO activists, what could be said to be the effect of CEO activism on society? Are there any consequences – positive or negative – of engaging in CEO activism for CEO activists? Does CEO activism lead to separate consequences for men and women CEOs in Ghana?

While sections of the extant CSR literature look at the consequences of engaging in CSR, I expect that the effects of CEO activism would be quite different from what we now know. This is so, not only because of some peculiarities of engaging in CEO activism generally but also because of the situational dynamics and the context of Ghana. Such considerations undergird the fourth research question of this book: *What effects have been produced by the resistance actions of CEO activists in Ghana?*

Some scholars have contemplated some of the consequences of CEO activism on CEOs who choose to serve as social activists. Some of these consequences have been described as not desirable for CEOs. While CEO activism is expected to become a global phenomenon, there is currently a gap in knowledge about how the phenomenon is shaping up in the developing world. Given the possible impact on businesses and CEO activists, what range of measures are taken by CEO activists to protect themselves?

Based on qualitative interviews, Chatterji and Toffel (2019b) suggest that CEOs activists could minimize some of the negative effects of their actions by paying heed to *when* they communicate and *how* they communicate. Are communication-related safeguards the only avenues open to CEO activists? Are the negative consequences of CEO activism only occasioned by communication challenges? What other safeguard options could be open to CEO activists? How does the sociocultural milieu in Ghana inform the safeguards employed by CEO activists in the country? These are some of the considerations that shaped the final research question in this study: *What safeguards do activist CEOs in Ghana employ to insulate themselves from the pushback they face because of their resistance actions?*

Thus, overall, the five (5) main research questions for this book have been presented, bearing in mind the specific sociocultural, economic, legal, and political context of Ghana. These research questions seek to illuminate significant links in the conceptual framework of CEO activism development, which explains key issues in the development of the activist stance by CEOs in Ghana.

Chapter 2

# Doing Well to Do Good: A Quick Map of the Field of Corporate Sociopolitical Involvement

## 2.1 Introduction

This chapter presents a review of relevant sections of the literature on corporate social advocacy. This includes discussions of several concepts that are related to corporate social advocacy. Important similarities and distinctions among the several concepts are examined, noting especially why the differences should matter to both scholars and practitioners. Some of the cognate concepts discussed include Corporate Social Responsibility (CSR), Sustainability, Political Corporate Social Responsibility (PCSR), Corporate Political Activity (CPA), Brand Responsibility (BR), Brand Activism (BA), Corporate Social Advocacy, and Chief Executive Officer (CEO) activism.

## 2.2 Corporate Sociopolitical Involvement

Historically, corporations and their brands have sought to gain competitive advantage and market dominance based purely on brand performance and the ability to exceed customer expectations (Kotler & Sarkar, 2017). However, owing to the fierce competitive clime in most markets, brand performance is no longer enough to assure a competitive advantage (Sarkar, 2019).

Traditional brand positioning strategies have become increasingly ineffective, due to several present-day market imperatives and factors, including higher concerns and expectations of significant market segments, such as Millennials and members of Generation Z. These sections of the population have strongly held concerns and worries regarding the world's biggest and most pressing problems, such as pollution, social inequality, climate change, and social injustice (Sarkar, 2019).

Indications are that present-day consumers are displaying a higher expectation of corporations (Cronin, 2018). While expecting corporations to deliver good products and services on the way to recording profits, consumers also now expect corporations to do much more than make consistent profits and returns for investors (Weber Shandwick, 2016, 2017). There is a greater realization among

CEOs on a Mission, 37–48

Copyright © 2023 Eric Kwame Adae

Published under exclusive licence by Emerald Publishing Limited

doi:10.1108/978-1-80382-215-020231002

corporations, governments, states, the civil society, and market segments of the need for corporations to maintain a careful balance between the profit maximization maxim with optimization of returns for people and the planet, as expressed in notions of the Triple Bottom Line (TBL) (Savitz, 2013). Linked to these are concerns for sustainable business practices, the need for corporations to achieve and maintain societal consent and legitimacy (Kotler & Sarkar, 2017).

Besides, in many societies the world over, there is a growing gap between the promises of governments and their ability to deliver much needed social services (Cronin, 2018). Most consumers expect corporations, their brands, and leaders to step up to the plate and fill this democratic gap/deficit, by taking up issue with some of the most important social, political, and environmental issues of the day (Cronin, 2018). Thus, customer segments such as Millennials are protesting online, and through street marches about many social issues (Valencia & Jones, 2018).

In the past, corporations could select which CSR programs to undertake. Nowadays, companies cannot afford to stand aloof or have the exclusive right to decide what social matters to stand for (Sarkar, 2019). The polarized political environment is creating opportunities for others besides politicians, pressure groups, civil society organizations, and advocacy groups to fill the democratic gap, by showing leadership on the big issues of the day (Kotler & Sarkar, 2017).

Corporate sociopolitical involvement presents itself in various hues and flavors. One of the least studied forms of corporate social advocacy is CEO activism. While CEO activism is mainly confined to the United States, it is expected to go global (Chatterji & Toffel, 2018). Weber Shandwick (2016) noted that more CEOs were taking public stances on societal issues that were not overtly tied to the financial bottom lines of their corporations.

A sizeable section of Americans (47%) believe that CEOs have a duty and a responsibility to speak out on contentious issues, despite the risks (and in view of the rewards) of weighing in on such issues (Weber Shandwick, 2017). Nearly 60% of Millennials think that business leaders have a greater responsibility to speak now than in years past regarding issues of wider social significance (Weber Shandwick, 2017).

Some examples of CEO activists are Lloyd Blankfein of Goldman Sachs, Jim Rogers of Duke Energy, and Eric Schmidt of Google (Chatterji & Toffel, 2015). Others have included Angie's List's CEO William Oesterle, and Dan T. Cathy of Chick-fil-A (Chatterji & Toffel, 2016). These CEOs and several others have become exemplars of corporate chieftains who have taken public stands on hot button social and environmental issues (Chatterji & Toffel, 2016; Weber Shandwick, 2016).

Americans are overwhelmingly supportive of corporate political involvement, with 88% of respondents agreeing that corporations have the power and responsibility to influence social change, and 78% agreeing that companies should act to address important issues facing society (Global Strategy Group, 2016).

## 2.3 Corporate Social Responsibility and Sustainability

CSR involves organizations assuming some level of responsibility for society, in ways that extend beyond their narrow profit maximization maxim (Pava & Krausz, 1996). CSR has undergone some ambiguity and ambivalence in the academic and professional literature (Dahlsrud, 2008). Despite the various semantic shifts, CSR is generally linked to the confluence of social and environmental responsibility within business operations and economic models (Moscato, 2016).

Davis (1973) conceptualized CSR in terms of an organization's consideration of, and response to, issues that extend beyond the limited economic, technical, and legal requirements of the firm, designed to enable the corporation to obtain social and environmental dividends, alongside their commitment to the usual economic profits that corporations seek in their operations. Thus, CSR entails corporate commitment to contribute to economic development, while improving the quality of life of employees, the environment, and society (Pompper, 2015).

Some scholars conceive of CSR as arising partly because of corporations whose success is directly linked to the health and well-being of communities and the environments within the immediate catchment areas of their operations, such as mining and oil companies (Moscato, 2016). Thus, such companies seek to implement diverse CSR programs, including good-paying jobs for locals, infrastructure, educational and recreational amenities, while committing to long-term sustainability.

While remaining an enduring business activity, formal articulations of business responsibility to multiple stakeholders are relatively new (Carroll, 1999). Increased public awareness of CSR activity is positively correlated to increased purchase intentions and a favorable corporate reputation (Wigley, 2008). Owing to its centrality to many organizational outcomes, CSR is sometimes seen as a route for a greater management role for public relations and corporate communications practitioners (Coombs & Holladay, 2009, 2012).

*Social responsibility* describes strategies and tactics aimed at ensuring that an organization (i) recognizes that it has linkages with multiple stakeholders, (ii) becomes aware of the economic, social, and environmental impacts of its operations and activities on members of its strategic constituency, and (iii) manages the wider impacts of organizations on society and the environment, with the view to serving the greater good (beyond the limited interests of owners and investors) (Pompper, 2015).

The terms "social responsibility" and "sustainability" have become core concepts in the lexicon of modern strategic communication because of the realization that organizations have multiple stakeholders, who have interests that may run counter to those of owners, investors, or shareholders (Coombs & Holladay, 2009; Ofori-Parku, 2015). Corporations are therefore required to operate according to higher demands than economic and legal requirements (Carroll, 1999).

In effect, social responsibility considers an organization's duty to help address such concerns as poverty eradication, climate change, promotion of human rights, employee health, and safety concerns (Coombs & Holladay, 2009). Social responsibility has been described as "the management of actions designed to affect an organization's impacts on society" (Coombs & Holladay, 2009, p. 94). CSR denotes the worldview that an organization has strategic linkages with a host of stakeholders who are affected by, and whose actions can also impact on the organization's ability to realize its objectives. Thus, beyond the economic responsibilities and obligations that an organization has toward its owners regarding financial performance, corporations must also recognize their duties to the environment and society at large (Coombs & Holladay, 2009).

Generally, there are two main classes of motivations for corporations to engage in CSR (Pompper, 2015). The first class of motivation involves strategic drivers, linked directly to corporate objectives and private self-interests/ enlightened self-interests. These include the cultivation of loyal employees, improved market shares, profitability, etc. The second motivation for engaging in CSR is altruism and related purpose-driven factors that are linked to catering to the greater social good.

Debates over CSR have been polarizing (Moscato, 2016, 2018). Friedman (1970) argues that the social responsibility of corporations is profit and to increase corporate profitability (Friedman, 2007). Kolstad (2007) also argues that social responsibility falls outside the profitability equation. Proponents of CSR point to some good business cases and links between CSR and the financial motives and incentives of corporations (Pompper, 2015).

Some scholars conceptualize CSR as a pyramid, with economic responsibility to investors as the base and the business imperative, serving as the imperative foundation of the corporation, before other goals (Carroll, 1999). Thus, despite the oft-cited social good of altruistic CSR, financial performance tends to be the ultimate criterion for evaluation and effectiveness (Dodd & Supa, 2014).

### 2.3.1 Sustainability

Related to "social responsibility" is the notion of "sustainability." Sustainability extends the idea of social responsibility in demanding that organizations secure their long-term viability by balancing the need to maximize profit for investors, with the need to positively impact employees, society, and the environment (Savitz, 2013).

The concept of sustainability thus seeks to align the competing interests of the plurality of members of an organization's strategic constituency. The goal is not to prioritize the profit-maximizing orientation, to the neglect of social and environmental interests (Savitz, 2013). To be sustainable, organizations must be externally focused in terms of securing the environment by creating environmental prosperity, promoting the welfare of people by creating social prosperity while remaining internally focused by way of securing its longevity and financial performance by creating economic prosperity for its owners (Savitz, 2013).

Sustainability focuses on ensuring prosperity for the organization, the environment, and the society at large. It differs from corporate philanthropy in requiring organizations to be profitable while supporting prosperity for society and the environment (Savitz, 2013). The belief is that pursuing environmental and social prosperity can fuel an organization's financial viability, hence the notion of the TBL (Savitz, 2013, p. 45). The goal is to identify a "sweet spot," the strategic overlap between a firm's business interests and its social and environmental interests (Savitz, 2013).

Some scholars suggest that CSR has fallen below wider social expectations in positively impacting society and the environment since it is primarily employed as a tool for the preservation of private firm value for investors (Sarkar, 2018). CSR is partly influenced by notions of the TBL, the sustainability framework envisioned by John Elkington (Elkington, 1999). Elkington had argued that rather than pursuing a single financial bottom line that privileges investors/owners, corporations should pursue three different bottom lines for (i) people (society/societal responsibility), (ii) planet (environmental sustainability), and (iii) profits (financial performance). Thus, Elkington's TBL measures the overall responsibility and sustainability of an organization's operations over a period.

Elkington's TBL was originally positioned as a triple helix of positive change for corporations and capitalism, through the production of meaningfully desirable outcomes for people (society), the planet (environment), and profit. Elkington recently "recalled" or disowned his own TBL framework in utter disappointment (Elkington, 2018), as CSR is often diluted by wider corporate self-interests and private profit priorities, without due concern for people and the planet (Sarkar, 2018).

Thus, CSR is not without its critics (Moscato, 2016). Some scholars challenge the plausibility of the argument that rises in industrial productivity (even with sustainable methods) can reduce current and future ecological externalities and negative social impacts (Foster, 2000). Again, CSR tends to preempt and circumvent democratic pressures for environmental regulation and public scrutiny of corporations, while fostering environmental degradation (Enoch, 2007).

### 2.3.2 CSR Criticized as Representing Forms of Corporate Inauthenticity

Besides, CSR faces several marketing-oriented strictures, linked to perceptions that CSR is merely a corporate veneer and strategy for deception and corporate hypocrisy, designed to mask organizational self-interest (Pompper, 2015). One of these criticisms is termed "*greenwashing*," referring to the tendency to promotional overhype of corporate environmental commitments and credentials (Sheehan & Atkinson, 2012). There is another critique of CSR as "*pinkwashing*," a marketing strategy that describes corporations and charities claiming to care about women's health issues such as breast cancer, even when those corporations and brands may, in fact, be directly associated with the causation of these diseases (McVeigh, 2012).

Others see CSR only as "*bluewashing*," the corporate proclivity to tout real or perceived partnerships with the United Nations Organization or any of its agencies or a brand's resolve to abide by the UN Global Compact, and profiting from such an image for promotional and economic gain by presenting a humanitarian image (Pompper, 2015). Still, some trend-watchers continue to identify and write about ever-evolving forms of inauthentic shows of corporate responsibility, contrived public relations stunts, and shady marketing-oriented brand associations.

While increasing numbers of consumers expect companies to genuinely help address societal and environmental issues, it has also been found that there is growing skepticism among customers about the social/environmental credentials of companies (Sheehan, 2019). Especially, customers are suspicious of the partnerships of some companies and brands with social movements, aimed at addressing issues concerning vulnerable groups in society, accusing such companies of an inauthentic form of public relations and brand communication termed *"wokewashing"* (Sheehan, 2019).

*Wokewashing* could be described as situations when a corporation, institution, or individual inauthentically promotes a cause by saying or doing something that signals its advocacy for a marginalized cause, just for show, publicity value, or some other hidden capitalistic rationale (Sheehan, 2019). Some analysts have cited instances where some companies and brands could only be seeking to catch a piece of a cultural moment, or even causing harm to the very vulnerable communities they purport to be supporting in their communications or advocacy (Adams, 2019).

## 2.4 Political Corporate Social Responsibility

PCSR conceptualizes corporations as veritable political actors while stressing the role and responsibility of organizations in alternative forms of government within the para-constitutional domain, such as public-policy networks and multi-stakeholder initiatives (Baur, 2011). Thus, it stands to reason that PCSR is more focused and narrower than CPA. Although PCSR may completely occur within "lobbying for good," it is implemented in the constitutional and para-constitutional sphere (Wettstein & Baur, 2016). The main similarity between PCSR and CPA is still the primary motive of serving the corporate private good, with the greater social good being an incidental add-on.

## 2.5 Brand Activism and Brand Responsibility

Moscato (2016) suggests that the lines between CSR and brand activism are blurring, as exemplified by the *DamNation* campaign of the adventure brand Patagonia. However, Kotler and Sarkar (2017) disagree, pointing instead to a shift from CSR to brand activism.

Kotler and Sarkar (2017) place the evolution of brand activism on a continuum, arguing that brand activism developed out of: (i) market-driven goals (cause-related marketing and corporate social marketing); (ii) corporate-driven (CSR/sustainability and PCSR); and (iii) values/corporate purpose-driven (brand activism, often occasioned by social, political, economic, legal, environmental, and business concerns).

These scholars also observe that brand activism is reflective of rising environmental, social, and governance (ESG) concerns (Kotler & Sarkar, 2017). It has further been suggested that the rise in brand activism stems from widespread disappointment in CSR (Kotler & Sarkar, 2019), as illustrated by the afore-stated marketing and cognate censures of CSR. Brand activism runs counter to the profit-maximization philosophy of corporations for investors and embraces a values-driven multistakeholder agenda for brands' concerns for society's future, the planet's sustainability, and justice for all (Lirtsman, 2017). Brand activism is unique in being driven by corporations' concerns for the biggest and most pressing problems that remain unresolved by CSR (Kotler & Sarkar, 2017, 2018a, 2018b).

In their typology, Kotler and Sarkar (2017, 2018a) identified six broad categories of issues/causes in brand activism. These include (i) social brand activism (including brand concerns regarding equality, LGBTQ, race, age, gender, education, etc.); (ii) political brand activism (including brand concerns for lobbying, campaign financing, etc.); and (iii) legal brand activism (including brand concerns for taxation issues and employment laws). The rest comprise (iv) economic brand activism (including brand concerns for minimum wage and related tax policies); (v) workplace activism (including corporate governance and corporate organization, CEO pay, worker compensation, labor and union relations, supply chain management, governance, etc.); and (vi) environmental brand activism (including brand concerns for climate change, land use, air quality, conservations, etc.).

Brand activism may be conceptualized as a continuum, with the sort of activism that brands engage in spanning from "progressive," through "neutral," to "regressive," relative to the classes of sociopolitical issues (Kotler & Sarkar, 2017, 2018a, 2018b).

Progressive brand activism involves brands working to make the world a better place. For instance, The Body Shop does not only sell top-notch cosmetics. The brand has a record of accomplishment for engaging in fair trade and environmental protection (Kotler & Sarkar, 2017). Ben & Jerry's says that its brand is all about peace, love, and social justice, but also sells ice cream (Sarkar, 2019). Patagonia is a staunch advocate for recycling, reusing, and protecting the environment (Kotler & Sarkar, 2017).

On the other hand, regressive brand activism involves brands working to turn back the hands of social and environmental progress, by pursuing policies that hurt the greater social good, engaging in deception and unsustainable practices (Kotler & Sarkar, 2018b). Generally, tobacco companies (Kotler & Sarkar, 2017) are deemed to be regressive, in engaging in business operations seen to be injurious to the health of populations.

A recent survey on regressive brands shortlisted some popular global brands, among many others (Kotler & Sarkar, 2018b). These included *Bayer* (for seeking to further monopolize the seed and chemical industry by merging with Monsanto, threatening to force even more small and family farms out of business globally), and *Beretta* (for making money from the manufacture of weapons; for appropriating the profits from arms sales to bankroll the National Rifle Association (NRA); and for resisting the gun safety movement).

*ExxonMobil* was cited for its long-standing public deception regarding climate change and for seeking to intimidate cities and states working to hold the company accountable. The *GEO Group*, for making its business to make money from the mass incarceration of people of color and immigrants at its private prisons while investing millions on lobbying and elections to protect its perceived unethical profiteering. *Goldman Sachs*, for its blatant exploitation of Puerto Ricans, through predatory loans (Kotler & Sarkar, 2018b).

*Nestle*, for its cheap exploitation of Michigan's groundwater just down the highway from Flint, where residents pay some of the highest rates in the country for poisoned water. Tobacco giant, *Phillip Morris International*, for starting a huge foundation to health wash its image and for its moves to derail the implementation of the global tobacco treaty. *Shell* came up for mention, for its role in the violent suppression of the Ogoni people in Nigeria's Delta Region and its continued blockade of a global compact on the climate. *Veolia* was mentioned for its hand in the lead crises in Pittsburgh and Flint, which have endangered thousands of people, particularly people of color and low-income communities (Kotler & Sarkar, 2018b).

With increasing political polarization and rising concerns about the serious issues in the world, customers expect brands to be progressive, rather than being regressive (Romani et al., 2015). The position a brand takes in its activism can have some consequences from its stakeholders. Generally, progressive brand activism is associated with "brand evangelizing" or recommendation by stakeholders, while regressive brand activism is associated with "brand shamming" and revolt by stakeholders (Kotler & Sarkar, 2018a, 2018b). For example, Abercrombie & Fitch was bashed by the public when its CEO made insensitive comments about plus-size customers. Burberry was also criticized when it emerged that it had used hazardous chemicals in its products (Romani et al., 2015).

While this is the expectation, it is generally better for a brand to take a stand, rather not at all, since corporate neutrality can be a risky strategy that stems from the perception that the corporation is insensitive and actually part of the world's problems (Kotler & Sarkar, 2018a).

Brand responsibility is closely related to brand activism. Brand responsibility is described as a progressive-leaning brand stance that demonstrates a brand's commitment to a crucial social mission or purpose, stemming from the very core of the brand DNA (not as an add-on or a contrived veneer-like activity or program) (Kim, 2018). Brand responsibility is a brand's resolve to contribute meaningfully to the creation of a better world by helping to solve some of the biggest global problems.

Responsible brands take leading roles in conscious conversations in the public sphere that border on such issues as social justice, inclusivity, diversity, and environmental protection (Lirtsman, 2017). Such social causes cannot be contrived but must be reflective of a genuine link between the brand's purpose and the locally relevant issues of the times. To engage in brand responsibility and brand activism, brands must be authentic in fitting the sociopolitical and environmental causes to the brand values and the brand origin (stories), while also embedding activism in the business strategy (Sarkar, 2019). Brands must also be courageous in taking public stances, creating activism campaigns, aligning with social movements, evangelizing, and even sacrificing the profit potential. Also, brands must have a consistent and unflinching resolve to serve the greater social good (Sarkar, 2019).

Brand activism is one expression of brand responsibility, and a corporation's response to the market's expectation of brands to stand for something, even if it means sacrificing some other market segments in order to resonate with core segments (Sarkar & Kotler, 2018). Brand responsibility is different from CSR because brand responsibility is not perceived as an add-on, but an authentic brand behavior that emanates from *continuity* (the brand's history), *credibility* (a track record of being results-driven and the ability to achieve social targets), *integrity* (inclination toward morally-based actions), and *symbolism* (meaningfully touching the lives of multiple stakeholders). For example, Jet Blue cut its airfares to encourage people to leave the Florida area before the hurricanes hit, while others increased their fares instead. Patagonia worked against the capitalist logic in advertising to encourage customers to buy less during the traditional Black Friday sales.

Brand responsibility and brand activism are regarded as shaking things up in business. Against the backdrop of CSR's growing perceived failure to deliver meaningful social impact, brand activism and brand responsibility are a set of disrupting strategies for the betterment of the world and meaningful break-throughs (Kotler & Sarkar, 2018a). Brand activism compels corporations, their brands, and leaders to have little choice in the matter, by putting the power in the hands of society and truly embedding brand responsibility in the core of the brand DNA (Sarkar, 2018). Thus, brand responsibility is conceptualized as different from CSR. While brand responsibility is regarded as purpose-driven, and stem-ming from the core of the brand's purpose, CSR is widely regarded as inauthentic, contrived, and a veneer-like add-on, aimed at corporate hypocrisy and realizing corporate private value (Kim, 2018).

Customers exhibit antibrand activism when brands are regressive or fall short of public expectation (Iyer & Muncy, 2009). Such antibrand activism may include sales boycotts, brand shamming, online activism, and diverse other forms of brand resistance. Customers may also engage in brand-focused activism, which involves the targeting of iconic brands such as Nike, Coca-Cola, and Nestle, with the view to getting such brands to reform their regressive practices (Dauvergne, 2017). It is noteworthy that unlike antibrand activism, brand-focused activism campaigns do not seek to destroy brands through such goals as sales boycotts. Brand-focused activism seeks constructive engagement with regressive brands, to get them to cooperate with activists to achieve reformations in their regressive practices and policies (Dauvergne, 2017).

## 2.6 Corporate Social Advocacy and CEO Activism

Dodd and Supa (2014) observed that "public stances regarding controversial social-political issues by executive leaders of major organizations (termed corporate social advocacy...) seem to be increasingly commonplace" (p. 1), situating the phenomenon at the intersection of two important areas of scholarship and practice, namely strategic issues management and CSR.

Heath et al. (2009) saw strategic issues management as:

> The amalgamation of organizational functions and responsive culture that blends strategic business planning, issue monitoring, best-practice standards of corporate responsibility, and dialogic communication needed to foster a supportive climate between each organization and those who can affect its success and who are affected by its operations (pp. 8–9).

At the heart of the concept of strategic issues management is the notion of organizational legitimacy, which Suchman (1995) saw in terms of a wide range of perceptions and assumptions that stakeholders have concerning an entity that those actions are the desirable, proper, and appropriate, as seen within the context of some shared systems of norms, values, belief, and definitions. Thus, strategic issues management permits for behaviors exhibited by organizations to be "legitimized by stakeholder perceptions of how that behavior fits societal and/or stakeholder group beliefs about the ways in which the organization should behave" (Dodd & Supa, 2014, p. 3).

As an emerging phenomenon, scholars are yet to agree on one label for the concept (Livonen, 2018). While some refer to the essentially the same phenomenon as Corporate Social Advocacy (see Dodd, 2016; Dodd & Supa, 2014, 2015), others label it CEO Sociopolitical Activism (see Hambrick & Wowak, 2021), and some term it Corporate Political Advocacy (see Baur & Wettstein, 2016; Wettstein & Baur, 2016). Still, others call it CEO activism (see Chatterji & Toffel, 2015, 2016, 2018, 2019b; Livonen, 2018). Despite the various labels employed, I am inclined to agree with those who employ the name "CEO activism" for the concept.

CEO activism involves CEOs publicly speaking up on sociopolitical and environmental issues that are not directly related to corporate profitability, including such issues as climate change, same-sex marriage, social injustice and inequality, gun control, etc. (Chatterji & Toffel, 2018). CEO activism is spurred by such notions as serving the TBL, CSR, brand activism, brand responsibility, and multistakeholder perspectives.

While CEO activism is essentially prevalent in the United States, it is expected to spread to other parts of the world (Chatterji & Toffel, 2017). CEO activism shares with CPA the idea of corporations seeking to influence politics. However, CPA is different from CEO activism. The concept of CPA entails lobbying to advance corporate self-interest or firm value (Hillman et al., 2004). However, CEO activism involves issues not directly related to the core business, and thus not salient to corporate objectives (Chatterji & Toffel, 2018; Nalick et al., 2016). CPA (lobbying of various forms) is private, taking place behind closed doors, while CEO activism is public advocacy (Livonen, 2018).

CEO activism is akin to PCSR in assuming it is not limited to the self-interest of corporations, but is also concerned with the greater social good. However, CEO activism and PCSR are different. While PCSR activities are externally driven but internally focused on the corporation's CSR policies and practices, CEO activism has an external focus, with corporate leaders seeking to instigate social change outside their corporations (Livonen, 2018; Nalick et al., 2016). CEO activism is also different from CSR by being involved in culture wars that are quite different from the noncontroversial activities in CSR (Scherer, 2013).

CEO activism is a relatively unique nonmarket strategy and a new form of CPA, yet to be fully conceptualized and operationalized (Baur & Wettstein, 2016) that presents new complications to the understanding of corporate nonmarket strategies and corporate social advocacy (Livonen, 2018). CEO activism is different from other forms of corporate sociopolitical involvement. The few scholars who have investigated CEO activism have coined different labels for it. While Dodd and Supa (2014, 2015) call it "Corporate Social Advocacy," Livonen (2018) and Chatterji and Toffel (2015, 2016, 2017, 2018) consistently refer to it as "CEO activism," and Hambrick and Wowak (2021) term it "CEO sociopolitical activism."

While the extant concepts of corporate sociopolitical involvement focus on the corporation and/the brand as the archetype, CEOs are, by definition, not incorporated. Again, although CEOs may spearhead other corporate and brand activism, this may not always be the case as CEOs may find themselves engaging in activisms, purely out of their personal conviction/passion for a cause. They may not have had the approval of their corporations for the public statements they issue as part of their activism. Besides, as observed by Kotler and Sarkar (2018b), corporate activism may find expression in various domains (beyond the social and the political). Thus, a more specific and heuristic label is required for the phenomenon.

Yet, the extant perspectives of brand activism, CSR, corporate social advocacy, and corporate political advocacy all assume the "corporate" imperative, while others continue to split hairs by labeling such involvements as "sociopolitical" (Hambrick & Wowak, 2021; Nalick et al., 2016), "political" (Baur & Wettstein, 2016; Wettstein & Baur, 2016), and "social" (Dodd & Supa, 2014, 2015), among others. I am persuaded to concur with Chatterji and Toffel (2015, 2016, 2017, 2018) and Livonen (2018) in referring to the phenomenon as "CEO activism." This labeling is not only direct and punchy but also more specific in describing this unique form of corporate sociopolitical engagement in the public sphere.

Although there is some history of corporate activism and of corporations seeking to wield some influence on public policy through CPAs such as lobbying, CEO activism is "newer and less understood" because there has been little, if any, research on it (Chatterji & Toffel, 2016). A review of the literature on corporate sociopolitical involvement reveals some ambiguity and ambivalence regarding a clear delineation of relevant concepts. For instance, there appears to be some conflation of some units of analysis in corporate activism, with the blurring of the diverse activism of corporations, their brands, and CEOs (Livonen, 2018). Both

Dodd and Supa (2014) and Chatterji and Toffel (2017) examined the effects of "corporate social advocacy" and "CEO activism," respectively, on selected organizational outcomes.

I find very appealing the approach adopted by Livonen (2018), Chatterji (2016), and Chatterji and Toffel (2015, 2016, 2017, 2018) in labeling the sort of corporate involvement that de facto takes place through (or is spearheaded by) the CEO as *CEO activism*. For instance, in its study of corporate reactions to the US travel ban on citizens of selected nations, Weber Shandwick (2017) found that for 84% of the companies that made public pronouncements on the matter, such corporate articulations were directly made by the CEOs, using their names.

This situation creates conceptual, epistemic, normative, and practical problems (Wettsten & Baur, 2016). Thus, for the avoidance of doubt, I believe a unique label must be consistently applied to the unique phenomenon that subsists when CEOs weigh in on wider social, economic, political, legal, and environmental issues that are directly not related to the profitability or operations of the corporations they lead. That concept must be labeled "CEO Activism," to help distinguish it from other forms of corporate sociopolitical activism.

Chapter 3

# This Is Why We Do It: Examining CEO Activism Motivations

## 3.1 Introduction

While political leaders are expected to comment on the matter, corporate leaders have not traditionally commented on such controversial social issues as race relations. However, this traditional order of things was turned on its head, as some CEOs weighed in on the thorny matter (Chatterji, 2016). Chatterji and Toffel (2016) suggest that after public pressure from the CEOs of Intel, Salesforce.com, and Unilever, Governor Nathan Deal of Georgia, a Republican politician, announced his intention to veto a "religious liberty" bill that would permit faith-based businesses and nonprofit groups to discriminate against same-sex couples. Apple CEO Tim Cook publicly opposed a similar bill in Indiana, at the end of which Governor Mike Pence, a Republican, signed a revised version of the law that specified that it would not allow discrimination based on sexual orientation or gender identity.

In the week following Independence Day in America in 2016, conversations were rife about race relations, following the fatal police shootings of African American men in Louisiana and Minnesota and the murder of some five police and pursuit officers in Dallas, Texas by an African American army veteran. This led to some protests and heated debates during the 2016 Presidential campaign in America. Dropbox's Drew Houston, Facebook's Mark Zuckerberg, and Apple's Tim Cook took to social media, tweeting out statements expressing solidarity with sections of the population angered by the police shootings (Chatterji, 2016). Companies such as Twitter, Pandora, and Square used the hashtag #BlackLivesMatter to support the movement. Also, Marc Benioff of Salesforce.com led the charge in the movement toward pay equality, by using his keynote address at Dreamforce, the company's annual gathering in San Francisco to highlight the issue (Chatterji, 2016).

Despite possible pitfalls and undesirable backlash, why are more CEOs taking a stand to wade into issues that may have no direct bearing on the corporate bottom line? This chapter explores some of the motivations and related factors that make the leaders of profit-seeking organizations feel the need to mix business with politics. This discussion will consider not only some general motivations but

CEOs on a Mission, 49–71
Copyright © 2023 Eric Kwame Adae
Published under exclusive licence by Emerald Publishing Limited
doi:10.1108/978-1-80382-215-020231003

also several specific factors. Given the unique African sociocultural milieu, the research participants offered several Afrocentric philosophies, concepts, and factors as motivations for CEO activism.

## 3.2 Examining CEO Activism Motivations

Generally, activist CEOs are thought to be motivated by a strong desire to belong to a growing armada of positive forces in the society who are resisting negative forces within the social system and helping produce some desired positive social changes (Adae, 2020). Such CEOs have been seeking to make a significant impact in such areas as embracing social difference, improving race relations, enhancing gender equality, and promoting socioeconomic development; areas of social life that may be unrelated to the core businesses of corporations (Chatterji, 2016; Chatterji & Toffel, 2016).

The extant literature discusses several specific CEO activism motivations. These include growing pressures on corporations and CEOs to take a stand on major issues within the context of a polarized sociopolitical climate, the personal convictions of CEOs, pro-social corporate values, stakeholder expectations, and related ideological inclinations, among other motivations (Nalick et al., 2016).

### 3.2.1 Pressure to Take a Stand in a Polarized Climate

Profit-pursuing corporations are finding it hard (and sometimes dangerous or unwise) to remain apolitical in the bid to personalize their brands to build stronger links to customers in an increasingly polarized political climate (Chatterji, 2016). Besides, most corporate leaders are having genuinely strong convictions about contemporary social issues, due in part to a new wave of business education that stresses social responsibility and sustainability (Josephs, 2019), and the general need for corporate leaders to think beyond maximizing shareholder value while serving multiple stakeholder perspectives (Pompper, 2015).

### 3.2.2 Driven by Personal Convictions

For some CEO activists, speaking up is driven by personal convictions such as religious beliefs, pandering to the wishes and aspirations of specific strategic constituencies such as Millennials, whether they are employees or customers, standing with and for the masses, and showing courage and sincerity (Chatterji & Toffel, 2018). Thus, there is a new breed of younger business leaders emerging who are favorably predisposed to social liberalism. More business leaders are aligned to the left side of the political divide and tend to identify with social and cultural issues, as opposed to economic issues only (Chatterji, 2016).

### 3.2.3 Motivated by Corporate Values and Fighting for the Common Good

In justifying their activist stance, some activist CEOs point to their corporate values (Chatterji & Toffel, 2018), while others suggest that they and their companies should have a higher purpose beyond financial profits or investor primacy concerns and the need to maximize shareholder value (Chatterji & Toffel, 2018; Gaines-Ross, 2017). Marc Benioff, co-CEO of Salesforce, has highlighted the need for present-day CEOs to step into the fray and take a stand not only for their investors but also for multiple stakeholders, such as their employees, their customers, their partners, the community, the environment, schools, and, indeed, the entire society (Chatterji & Toffel, 2018).

It appears that the increased penetration of social media has transformed and challenged the social activism landscape in numerous fundamental ways. Emergent digital and social media platforms have been metaphorically compared to a microphone that is always activated and turned on, and making corporate silence ever more conspicuous whenever battle lines form regarding controversial social, environmental, and economic issues (Chatterji, 2016). In such situations, corporate silence is often seen as acquiescence or tacit endorsement for whatever positions sections of the public do not agree with. Consequently, the hyper-partisan and hyper-plugged-in society has had the proclivity to fuel and amplify CEO activism.

### 3.2.4 Driven by Stakeholder Expectations and Ideological Inclinations

Nalick et al. (2016) argue that there are three main classes of motivations for corporations and their CEOs becoming involved in sociopolitical issues, including (1) betting on future stakeholder benefits, (2) responding to current stakeholder pressures, and (3) pursuing ideological inclinations. These scholars note that a myriad of conditions and factors within the institutional context however serve to determine the extent to which a corporation would become involved in such sociopolitical issues, including general political mechanisms, stakeholder participation levels, and related mechanisms, treatment of firms by external entities, ownership structure, executive prominence, availability and the quality of message outlets, and the prevailing/available managerial mechanisms.

Livonen (2018) appears to be extending these perspectives of Nalick and his coworkers (2016) by proposing additional factors that may determine the nature and extent of the engagement in or reception of CEO activism, including (1) the characteristics of the CEO, (2) the features of the organization and industry, and (3) the characteristics of the focal issue and the social movement. In this vein, Livonen (2018) opines that CEO characteristics that may influence participation in and reception of CEO activism include such traits as CEO personality factors, celebrity status, social engagement, and personal background. Firm and industry characteristics include the social responsibility of the firm, the identity of the industry, the firm and/or industry reputation, and financial performance. Relevant characteristics of the issue/movement include the movement/issue phase, movement/issue content, and the movement/issue audience and type of approach.

While many see corporate involvement in sociopolitical issues in positive/glowing terms, others see a dark underbelly in corporate sociopolitical involvement. Take for instance, Baur and Wettstein (2016) and Wettstein and Baur

(2016), who distinguished between "corporate political activity" and "corporate political advocacy," positioning the latter within the domain of corporate political involvement, and normatively as part of corporate social responsibility. These scholars observe that *corporate political activity* is akin to diverse forms of lobbying and is motivated by the pursuance of corporate self-interest and enlightened self-interest (Wettstein & Baur, 2016). However, they argue that *corporate political advocacy* is driven by the pursuit of wider social and environmental goals and ideals not directly related to the financial bottom line and the operations of the corporation.

These scholars further suggest that other criticisms of wider *corporate political advocacy* may include (1) concerns regarding the deeper underlying corporate motivations and the covert business case for *corporate political advocacy*; (2) the issue of potential alienation of certain members of a corporation's strategic constituency (such as employees, suppliers, or customers) due to the polarizing nature of sociopolitical issues; (3) the infusion and intrusion of corporate ideology in the consumption realm; and (4) debates regarding which values offer legitimate grounds for *corporate political advocacy* (Wettstein & Baur, 2016).

With the surge of corporations engaging in one form of corporate political advocacy or another, Wettstein and Baur (2016) discuss some practical challenges for managers and other decision-makers. "We suggest that there are three basic conditions to a legitimate advocacy campaign, which managers should assess thoroughly and sincerely before deciding to throw the weight of the company behind a specific cause. They are consistency, plausibility, and authenticity" (Wettstein & Baur, 2016, p. 221).

## 3.3 Opening Newer Pages: Examining Alternate CEO Activism Motivations

While the preceding section has presented some general and specific motivations of CEO activism, as contained in the extant literature. It stands to reason that since the current corps of research literature on CEO activism has largely excluded African cases, philosophies, and worldviews, the extant motivations of the phenomenon have largely displayed a Western and Eurocentric focus and an ideological stance that has favored modernist perspectives to the exclusion of alternative standpoints.

This book purposes to broaden and deepen the current understanding of CEO activism motivations by the application of alternative theoretical lenses such as *Afrocentric philosophies* (see Pompper & Adae, 2023) and *postmodern values in public relations* (see Holtzhausen & Voto, 2002). What fresh motivations and contributions could emerge by the application of alternative theoretical and conceptual lenses?

The next section discusses the major emergent themes regarding what the participants in this study disclosed as their motivations for developing the activist stance and/or for continuing to engage in CEO activism within the Ghanaian non-Western context. As will emerge, these reflect some alternative and largely non-Western motivations, previously unarticulated in the literature, including the influences of *Caritas, Ubuntu, Africapitalism*, and some postmodern concepts.

Overall, it emerged that CEO activism within the Ghana African context was strongly motivated by a complex web of factors relating to *Caritas* and the indigenous African moral philosophy of *Ubuntu*. Many of the CEOs who participated in this study indicated that their activist stances had been spurred by predispositions to be helpful, loving, caring, charitable, and benevolent, derived from faith-based or religious doctrines.

For most participants, CEO activism was motivated by a strong commitment to place struggles for the common social good above the quest for sectional private interests and financial profits only for companies and their investors. Such socially oriented motivations tended to privilege relationship-building above the pursuit of individual interests, by acting in ways that promoted justice, mercy, equity, and fairness in society, because these were God-given expectations for the strong and powerful in society.

Most of the participants disclosed some *Ubuntu*-related motivations for engaging in CEO activism. These informants spoke of these motivations in ways that displayed worldviews that went against the Western capitalist logic that typically favors stiff competition and personal capital accumulation, at the expense of standing up for the vulnerable in society; being a voice for the voiceless; spurring socioeconomic development; relating well with others; seeking multiple stakeholder interests; and promoting social diversity, equity, inclusivity, and justice.

### 3.3.1 Motivated by Caritas

Faith or belief in God and caring for others because it is a divine instruction were strong themes that emerged as the bases for the actions of most of the CEO activists in this study. Irrespective of their gender, age, ethnicity, marital status, or indeed, other social identity markers, most informants in this study indicated that their activism was grounded in their personal faith in God or a supreme being, and their belief in working for the welfare of the society. For instance, Participant #24, CEO of an agro-processing firm, declared that their activism was driven by their belief in God, a faith that grants them the courage to stand up for whatever they believed in:

> We must believe in God and be fearless in fighting for just causes. You must seek to make a positive impact; a great difference in the lives of people.

Similarly, Participant #15, CEO of a media corporation, disclosed that their activist stance was strongly driven by their personal belief in fulfilling a Godly assignment:

> My activism is firmly grounded in some deeply held personal beliefs ... that we are in this world on assignment. While some

have come to help others climb, others are here to support others, and still, others have come to lead the way. I believe that, if I can support or lead the way for others to follow, it is a good thing for me.

Referring to sections of the Bible (Matthew 7:12), Participant #14, who was CEO of an association of bulk oil distributors during data collection for this project (but who currently holds varied agribusiness investment interests) believes in corporations and the powerful in society to be motivated by the desire to render service to others, rather than service to the self. They enjoined all to love and be each other's keepers, stating that this worldview had sparked in them the need to have an intergenerational mindset into sharper focus, where notions of prudent resource utilization, a stewardship mentality, and sustainability rang true:

> The Holy Bible says that whatsoever you would like others to do unto you, do it even so unto them. So, whenever others can, I would wish that they would be able to build and keep a world that would make me thrive. When I can, I would do the same for others. We owe it to generations yet to come, to leave behind for them a society that is in a more viable shape than we found it.

### 3.3.2 The Influence of Ubuntu

Several informants disclosed that their social resistance activities were grounded in a *Maa-tic* worldview (see Asante, 2007), based on such virtues as truth, justice, harmony, righteousness, balance, order, reciprocity, and propriety (see Asante & Dove, 2021). *Maaticity* is linked with a value system that required human social actors to be compassionate and have deeper senses of empathy for their fellow members of society on the path of righteousness, accepting that "there can be difference without othering," (p. 194), and reprogrammed into being human beings where there is "the construction of an ethical human being, never unnerved by the assaults of race, . . . a human freed from human family quarrels brought on by religion, race, creed, and doctrines of domination" (p. 190).

For instance, Participant #19, CEO of an IT firm, expressed the view that empathetic traits had a strong influence in conditioning them to always put themselves in the shoes of some of the most vulnerable in Ghanaian society, and to speak for the underprivileged:

> I have great empathy and I believe in walking in someone else's shoes. We live in a developing world, and there're many problems, so I feel I must make a difference because I care for others.

It was found that such feelings of compassion and empathy were connected to some community-focused worldviews about progress and prosperity. Many participants described notions that limited progress and prosperity to material accumulation as fundamentally flawed. It emerged that the notion of progress and prosperity related to a basket of indicators that reflected the quality of life of the community. Many participants described how they typically felt about learning about the problems faced by the vulnerable in society.

It was learned that when many of the informants in this study found themselves in situations where they realized that the vulnerable in society faced issues beyond their control, a common feeling was one of empathy that served to ignite in the activist CEO the desire to personally assist in bringing about a solution to the perceived problem(s). It was found that some CEOs in this study felt a sense of duty to advocate on behalf of the less powerful in society, whenever necessary. As disclosed by Participant #20, CEO of management accounting firm, the need to speak on issues that confronted the vulnerable sections of Ghanaian society had driven them to seek numerous media opportunities:

> Whenever I notice such horrible situations, I feel I owe it a duty to speak out on behalf of the less privileged and the less powerful in society. Usually, I would arrange a media briefing to enable me to speak to the issues at hand.

### 3.3.3 Motivated by Personal Values and Beliefs

Numerous participants revealed that their activist stances were driven by their personal beliefs in the shared well-being of Ghanaians. Thus, some participants stated that they engaged in CEO activism because of the desire to ensure the security and viability of the entire society. It emerged that such sentiments were driven in part by the passion for Ghana and a *we-mentality* that fueled the belief that whatever affected any Ghanaian had the potential of affecting everyone else.

For Participant #13, CEO of various firms involved in film production, promotion, and distribution, it was such a realization that made it especially difficult to focus on business as usual and be unconcerned about the subnormal state of socioeconomic development in Ghana. Describing themselves as an *Africanist* and a *Globalist*, they spoke of their activism as being grounded in their personal belief in the human spirit and the need to be socially responsible. According to this participant, the overriding and greater purpose of their business was to serve as a tool for driving social change:

> These external things [protest actions] are really internal. I am an Africanist and a Globalist, and I believe that society can be better. I am here for a purpose, which I am trying to achieve through my business and social causes. Being a CEO, you have to stand up and fight for others. It is a calling!

It emerged that the values of truth, integrity, honesty, fairness, justice, and doing things right were some of the personal convictions and belief systems that motivated the actions of most of the CEOs in this study. Most informants pointed to their early socialization within the family system, Ghana's school system, and the church, as strong forces in helping them deeply embed these values as part of their moral compasses. For Participant #24, the value of upholding the truth and doing things right had been part of their socialization and had effectively guided their actions in the direction of upholding equity, fairness, good, and justice:

> I was brought up like that. The motto for Wesley Girls High School [her alma mater] says, *"Live Pure, Speak True, Right Wrong, Follow the King."* These values always make me want to stand for justice and fairness for everyone.

Participant #24 urged Ghana's elite to believe in God and be courageous in the fight for the common good, even to the point of death: *We must believe in God and be fearless in fighting for just causes. We must not fear to lay down our lives for the good of society.*

Some participants believed that it was every Ghanaian's national duty to be involved in building a country that was worth living in. Interestingly, some participants saw this as a divine duty, which sometimes meant rejecting opportunities to migrate or hold citizenships of other nations. In this regard, Participant #8, the Managing Partner of law and business advisory firm, observed that:

> This is where God in His Wisdom decided to place me. I have never dreamt of being a citizen of another country. I have had many opportunities to do that, but I have never taken them. This is the reason why I need to make this country better.

The interviews showed that a range of personal characteristics motivated some of the participants to engage in CEO activism. These characteristics included their family traits and conditions, education, a background of adversity, and past roles as student activists. Several of the participants indicated that the activist stance had always been a part of their backgrounds. Typically, being a student leader played a major role in predisposing participants to their current role as CEO activists. Some explained that youth or student activism placed them in a situation where they had to seek diverse mechanisms for effecting positive social changes, as related by Participant #14:

> My activism started in my student days as a student leader. I'm quite a curious person ... I like to question issues and to probe deeper for better solutions to the problems facing society. You are looking at mechanisms to constructive change.

For Participant #24, the development of their activist voice as part of their growth and development as an individual. However, they believed that factors such as their family and upbringing, as well as their early education together enabled them to develop the activist stance. They particularly mentioned their family orientation that underscored the need to uphold truth and integrity as influencing their activism:

I was born into a home where truth and honesty were paramount. At school, things were done in a certain way; the right and the truthful way.

For several informants, the motivation for becoming activists was a matter of living up to some perceived family tradition. Here, some informants told stories about how their parents (especially fathers) and grandparents (grandpas) were activists during Ghana's colonial or precolonial eras. Participant #8's appetite for activism was a family trait. They recounted some activities of their grandfather, who always sought to be upright and fought for social justice:

It is in my genes ... a family trait. My grandfather had the reputation of being extremely prim and proper. My father always believed in playing your part. He had an anti-establishment and activist streak in him that I find in my life too. Growing up, through school, work, and all that, this pattern has always been a part of me. I feel that it is what we need to do to build our nation into one worth living in.

Still, some participants offered some deeply personal motivations that had to do with the inner desire to have a positive social impact. Participant #20s motivation derived from the need to look out for the interests of others and ensure that the average Ghanaian made the right decisions in financial and investment matters. This participant had a spiritual view of their motivation when they noted that there was an afterlife and that there was going to be a day of reckoning when everyone's impact on Earth would be accounted for, based on how much they supported others:

My motivation is very personal. When I sleep, I say to myself that when people leave this earth, I don't think we will be measured by the material property you had, but by the impact, we made on people's lives. I am driven more by the need to look out for the interest of others.

Others expressed the idea of speaking out for the vulnerable in somewhat philosophical terms. Thus, it was not good enough for the few members of the society who managed to emancipate themselves socioeconomically to remain unconcerned about the plight of most Ghanaians who continued to fall through the cracks. Participant #4 captured their views about working for the well-being of the entire society:

I believe that you cannot be a rich man in a poor country. It is this conviction that drives me to engage in all these activities for the common good of our society. You know, Bob Marley rightly stated in one of his songs, "When the rain falls, it doesn't fall on one man's house." I have great satisfaction from seeing myself involved in things that are enhancing the welfare of the collective.

### 3.3.4 Motivated by Africapitalism

*Africapitalism* was coined by Nigerian business magnate Tony O. Elumelu (2012) as a call for corporations to embrace social development by partnering governments, the public sector, the private sector, civil society organizations, donors, and philanthropic organizations to transform Africa (Tony Elumelu Foundation, 2019). In Ubuntu, an individual's identity is closely entwined with those of their society (Amaeshi & Idemudia, 2015), and one's social value is proportional to one's ability to empower others (Mbigi, 2007).

Africapitalism is an expression of *Ubuntu* values in underscore the idea that the ultimate social role of the corporation and its agents is not exclusively to serve the interests of investors (Amaeshi & Idemudia, 2015), but the advancement of meaningful social development (Norren, 2014), and the promotion of the greater good (see e.g., Quelch & Jocz, 2008). Like *Caritas*, *Africapitalism* promotes a corporate culture that embraces DEI and sustainability by integrating business economic goals, social ends, and environmental concerns (Lutz, 2009).

*Africapitalism* is driven by four unique worldviews that set it apart from neoliberal capitalism: (1) a sense of progress and prosperity, (2) a sense of parity, (3) a sense of peace and harmony, and (4) a sense of place and belongingness. By entailing *doing good to do well* (Amaeshi & Idemudia, 2015, p. 218), *Africapitalism* is consistent with difference and DEI and CSR/Sustainability and is in tune with *Caritas* and *Ubuntu* values that encourage the influential and wealthy in society to stand up and fight for the progress and well-being of the entire society.

It was found that CEO activism in Ghana was not only motivated by the desire to uphold some notions of *Africapitalism*. Most study participants shared views that were consistent with some postulates of *Africapitalism* such as unique understandings of such ideas as a sense of progress and prosperity, a sense of parity, a sense of harmony, and a sense of place and belonging.

Several participants shared the belief that the private sector in Africa had a renewed role to play in the continent's development, by taking a more central place in catalyzing Africa's development by partnering with the public sector, civil society organizations, donors, and the development community in driving positive change in Africa. Some saw the role of Ghana's private sector as becoming more socially responsible and partnering with the government, local communities, and civil society organizations in delivering the needed level of progress and prosperity for the common good.

For some participants, a strong pathway by which Africa's private sector could help share the fruits of progress and prosperity for the greater good related to the role of companies in building traditional authority structures. Here, some informants believed that companies could develop the capacities of traditional chiefs and leaders in Africa to better support the socioeconomic development agenda of Africa.

Many of the participants believed that the private sector in Africa had an important role to play in ensuring that the fruits of progress and prosperity were shared equitably and for the common good. They described important roles that could be played by the private sector in contributing to the creation of shared value in ways that promoted equity, diversity, and inclusivity. Many informants noted that the achievement of social inclusivity ought to be regarded as a pre-requisite for Africa's private capitalists to be able to freely enjoy the fruits of their capital. An overwhelming number of participants expressed the need for African countries to seek greater inclusivity and parity, especially in terms of granting the youth real opportunities to enhance and realize their dreams.

Several participants thus called for egalitarian measures to address the needs of the marginalized in society. Many called for policies that promoted inclusivity and urged companies to implement more social responsibility programs that addressed the wide divisions in society, highlighting the centrality of education in such a process. A good number of participants noted that achieving the needed depth of harmony called for the increased realization that an overriding purpose of humans was the creation, nurturing, and maintenance of relationships and experience, including having regard for our mutual interdependence with the environment, generations yet unborn, as well as the invisible realm.

Sharing more insights on how creating and sharing valuable social relationships and experiences would promote a greater sense of harmony, several participants advocated for a return to the age-old African social value of reciprocity that served to preserve many traditional African societies. Most participants were quite unanimous in indicating that good leadership across all strata of society had a pivotal role to play in moving society in the direction of having more balance between economic prosperity, social wealth, and environmental safeguards. They also expressed the view that corporate advocacy was essential in promoting sustainable development.

Some participants intimated that Africans needed to reexamine the blind copying of destructive competitive tendencies of Western capitalism since most of such tendencies undermined harmony on the continent. For those that shared such views, the *survival of the fittest* competitive philosophy inherent in neoliberal capitalism was antithetical to traditional African notions of peace and harmony.

Clearly, *Africapitalism* emerged as a major theme in the study, highlighting this novel inclusive capitalism ideology as a pivotal motivation for CEO activism in Africa. Owing to the copious insights generated surrounding this management ethos, Chapter Four is devoted to a more exhaustive discussion of *Africapitalism* and its interpenetrations with CEO activism in Ghana.

### 3.3.5 *Motivated by Postmodern Values*

It emerged also that some extant postmodernism values in contemporary public relations (see Holtzhausen & Voto, 2002) served as motivations for some of the participants, including notions of organizational politics; micropolitics and alliances; postmodern biopower; dissensus and dissymmetry; and local and situated ethics and decision-making.

### 3.3.5.1 Postmodern Biopower and CEO Activism

Informants generally felt empowered to undertake the kind of activism they wished to engage in, and to the extent, they wished for. Many of the CEOs disclosed that they felt they had the inner power to conceptualize and roll out activist campaigns designed to resist oppressive systems within the Ghanaian social system that worked against the interests of the vulnerable in society and/or retarded social development.

Several informants expressed the view that they had the capacity and ability to leverage their statuses and roles as CEOs in Ghana to serve as social activists, working to drive society in a positive direction. In recognizing their power to effect positive social change, most informants perceived their roles as activists as comprising standing up to dominant power centers in Ghana, especially the government. In this vein, many of the participants displayed a keen sense of awareness as conscious participants who wielded the power to resist dominant centers of power in Ghana, such as the interests of owners of businesses and other sections of the business community in the country.

In discussing their sense of personal power, many of the participants felt they were doing much more than they could have hoped for. Indeed, for this group of participants, there was no limit to their ability to envision and implement any form of social resistance activity. Participant #10, Managing Partner of a law firm, emerged as an exemplar for those who believed that their power to engage in any form of activism was not unlimited, even though working as a CEO activist was a part-time activity. However, this participant felt that not all activists in Ghana felt empowered in their roles and called for more effective pressure groups to join the struggle for the common good. They called for more citizens of Ghana to see the need to be active in-between elections:

> I am doing more than enough, as a spare time activity. Every Ghanaian ought to occupy their space and speak up against things they don't like. If we have more people speaking up and constructively engaging the government intellectually on critical issues, Ghana would work better for all.

It was found that the perception of personal power to engage in CEO activism emanated from several sources, factors, personal characteristics, and social situations. For instance, the power to be active was derived from their executive management positions. For Participant #5, CEO of a savings and loans company, their high-profile status was a strong influence on their perception of power to engage in activism. They added that this had had such an enduring influence on others' perceptions of their capability and that they felt they wielded a strong influence in Ghana:

> I have the power to push for the sort of change that must happen in Ghana. My public profile has been helpful in my activism. People would listen to you because of who you are … they would go along with you, follow the positions you espouse, and accept your recommendations.

Although generally, there was a feeling of having the power to engage in activism as desired, some participants felt that they could not undertake their activities to the extent desired. For these informants, there were some limitations, due to such factors as time and the complexity of managing or aligning discordant stakeholder interests and loyalties. Participant #14 was one informant who shared some feelings about having to sometimes act against the interests of the members of the petroleum chamber they headed:

> No, I don't feel that I have enough power to do the kind of activism I would like to do, to the extent that I wished for. I feel limited by time … constrained by the need to manage all related interests, which may be conflicted.

### 3.3.5.2 Micropolitics, Alliances, and CEO Activism

Many of the informants in this study were conscious of the potency of enhancing their power and influence as CEO activists by forming all manner of alliances. Although most participants had a conscious appreciation of their abilities to take action, some felt that there was only so much an individual could do by way of solo actions. Those who felt this way wished they had the support of other CEOs.

Participant #17, a serial entrepreneur and CEO of a holding company with specialized subsidiaries in human capital development, management consulting, food and beverages, shared some pessimism regarding the growth of CEO activism in Ghana, partly because of the lack of support from others for the activist CEO. To them, many benefits could be derived from the critical mass and group dynamics of joint actions by CEOs:

> As an individual, I can only do so much in my small corner, sharing my thoughts about issues that matter to me. I think as a collective, we have more power. A lot of the time, I have found that power in the collective. People hesitate to voice out when others do not stand in solidarity with them.

It was found while several participants undertook their actions as solo enterprises, an overwhelming number of them tended to identify various layers of micropolitical power, both within and outside of their organizations. Such strategic alliances were found to be with like-minded individuals and groups that could assist the work of the activist CEO in one way or the other.

For instance, some internal alliances were found to be with boards of directors, individual directors, members of management, and selected employees. For instance, it emerged that Participant #5's work as a CEO activist was greatly enabled by the support he enjoyed from the Board of Directors of their firm but also the instrumentality of one of the directors of the company.

Most of the informants indicated that they felt that they had significant abilities to undertake their actions partly because of the support they received from various quarters or allies, including board members, other CEOs (be they activists or not), and other members of the C-suite. Participant #20 indicated that their sense of empowerment emanated from the active roles played by their employees in their activist campaigns:

> I feel empowered and emboldened because I have the total support of my team. My employees are a part of my campaigns ... they assist me in my campaigns ... helping with my presentations and putting publicity materials together, thinking through speaking points, and anticipating questions and rebuttals.

Other participants spoke of the instrumentality of the *Kitchen Cabinet*, comprising selected members of staff, management, and directors, who played various roles in supporting the work of some of the CEO activists in this study, ranging from helping to identify issues, defining messaging strategies, serving as researchers and a listening post, critiquing and preparing CEOs to speak effectively, and participating in postmortems and debriefing sessions.

It emerged that some participants had sought to build power bases for their actions, by forming external alliances with other like-minded individuals, for various purposes. For instance, participants such as Participant #1, Participant #11, Participant #21, Participant #2, and other women activist CEOs had seen the need to belong to the Executive Women Network (EWN), to promote the interests of the corporate woman in Ghana, while standing with the vulnerable in the society.

### 3.3.5.3 Organizational Politics and CEO Activism
Generally, participants' responses supported postmodern notions of companies as political systems, where power was regarded as an important resource that could be employed for positive social and organizational outcomes. In playing the corporate political terrain to their advantage, it emerged that although they were part of the power centers within their organizations, many participants saw the need to sometimes refuse to align with the power bases not only within the organizations, such as boards of directors and management teams, but also powerful power centers within the country, such as the Government of Ghana.

### 3.3.5.4 Local and Situational Ethics and Decision-Making
Although participants belonged to the dominant classes within their organizations and the wider Ghanaian society, they were prepared to go against the grain in sometimes opposing interests of powerful sections of society, such as the

government, investors, and the corporate interest. For instance, it was most participants' significant rejection of certain norms and the privileges of dominant power structures in the society that motivated most of them to stand with marginalized groups within Ghana, such as the poor, the vulnerable, minorities, and marginalized groups.

It turned out that their actions as CEO activists were driven by the need to take actions, based on the requirements of particular situations, and in ways that convinced them that such decisions were most ethical and human, under the circumstance. It was learned, for instance, that most of the informants were positively predisposed to ideas of diversity, equity, and inclusivity. Such orientations were found to produce responses that emboldened most of them to resist influences in power within the Ghanaian society that excluded the voices of marginalized people within the society.

For an overwhelming majority of the participants, the motivation for CEO activism was a strong desire to consider the interests and views of multiple stakeholders in their decisions. In fact, for most informants, it was the need to represent the interests of multiple stakeholders – rather than the strategic corporate interests of financial profits for investors – that kept motivating them to become activists.

It turned out that, for the most part, the CEOs who participated in this study considered the interests of others, besides the interests of investors, in their situational decision-making processes. A common theme that emerged was that, for some of the participants in this study, while the interests of the owners of businesses in making money or profit remained the primary determinant of business decisions, there was also the realization of the need to make a bigger impact in society by considering the needs of other stakeholders. For these informants, this goal made it imperative for private businesses in Ghana to become more open-minded in considering the interests and needs of many other stakeholders.

In fact, all participants in this study displayed a tendency to embrace diversity, equity, and social inclusivity. While traditionally, ethnicity had been viewed as one of the bases for social stratification in Ghana, all the informants in this study noted that they did not subscribe to social distinctions based on ethnicity. In affirming their support for social equity and inclusivity, some of the informants spoke of the importance of diversity in progressive organizational and social processes. As Participant #20 observed, diversity was necessary for providing suitable levels of multiple perspectives needed for social and organizational advancement. This participant thus indicated a culture within their organization that embraced social diversity and inclusivity:

> If your position is that everyone must think like you and do things like you, then we are not going anywhere as a society. We need diversity and social inclusivity to advance society. Traditional Ghanaian philosophy says that *"All the fingers of the hand are not the same."* This underscores the need for difference and diversity in society.

Several reasons accounted for this pattern of ethnic blindness. For most of the CEOs in this study, the recognition that their diverse ethnic backgrounds and those of virtually every Ghanaian had a role to play helped explain this openness to diversity. For instance, Participant #10 referred to their "impure" ethnic, international, and racial lineage that made him refer to his children as the "United Nations":

> I am one of those ethnically impure people you can find, coming from a mixture of about five or six ethnic groups in Ghana. I am part-*Akyem*, part-*Fante*, part-*Asante*, part-*Larteh*, [all ethnic groups in Ghana], part-*Malian* [referring to the West African nation of Mali], and part-*Portuguese*. So, which of these am I going to identify with, and which do I look down on? I call my children *'United Nations'* because of their mixed ethnicities and lineage. I recently traced my Portuguese ancestry and realized that I could get a Portuguese passport.

Gender diversity was likewise valued. For Participant #10, being raised in a home that involved living and relating with more women than men influenced his openness to gender diversity and overall positive attitudes to women, despite being a powerful man in a patriarchal Ghanaian society:

> I have no negative attitudes toward women. My parents had me and five sisters. My dad passed on at a relatively young age, so I was raised by my mum and my sisters. I have a wife and two daughters, my wife has only sisters, and I have only one son. A person's social identity does not influence me per se.

Some participants in this study had a Biblical turn of mind in expressing their support for diversity and social inclusivity. In this regard, some spoke about the need to avoid discrimination since all humans were children of God. Participant #21, CEO of the ad agency and a specialty décor supply firm, remarked that:

> We are all human beings and children of God, so I want to accept them for who they are, where they are coming from, however they choose to identify themselves, and when we have to work together, I see how best we can do that, without worrying too much about the labels.

In expressing their tolerance for people from diverse backgrounds, several participants alluded to the fact that it was not their place to judge others. According to Participant #19, although many things pointed to the fact that many sections of the Ghanaian society were not tolerant of diversity, their open-mindedness and a keen sense of curiosity have tended to favorably predispose them to notions of diversity, equity, and social inclusivity in Ghana:

I'm very opened-minded and I'm generally curious to understand how they live their lives because I need curious individuals. This openness and curiosity influence my activism because it enables me to tailor my messages to the audience.

Many participants expressed the view that embracing equity, diversity, and social inclusivity was important in harnessing the total human capital potential of Ghana for rapid national development. Participants testified that no matter their social identity, everyone had an important social function, and should, therefore, be brought on board and given the chance to contribute to society, based on their merit and capability. Participant #6, CEO of a group of players in the telecommunications sector in Ghana, spoke against patterns of discrimination and in favor of social justice for all in Ghana:

I think everybody has a place in society and should be given a chance. The fact that you are physically challenged doesn't mean you're useless. The fact that you are a woman doesn't mean you shouldn't be given the same advantages as men. I believe in equity, giving people the opportunity, and empowering people to speak out and be heard. However, people should be responsible for their freedom of speech.

Although many participants in this study said they were unopposed to sexual minorities in Ghana, such as members of the LGBTQ+ community, they would like their embrace of sexual minorities to remain at the personal level. None of them agreed to the suggestion of engaging in activism for the promotion of same-sex marriage in Ghana, citing cultural barriers. For instance, Participant #18, CEO of a group of financial institutions, shared that they did not personally endorse LGBTQ+ rights in Ghana and would not make same-sex rights the focus of any of his campaigns, although they foresaw a CEO in Ghana publicly declaring so, quite soon in Ghana:

I don't have any hard feelings against it, but I don't think it is a culture that we should introduce formally into our setting. It is not an agenda I would like to pursue, as in making a public statement about. I see a time when a business leader in Ghana would come out to declare that he is gay.

Participant #15's stance, relative to the LGBTQ was one of hard-nosed intolerance. For them, it was an aberration for one to be sexually attracted to people of the same sex. For them, issues concerning same-sex relationships and marriages were nonissues within Ghana, and were of less priority to Ghana's developmental needs:

It is something that shouldn't come to this part of our world because we have bigger problems that need to be solved.

> LGBTQ is like when you solve all your problems and there is nothing more to do. A teacher is walking 12 hours just to be able to teach, don't talk to me about LGBTQ; it doesn't even cross my mind.

### 3.3.5.5 Dissensus, Dissymmetry, and CEO Activism

The CEOs who participated in this study displayed a strong willingness to embrace conflict and tension, whenever necessary, in their efforts to effect changes in society. In doing so, most of them showed the ability to seek out issues within the society they disagreed with and to oppose all manner of individuals and organizations in Ghana. It emerged that most participants saw disagreement and conflict as integral to their role as CEO activists. As indicated by Participant #8, there would be no need for their agitation if CEO activists agreed with everything in the system:

> You're like a professional quarrelsome person. You're always arguing about something. Conflict comes with the territory – if we agreed, then there would be no need to agitate. However, you come to it with humility. The drive for engaging in CEO activism was the existence of social injustices in Ghana that disagreed with the expectations of most participants regarding what the social order in Ghana ought to be. Many participants felt that social resistance, in the form of CEO activism, was necessary for addressing social injustices.

### 3.3.6 Motivated by a Bright Outlook on CEO Activism

It was found that most of the CEOs who took part in this study were motivated by their perception of an outlook on CEO activism in Ghana. For some of the informants, such motivations related to their belief in the power of CEO activism and its increased relevance in addressing some of the challenges facing Ghana.

Despite the many physical attacks, business disadvantages, and the diverse forms of pushback they suffered, most of the CEOs in this study believed that Ghana was worth fighting for. For many participants, such as Participant #10, it was important to keep engaging in CEO activism because there were always new issues emerging that needed to be addressed, including public sector corruption and public sector reforms in Ghana:

> We have to keep fighting because the problems are not over. We are still going to carry on our fight against public sector corruption in Ghana and see how best we can influence the discourse where that is concerned and push for positive changes in our public sector.

Several participants revealed a resolute posture to keep driving socioeconomic changes within Ghana. For instance, Participant #14 partly inspired the title of this book when they described themselves as "a man with a mission," and saw themselves only continuing with their work of being a voice that drove positive socioeconomic, business, political, and cultural changes in Ghana:

> I'm a man with a mission. I'm a driver of socio-economic change, and I don't see what can stop this mission. I try to drive positive social change from any angle possible. I am always on the move. Although I struggle sometimes, I always try to survive so that I can help realize the vision of driving social change.

Several participants expressed the desire to engage in even more activism. Others expressed similar sentiments about stepping up their level of activism, especially agitating for greater reforms in Ghana's public sector. For such CEOs, the urge to do more was linked with aging and the desire to accelerate the rate of positive changes in Ghana.

### 3.3.7 Motivated by the Desire for Social Change

Many of the participants disclosed that their appetite for becoming and engaging in CEO activism in Ghana was borne out of their strong dissatisfaction with the continued underdevelopment of Ghana, despite the immense human and natural resources of the country. It was found that, for most of the participants, a significant motivation for engaging in CEO activism was a strong desire to see an effective transformation of Ghanaian society into a state judged desirable. Thus, generally, most of the participants spoke about desiring to find themselves in the camp of the positive social forces that were working to transform Ghana for the better.

For instance, in the case of Participant #7, CEO of a car care company, the motivation was the desire to champion a cause for the greater good, in which a whole new generation of entrepreneurs would emerge in Ghana. They indicated that their goal for engaging in social resistance actions was not to become wealthy as a businessperson, but rather for contributing to the general good of society through creating independent-minded young people who would be bold to pursue lives as business owners:

> I have been doing this since 2013. Money has never been the goal of my campaigns. My focus is on empowering the youth to think of business and entrepreneurship within the informal sector.

It was a deep sense of public-spiritedness to work and fight toward social development that served as the motivation for some participants. As indicated by Participant #8, the hunger for activism was the general desire to speak up about social problems and issues they deemed unacceptably wrong:

> When you find something going wrong, I like to take action or
> pushing it to whoever needs to take care of it. I have done all kinds
> of things on the way to the national level to help maintain some
> decency and a certain normal level of life for the members of the
> society.

Many CEOs in this study believed that business leaders had important parts to
play in making or driving the change they wanted to see in Ghana. Thus, an
important motivation for engaging in CEO activism was the need to become more
socially responsible as a business leader and to lead in driving change in society,
including being the voice of the voiceless in society. Participant #2, Managing
Director and Head of Firm Resilience at a major global financial institution,
stated the need for businesses to look beyond the profit motive and their strategic
interests only. According to them, businesses had an increasingly pivotal role to
play in the wider society:

> ... as businesspeople, we have a role to play to improve society
> and help society make progress. We can drive positive changes in
> society with our know-how, our high-caliber human capital, our
> proven business models, and so on. It is about using business to
> push forward the agenda of progress in Africa.

### 3.3.8 Motivated by Personal and Calculated Business Decisions

It was learned that some participants' roles in CEO activism were either motivated by a calculated business decision or occasioned by enlightened self-interest.
Some participants testified that there could be minimal business factors, in
motivating their activism. However, those that shared this view saw the enlightened self-interest in the general growth and well-being of the entire country as the
overwhelming driver. According to Participant #14, whose views typified those
that shared the idea of a limited business motive for activism, it made much sense
to have a remote business motive in a brighter and prosperous Ghana:

> If any, there's very little of a calculated business decision
> concerning my activism. A brighter and a better Ghana will also
> help my business. However, I don't think about that – it is not even
> a primary driver for me. It is an obligation that comes with your
> social standing.

Several other participants described some personal motives and gratifications
for engaging in CEO activism. These personal rewards for engaging in activism
included the camaraderie enjoyed through close relationships with other CEOs;
the networking and business dividends, among several other motivations. For
instance, Participant #1 noted that:

> Please don't get me wrong. I get a lot out of activism myself. Especially, the six founders of the EWN are my "sisters" and we stand by each other. Off the top of my head, I have the CEO of Airtel Ghana, the CEOs of Vodafone Ghana, Barclays Bank Ghana, Standard Chartered Bank Ghana, and UBA Ghana, etc. – all of them are powerful leaders of important organizations in Ghana. Since they are part of my network, I can just make a phone call and great things would happen for me.

It emerged that for some CEOs who participated in this study, CEO activism was a part of an overtly calculated business strategy. Those participants who affirmed an avowed business motive for engaging in CEO activism indicated several business advantages that could be derived from the social resistance activities of the CEO. Such business ends were diverse, ranging from the need for competitive advantages; driving greater profitability; building strong corporate brands, reputations, and brand positionings; and earning free or cheap media publicity and social profiling for the activist and the company.

Others saw CEO activism as comprising a core to the business strategy. Participant #5 spoke about the deliberate decision at their savings and loans firm to embed CEO activism within the corporate strategy. They disclosed, for instance, that their company had derived immense competitive advantages from their role as an activist CEO, achieved through the company's ability to mobilize investible funds from the marketplace, at rates significantly lower than the company's competitors. Specifically, they revealed that by being a significantly socially responsible and a thought leader in working for the common good because of their activism, their company was able to record markedly greater levels of profits, by courtesy of the wider spread between its cost of funds and the interests it charged on the loans it granted to its customers:

> It has a direct relationship with our profitability. As a financial institution, we trade in money. My economic activism builds the business's brand and enables us to mobilize funds at least two percent below the market rate. So, if you take it that our profit is US\$ 2 million, that translates straight into the bottom line.

Participant #5's genre of CEO activism was deemed to be for the purpose of achieving some strategic objectives for his company. They indicated that, from the outset, the company sought to derive some competitive and brand equity dividends from CEO activism. This study collaborator indicated that for them and their team, it was a win-win activity, as CEO activism produced some corporate and branding benefits while allowing them to fulfill their personal and social responsibilities.

## 3.4 Discussion

This chapter has presented the major themes relating to CEO activism motivations emerging from in-depth interviews with the 24 CEO activists purposively selected for this study.

It was found that numerous factors served as motivations for the informants to become CEO activists and to continue working as activist CEOs, including some personal values; calculated business decisions; postmodernist notions such as organizational politics, micropolitics, and alliances, biopower, dissensus and dissymmetry, and local and situational ethics and decision-making; a bullish outlook on CEO activism; and notions of *Africapitalism and Africonsciousness, Caritas*, and the *Ubuntu philosophy*.

Some of the findings are consistent with extant motivations for CEO activism, such as those of Chatterji and Toffel (2018) and Chatterji (2016) regarding the desire for social change; the influence of personal convictions; the need to serve the interests of multiple stakeholders; and the influence of corporate values. Some of the findings in this study also mirror aspects of the views of Nalick et al. (2016), particularly the argument that CEOs were motivated by optimism for future stakeholder benefits, responding to current stakeholder pressures, and pursuing some ideological inclinations.

However, some of the findings in this study extend our understanding of the motivations of CEO activists in new directions. Besides providing fresh (hitherto nonexistent) evidence from the emerging markets context of Africa to the literature on CEO activism, the research also makes some significant basic contributions. The findings introduce the notions of Caritas, Ubuntu philosophy, and Africapitalism as motivations for CEO activism. The extant literature on CEO activism was devoid of such concepts as serving to motivate CEOs to become social activists. These concepts and values open opportunities for the deeper examination of more specific pathways through which they could serve as motivational factors in CEO activism.

Chatterji (2016) and Chatterji and Toffel (2018) suggested that the leanings of some CEOs to the left side of political ideology could be a motivation for CEO activism. However, these scholars failed to provide empirical support for such an assertation. Again, the extant literature on CEO activism have tended to adopt a right-wing and a modernist perspective that has sought to argue that among the major motivations for CEO activism has been the impact on organizational outcomes of CEO activism (see Chatterji & Toffel, 2018; Dodd & Supa, 2014, 2015, etc.).

The findings in this study, perhaps for the first time, establish a strong connection between postmodernism and CEO activism. Particularly, it has made the case for the influence of selected postmodern values in public relations (Holtzhausen, 2000; Holtzhausen & Voto, 2002), serving possible motivations for CEO activism.

An area of theoretical contribution is the provision of some nuances in how the pursuit of strategic personal and calculated business goals could serve as motivations for CEO activism. In this, the findings point to varying degrees of corporate motives, personal motives, and the pursuit of enlightened self-interest. Yet, the findings suggest the addition of CEOs' optimistic outlook on the pursuit of CEO activism as a motivation factor for CEO activism.

These findings aid the explication and development of the CEO Activism Development Model. Besides affirming the significance of motivations for CEO activism, it develops the working model by providing a range of specific motives that the CEOs in Ghana who participated in this study articulated. The impact of these findings is depicted in Evolution One of the working CEO Activism Development Model, as shown in Fig. 3 (below):

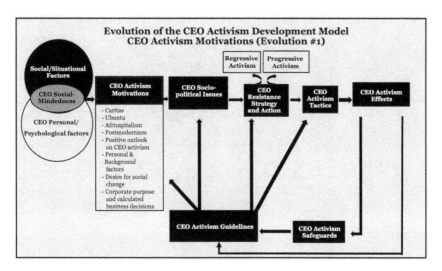

Fig. 3.    Evolution #1 of the CEO Activism Development Model, Indicating CEO Activism Motivations. *Source:* Author (2023).

Within the context of the working model for this study, the findings regarding the motivations for CEO activism are occasioned by the generation of social-mindedness of CEOs, following the interaction of personal/psychological forces with social/situational factors. Such motivations for CEO activism are deemed to then lead to the selection of sociopolitical issues/causes that CEO activists advocate, as shown in Fig. 3 above.

Given that the concept of Africapitalism emerged as a major motivation of CEO activism in Ghana, the next chapter is devoted to a discussion of the forward and backward linkages between Africapitalism and CEO activism. It also examines the extent to which discourses surrounding CEO activism are contributing to the institutionalization of Africapitalism among corporations in Ghana.

Chapter 4

# Walking the Talk: Africapitalism as a Major Motivation for CEO Activism

## 4.1 Introduction

Phillips et al. offered what they termed "a discursive view of institutions" (see 2004, p. 646) in which they sought to address some lopsidedness in institutional theory, relating to some limitations in its approach to analyzing processes of institutionalization (see e.g., DiMaggio & Powell, 1983). To Phillips and colleagues (2004), institutional theory suffered from the fact that it accorded very scanty attention to the importance of language in processes of institutionalization and moved for the bolstering of institutional theory with some insights from discourse analysis, aimed at highlighting the pivotal role of language in institutionalization and yielding some benefits of "reconnecting institutional theory to a concern with power and politics" (2004, p. 648).

These scholars argued for the development and adoption of a discursive model of institutionalization, based on their position that "whereas we institutions are constituted through discourse and that it is not action per se that provides the basis for institutionalization, but rather, the texts that describe and communicate those actions" (Phillips et al., 2004, p. 635). Thus, language and texts serve as basic foundations for influencing and understanding the actions of others, especially within organizational contexts.

For decades, there have been strident discussions concerning the business–society relationship. Such efforts that have tended to reimagine the critical role of business in Africa's development have spawned the formulation of diverse concepts (Amaeshi & Idemudia, 2015). One such concept is *Africapitalism*, a notion that was coined by Nigerian businessman and economist Tony O. Elumelu (2012) to undergird the significant role of the private sector to the socioeconomic development of the African continent.

According to Elumelu, the chairman of several corporations, including Heirs Holdings, the United Bank for Africa (UBA), Transcorp, and the Tony Elumelu Foundation, Africapitalism is an economic philosophy that highlights the leading role of Africa's private sector in the socioeconomic development of the continent (Elumelu, 2012; Tony Elumelu Foundation (TEF), 2019). This philosophy is a call for businesses to be innovative in getting involved in the business of social

CEOs on a Mission, 73–85
Copyright © 2023 Eric Kwame Adae
Published under exclusive licence by Emerald Publishing Limited
doi:10.1108/978-1-80382-215-020231004

development by partnering with governments, donors, and philanthropic organizations in the positive transformation of Africa (TEF, 2019).

It is expected that *Africapitalism* will "ultimately help businesses become more profitable as the communities they serve become well-off consumers, healthy and better-educated employees, and even entrepreneurs who go on to become suppliers and service providers" (TEF, 2019). *Africapitalism* is borne out of the enlightened self-interest of businesses since the success of business organizations in Africa is linked up with the progress and well-being of communities in which they operate (Elumelu, 2012).

Despite the high hopes and expectations of Africapitalism, conceptualized as a genre of inclusive capitalist logic aimed at meaningfully contributing to rapid socioeconomic development in Africa, there appear to be some doubts about this happening. Adegbite et al. (2020) wonder whether *Africapitalism* will work, and asks some hard questions of the functionality of this brand of capitalist ideology in addressing issues of diversity and development across Africa. Making a case for a more realistic approach to Africa's developmental challenges, Adegbite et al. (2020) pose six key criticisms that must be addressed in order to give *Africapitalism* a fighting chance to work for the benefit of Africa.

Based on the expectation that CEO activism in Ghana is motivated by *Africapitalism*, and the idea that CEO activism is already an expression of *Africapitalism*, this chapter examines the extent to which *Africapitalism* has already taken hold as a management ideology in Ghana. Further, this chapter investigates how discourses by business leaders surrounding CEO activism are contributing to the institutionalization of the phenomenon.

## 4.2 Africapitalism, a Home-Grown Pathway to Africa's Development?

It has been suggested that the significance of *Africapitalism* is accentuated by Africa's unfortunately long history of triggers of deep-seated underdevelopment, including colonialism, poor leadership and bad governance, crippling poverty, weak institutions, and distressed civil societies (Amaeshi & Idemudia, 2015). The centrality of *Africapitalism* is further heightened by Africa's developmental and governance challenges, and the view that the continent needs to employ a unique economic philosophy and business model for its own development.

This call rings truer, especially as efforts to kick-start Africa's development have been compounded by the multinational corporations, foreign governments, aid agencies, international nongovernmental organizations, and international donors, many of whom have made Africa's development a booming business venture for their own gain (Amaeshi & Idemudia, 2015).

Especially, many multinational corporations in Africa have often found themselves implementing social intervention programs, as part of corporate social responsibility (CSR), most of which have failed to produce the desired currents of social development (see Idemudia, 2014). Thus, within the context of Africa's continued crisis of development in the face of the impotence of governments and the business sector to deliver much-needed social development (Amaeshi & Idemudia, 2015), some scholars have advocated for greater partnership among such actors as the state, business, and civil society (see Idemudia, 2014; Mirvis & Googins, 2018; Richey & Ponte, 2014).

Some have suggested that Africapitalism is reflective of the African philosophy of *Ubuntu* that holds that the ultimate purpose of corporations, and their management is not to benefit only one group of people, nor is it for the gain of diverse collectivities of people (as posited by stakeholder theory, for instance) (Amaeshi & Idemudia, 2015). Ubuntu philosophy asserts that the ultimate purpose of business is the benefit of the community and the greater good (Lutz, 2009; Norren, 2014).

Generally, Ubuntu values include (i) respect for the dignity of others, (ii) group solidarity, (iii) participation, (iv) sharing, (v) the spirit of harmony, and (vi) interdependency (Mbigi, 2007). Thus, Amaeshi & Idemudia (2015) suggest that Africapitalism is built on at least four Ubuntu values and senses regarding how the world ought to work, namely (i) a sense of progress and prosperity, (ii) a sense of parity, (iii) a sense of peace and harmony, and (iv) a sense of place and belongingness.

In reflecting Ubuntu (African traditional humanism) values, "Africapitalism implies the restoration of African-ness in capitalism, reflecting the economic and social practices implicit in African culture and tradition" (Amaeshi & Idemudia, 2015, p. 215). While not completely against self-prosperity and self-interest, Ubuntu places a burden on the rich to show communal relevance by helping to elevate others and the entire community (Karsten & Illa, 2005; Littrell et al., 2013; Lutz, 2009).

In Ubuntu philosophy, an individual's identity is inexorably linked up with the matrix of his/her society (Amaeshi & Idemudia, 2015), and that one's personal, economic, and social value is directly proportional to one's ability to empower and liberate others (Mbigi, 2007). Thus, just like Caritas, the notion of Ubuntu-derived *Africapitalism* provides a backdrop for a corporate culture that conditions corporations to pursue sustainability by seeking their profitability, while also advancing social and environmental ideals (Lutz, 2009).

*Africapitalism* pursues a sense of progress and prosperity by focusing on achieving financial profitability together with social wealth, in ways that transcend material accumulation and includes the psychological and social welfare of all stakeholders (Amaeshi & Idemudia, 2015). This orientation seeks to promote the creation of both financial and social wealth. Thus, progress and prosperity are not conceptualized as the absence of poverty. Rather, they are seen holistically as referring to the creation and maintenance of a matrix of conditions for a fulfilling life for all in society, including good quality and accessible health, education, social capital, and strong and democratic institutions (Brundtland, 1994).

Second, Africapitalism involves a sense of parity, referring to the imperative of seeking social equity, inclusivity, and diversity, and ensuring that wealth accumulation and its distribution are equitable and fair to all parties (Amaeshi & Idemudia, 2015). In Africa, inequity has been described as "the new poverty," the absence of liberalism, and "the entrenchment of crony capitalism and corruption" (Amaeshi & Idemudia, 2015, p. 216). Africapitalism provides a ray of hope in curing these roots of poverty by promoting social inclusivity and equity and in advocating for corporations that seek to adopt a multiple stakeholder orientation.

Third, in seeking a sense of peace and harmony, it has been suggested that Africapitalism can help address the influence of the Schumpeterian drive for creative destruction, self-interest, and the never-ending bouts of struggles, competition, and contestations between places and spaces, generations, regimes, and in other spheres that have marked present-day capitalism (Amaeshi & Idemudia, 2015). This orientation advocates for the negation of contestations, conflicts, and struggles that characterize capitalism (Amaeshi, 2018). Africapitalism is in sync with the pursuit of the values of balance and harmony and drives for holistic human development. Africapitalism advocates for the creation of private wealth, but with due consideration of the production of social capital for all in a harmonious and balanced manner.

Finally, Africapitalism departs from the ideals of global capitalism, by embracing a sense of place and belongingness. Global capitalism takes place for granted, prioritizes cost, and encourages outsourcing and capital flight in the direction of cost minimization (Amaeshi & Idemudia, 2015); thus, "place is consumed" (p. 217). On the contrary, Africapitalism heightens a sense of rootedness and promotes a sense of *topophilia* (Tuan, 1977, 1974) by its linkage of people and place (Duncan & Duncan, 2001). This consciousness may be expressed in economic patriotism (seeking the development of one's community or homeland) (Clift & Woll, 2012) and the pursuit of national development (Audi, 2009).

*Africapitalism* actively advocates for the eager consideration of the African context in prescribing solutions to the continent's developmental challenges (Amaeshi, 2018). Thus, *Africapitalism* is also a reflection of corporate patriotism in which corporate behavior is oriented toward contributing to the welfare of citizens and the community while garnering support from stakeholders such as customers, the media, and others (Puncheva-Michelotti et al., 2014).

In tandem with tenets of postmodernism that reject meta-narratives, Amaeshi and Idemudia (2015) argue that *Africapitalism* is a linguistic project that questions conventional wisdom "and repositions the development of Africa in the world firmly as an indigenous project in which Africans will play significant, active roles" (p. 218); it is "Capitalism by Africa-oriented entrepreneurs for Africa" (p. 219). These scholars see *Africapitalism* as a force for Africa's sustainable development that stresses the role of the emotions, sentiments, and actions of rational economic actors, including the entrepreneurs and corporate executives of Africa.

By entailing "doing good to do well" (Amaeshi & Idemudia, 2015, p. 218), Africapitalism is consistent with ideas such as CSR, corporate citizenship, the bottom of the pyramid, and the triple bottom line. Amaeshi and Idemudia (2015) however argue that Africapitalism is distinctive in that these cognate concepts seek to tackle some challenges of firm profit maximization but falling short of getting to the very heart of the problem, which other scholars have traced to the issue of individualism (Lutz, 2009).

*Africapitalism* addresses this issue head-on by casting the corporation as representing a community that evokes a sense of belonging in its members and other stakeholders, an attribute that concepts like CSR ignore (Amaeshi & Idemudia, 2015). Africapitalism's highlighting of the instrumentality of place and emotion in capitalism also position it as providing a transformative agenda for the role of corporations in Africa's development, and a clarion call for all people who share an emotional attachment with Africa. It is a "deceptively simple notion, but a powerful one that has the potential to remake a continent, and put Africa on an equal economic footing with the rest of the world ... embodies a private-sector-led approach to solving some of Africa's most intractable development problems" (Amaeshi, 2018).

The phenomenon of CEO activism appears to be an important expression of *Africapitalism* and postmodernism. CEO activism underlines *Africapitalistic* calls on Africa's private sector to play active roles in the continent's socioeconomic development. This trend is in keeping with *Ubuntu* values that enjoin the more powerful and successful people in society to care about and to work to empower the weaker segments of the community.

In Ghana, both men and women CEO activists engage in various forms of activism. CEOs have taken public stances on an increasing array of contentious issues within contemporary Ghanaian society. Such issues have included the planned introduction of Comprehensive Sexuality Education (CSE) in the elementary, junior high, and senior high schools in 2019, financial and economic crimes, political vigilantism, media freedom, public finance and economic mismanagement, and educational reforms, among other issues.

While some CEOs in the country have engaged in solo activism campaigns, others have done so as a group. Present-day activists in Ghana include Kenneth Thompson (economic mismanagement of the national resources); David Ampofo (social injustice and political reforms); Emmanuel Awumee (youth empowerment); Dr. Kwesi Nduom (poverty alleviation, wealth creation, and jobs); and Kenneth Ashigbey (environmental protection). Kofi Bentil is CEO of law and business advisory firm, Lex Praxis. Bentil has been advocating for various civil rights issues, including the Right to Information Bill, better economic management, governmental transparency and accountability, and environmental conservation. Senyo Hosi, CEO of the Ghana Chamber of Bulk Oil Distributors (GCBOD), has been taking public stances on economic and social development matters in Ghana.

Some women have broken the glass ceiling and now serve as CEOs of diverse organizations in Ghana (IFC, 2018) and are playing activist roles as CEOs by mobilizing not only as individuals but also as groups to challenge and change their socioeconomic and political situations (Badri & Tripp, 2017). These have included Juliet Yaa Asantewaa Asante (political party vigilantes and election-related violence).

Others are some leading members of diverse professional women's groupings, including the Executive Women Network (EWN), Women in Media (Ghana), Women in Broadcasting (WIB), and Women in Public Relations (Ghana). These professional women include Edith Dankwa (Group CEO of the Business & Financial Times Group), Lucy Quist (former CEO of telecommunications company Airtel Ghana, and founder and current CEO of business advisory firm Quist Blue Diamond), and Dzigbordi Dosoo (CEO of beauty and wellness group Allure Ghana).

Others are Yvette Atekpe (Regional Managing Director of Internet Solutions Ghana), Esther Cobbah (CEO of communications advisory firm StratCom Africa), Maidie Arkutu (Chairman & Managing Director, Unilever Francophone Africa), Pearl Esua-Mensah (CEO of the Ghana Deposit Protection Corporation, and President of Ashesi University Ghana), Dr. Joyce Aryee (former CEO of the Ghana Chamber of Mines), Fredua Duplan (former CEO of Nestle Ghana, and current CEO of Nestle Pakistan), and Sheila Minkah-Premo (Managing Consultant at Apex Law Consult Ghana).

Oheneyere Gifty Anti, CEO of GDA Concepts, a media production company has been advocating for improved social protection and inclusivity in Ghana. For well over a decade now, she has been producing and transmitting a television program called "The Stand-Point" that has become an advocacy platform for the vulnerable in Ghanaian society.

These women are driven to empower women in Ghana to increase their influence and participation not only in Ghana but also internationally. They work to influence and drive policy changes that increase the representation of women in senior leadership positions in Ghana while promoting women's rights in support of the United Nations Sustainable Development Goal Five (5) on gender equality and empowerment for all women and girls.

Generally, these CEOs have seen the need to publicly speak up about diverse sociopolitical matters while seeking to drive change from their high perches atop the C-suite. Even when such activist CEOs in Ghana such as Kenneth Thompson weigh in on economic issues facing the nation, it appears that the objective is not only to help engender a more business-friendly economic system in Ghana but also to see the government pursuing sound economic policies that would spur economic growth and produce better life chances and improved quality of life for the generality of Ghanaians.

These activist CEOs are motivated to seek the greater good. As the incidence of CEO activism may be new in most non-Western parts of the globe (Chatterji & Toffel, 2016), one can argue that the phenomenon may not be so new in Ghana since it may well be a modern reexpression of age-old elements of the Ghanaian/African cultural values. Could an effort to reminisce about such ancient African cultural traits effectively navigate us in the direction of a glorious future for CEO activism?

## 4.3 Examining Africapitalism as a Special Motivation for CEO Activism

Many participants shared the belief that the private sector in Africa had a renewed role to play in the continent's development, by taking a more central place in catalyzing Africa's development by partnering with the public sector, civil society organizations, donors, and the development community in driving positive change in Africa.

### 4.3.1 A Sense of Progress and Prosperity

Some saw the role of Ghana's private sector as becoming more socially responsible and partnering with the government, local communities, and civil society organizations in delivering the needed level of progress and prosperity for the common good. As articulated by Participant #11, CEO of a major player in electric power generation, the time for companies in Ghana to step up their social responsibilities and close ranks with various stakeholders was long overdue:

> Companies can do more in driving progress and prosperity by seeing the welfare of society as part of their responsibility. It's not just about the corporate bottom line but having the responsibility to bring the community along.

For some participants, a strong pathway by which Africa's private sector could help share the fruits of progress and prosperity for the greater good related to the role of companies in building traditional authority structures. Here, some informants believed that companies could develop the capacities of traditional chief and leaders in Africa to better support the socioeconomic development agenda of Africa. Participant #20 believed that, besides their roles in providing tax revenues and employment opportunities, private companies could upgrade the knowledge of traditional leaders in Africa to play more potent roles in educating the citizens at the local and community levels:

> A profitable company can support traditional leaders. The traditional leaders and our traditional institutions should be strengthened to play more effective roles in social change and socioeconomic development.

Some felt that more attention needed to be focused on lifting Africa's subsistence sector, even as efforts were being made to rapidly transform the continent. However, a few of the participants believed that a major factor militating against the realization of progress and prosperity across Africa was the inconsistency with which governments across the continent had been seeking to drive the developmental agenda. Some participants expressed the idea that to share the burden of promoting progress and prosperity through consistent pushes across the continent, the private sector must partner with governments and civil society organizations.

### 4.3.2 A Sense of Parity

Many of the participants believed that the private sector in Africa had an important role to play in ensuring that the fruits of progress and prosperity were shared equitably and for the common good. They described important roles that could be played by the private sector in contributing to the creation of shared value in ways that promoted equity, diversity, and inclusivity.

Many informants noted that the achievement of social inclusivity ought to be regarded as a prerequisite for Africa's private capitalists to be able to freely enjoy the fruits of their capital. As articulated by Participant #14, a deeper sense of equity, justice, diversity, and social inclusivity should precede the private businessperson's ability to contemplate an open enjoyment of their progress and prosperity:

> Equity, inclusivity, and fairness are prerequisites for you as a businessperson to fully enjoy the fruits of your capital. When there is fairness and equity, you can cruise about in your top-spec automobile, without looking over your shoulders. If the society lacks equity for all, you risk having the poor masses pouncing on you.

In reechoing similar sentiments, Participant #16, CEO of a talent development company, observed the need for African countries to seek greater inclusivity and parity, especially in terms of granting the youth real opportunities to enhance and realize their dreams:

> If we don't create avenues for young people to feel that there're ample opportunities for them, they will probably take missiles and other weapons and attack those of us parading about in nice cars and living in nice homes.

Several participants thus called for egalitarian measures to address the needs of the marginalized in society. Participant #9, CEO of an insurance group, called for policies that promoted equity, diversity, inclusivity, and social justice and urged companies to implement more social responsibility programs that addressed the wide divisions in society, highlighting the centrality of education in such a process:

> Education is a factor that can help to bridge the gap. The education gap needs to be closed and more investments made in infrastructure and critical areas to support access to education.

Some participants advocated for more media publicity for the role of CEO activists in Ghana, seeing modest contributions of some companies in Ghana to promote greater equity, diversity, and social inclusivity as largely unnoticed. Some of them were of the view that the private sector had more to do in terms of scaling up investments, supporting other institutions working to promote social inclusivity, and speaking truth to power. For Participant #19, achieving a critical mass of private companies working for the realization of greater equity, diversity, and social inclusivity was essential in this effort:

The private sector must be bold in speaking truth to power. Ghana's private sector should be brave to call out leaders and other public office holders found not to be doing the right thing.

Many of the CEOs saw endemic corruption in Ghana as a strong force that had negated efforts to promote parity and shared value for the people. Indicating what she saw as part of the reason for its existence, Participant #24 described corruption as the present-day "scourge" that was holding back the hands of Africa's progress:

Corruption is a scourge because everyone thinks they should have a large part of the national cake. We must find ways of fighting corruption. People must understand that they won't die of hunger.

Some informants believed that creating social wealth for all stakeholders required a special focus on improving the life chances of all Ghanaians. For Participant #10, such moves must be genuine and should not exclude any social stratum:

It requires a special focus on creating and improving the life chances of all, including the youth who live in the remotest villages. In the early 1950s, my father was able to enter Mfantsipim School (one of the top senior high schools) straight from my humble village of Akyiase. Not so today. This must be addressed.

### 4.3.3 A Sense of Harmony

Some of the informants advocated for sustainable development in Ghana and the pursuit of the Triple Bottom Line, where the entire society would have the mindset that corporate profits should be pursued, but with due consideration of present and future generations and with adequate regard for the protection of the planet.

A good number of participants noted that achieving the needed depth of harmony called for the increased realization that an overriding purpose of humans was the creation, nurturing, and maintenance of relationships and experiences. In this regard, it was shared that a big part of living on the planet Earth was for relationship-building, loving one another, and community-building, as articulated by Participant #24:

We're here for relationships and experiences ... to love one another. We're not here to serve mammon. We're here to feel the grace-creation in which we find ourselves and to experience love and relationships.

Sharing more insights on how creating and sharing valuable social relationships and experiences would promote a greater sense of harmony, several participants advocated for a return to the age-old African social value of reciprocity that served to preserve many traditional African societies.

The participants in this research were quite unanimous in indicating that good leadership across all strata of society had a pivotal role to play in moving society in the direction of having more balance between economic prosperity, social wealth, and environmental safeguards. They also expressed the view that corporate advocacy was essential in promoting sustainable development, as shared by Participant #12, former CEO of a major power authority in Ghana:

> Strong advocacy should come from corporate citizens, making sure that it is working with the government to understand and help them in areas where they need to be spending the money. We cannot leave the government alone to do that.

Some participants intimated that Africans needed to reexamine the blind copying of destructive competitive tendencies of Western capitalism since most of such tendencies undermined harmony on the continent. For those that shared such views, the *survival of the fittest* competitive philosophy inherent in neoliberal capitalism was antithetical to traditional African notions of peace and harmony.

Participant #20 advocated for a rejection of destructive discordant competitive tendencies of Western capitalism, and a return to traditional African philosophies that tended toward conciliation and cooperation, rather than competition:

> Africa should look more at cooperation rather than competition ... that is our culture as Africans. We need to rediscover our values. We are traditionally people who seek and work toward the welfare of the entire society.

### 4.3.4 A Sense of Place and Belonging

It turned out that the strong identity felt as Ghanaians/Africans comingled with the need to see Ghana develop, served as a strong driver of the work of many of the activist CEOs who participated in this study. For instance, Participant #20 indicated that their work as a CEO activist was largely influenced by their strong desire to see Ghana join the comity of developed nations of the world:

> I am a CEO activist because I want my business to thrive, even when I am no more. So, I am pushing for the advancement of society, not for my own sake, but the sake of future generations. You cannot belong to any other place but Africa, where you were born ... where you belong ... where your umbilical cord is buried ..., so you'd wish that your Motherland would also prosper and

have a high level of progress, prosperity, and development. That's why we do what we do as CEO activists.

For Participant #8, Ghana was his only Motherland and was the only country they belonged to. Owing to this tera-bonding, they found it necessary to do whatever they could to make the country a better home for all Ghanaians:

> All those migrants who have been dying on the Sahara Desert or drowning in the Mediterranean Sea in their bid to leave Africa for perceived greener pastures in Europe wouldn't be dying if we all tried to make Africa a better place for us all. Ghana is the only place I can call "home," so that I don't have to ever leave it to go anywhere else.

For several other participants, this feeling was expressed in terms of some deep pride in identifying as Ghanaian. Using some experiences surrounding the birth of his second daughter, Participant #18 spoke about their pride in being a Ghanaian:

> I like to say I am a proud Ghanaian. When my wife was pregnant with my second daughter, she was in the UK with her sister. My mother-in-law wanted my wife to give birth in the UK, but I insisted that I wanted my daughter to be born in Ghana.

Thus, several participants disclosed that Ghana was the only place they could call home and that all of its citizens were duty-bound to address developmental challenges facing the nation. In the words of Participant #16, CEO activism in Africa ought to be distinct from the expressions of the phenomenon elsewhere. The object of CEO activism in Africa related to leapfrogging Africa's developmental agenda:

> CEO activism is more relevant in Africa than anywhere else because we're left behind in development. Others may engage in CEO activism out of altruism, but in Africa, we must do so out of urgency and necessity to leapfrog our development, while ensuring social justice.

Many participants said that their love for Africa was the reason why they became CEO activists. Participant #14 explained that Africa was the only continent for Africans and Africanists and that no matter how much Africans tried to belong elsewhere, those other places would never be their true homes. It was therefore essential for the current generation of Africans to ensure the continent's preservation and sustainable development:

> My love for Africa is the reason why I am a CEO activist. I am African and this is where I belong ... I owe it to the generations that have graced me the opportunity and more the responsibility to

be African and to be on this land to account for my time and ensure that the land that they've leased to me, will be handed over in much better shape than we found it.

For Participant #13, it was their love for Ghana and their pride in being an African that sparked their desire to be a CEO activist. They explained that it was their consciousness of being an African, and the confidence in their ability to help make some positive contributions to Africa's social transformation that kept their activist spirit alive. They expressed their belief in staying relevant by helping to find home-grown solutions to Africa's developmental problems. They noted that they were born in Africa to be an important part of solving the biggest problems facing Africa:

My belief in Ghana and the love and pride I have in being Africa has everything to do with my activism as a CEO. I think the whole African consciousness; being a Black person; taking great pride in being who I am; and the fact that I know I can make an impact in my community ...

## 4.4 Discussion

Against the backdrop of the African continent's continued struggles to develop, Africapitalism has been mooted as an innovative home-grown inclusive capitalist philosophy that could support the socioeconomic transformation of the continent by supporting the increased role of private sector players on the continent of Africa (see Amaeshi & Idemudia, 2015). Despite these strong initial hopes and expectations of Africapitalism, some scholars have virtually described the concept as utopian. Subjecting the concept of Africapitalism to serious stricture, Adegbite et al. (2020) wondered as to the workability of the concept.

Phillips et al. (2004) argued for a discursive approach to understanding institutionalization processes, based on the belief that it is not actions, in and of themselves, that serve as the foundation for institutionalization, but rather that such processes are realized through the agency of texts and language describing and communicating those actions. Thus, this study sought to investigate the concept of Africapitalism as a special motivation of CEO activism in Ghana, on the way to examining the extent to which continuous discussions on Africapitalism among business leaders could be seen to be helping institutionalize both Africapitalism and CEO activism.

Overall, it was found that CEO activism in Ghana was not only motivated by the desire to uphold some notions of *Africapitalism* but also that CEO activism in the country was an expression of Africapitalism. Many of the participants shared views that were consistent with some postulates of Africapitalism such as unique understandings of such ideas as a sense of progress and prosperity, a sense of parity, a sense of harmony, and a sense of place and belonging.

Further, contrary to doubts in sections of the literature about the mere paper beauty of the concept of Africapitalism (see e.g., Adegbite et al., 2020), the findings support the discursive notions of institutionalization articulated by Phillips et al. (2004). It was learned that Africapitalism has already taken hold as a workable business ethic and that many business leaders have started working according to the Africapitalism ethic. One expression of the power of Africapitalism can be found in the effective ways in which it is spurring notions of inclusive capitalism and promoting CEO capitalism in Ghana. The concept of Africapitalism is scarcely a perfect business idea. While it is still a diamond in the rough, this study has demonstrated that the concept has already taken hold within the business community in Ghana and is serving as an important impetus for CEO activism.

# Chapter 5

# This Is What We Fight for: Examining CEO Activism Issues

## 5.1 Introduction

Some scholars have conceptualized corporations, their executives, and the brands in the corporate stable as having the capacity for engaging in activism (Hillman et al., 2004). Thus, there is a slowly increasing corps of scholarly work that focuses on profit-seeking corporations now seeking to serve multiple stakeholder interests, by engaging in one form of activism or another (Nalick et al., 2016) on political issues (Baur & Wettstein, 2016; Wettstein & Baur, 2016), social issues (Dodd & Supa, 2014, 2015), and environmental issues (Moscato, 2016; Ofori-Parku, 2015). For instance, Ben and Jerry's taking a public stance on the issue of gay marriage, based on its core brand purpose and belief in social justice. There have been similar trends in the environmental realm, where corporations have been proactive and vociferous in campaigning regarding damming (Moscato, 2016), climate change (Moscato, 2018), and oil production (Ofori-Parku, 2015).

Nalick et al. (2016) conceptualized sociopolitical issues as "… salient unresolved matters on which societal and institutional opinion is split, thus potentially engendering acrimonious debate across groups" (Nalick et al., 2016, p. 386). Such sociopolitical issues are characterized by several elements. Usually, there is a lack of societal consensus because such issues border on "contentious unsettled social matters on which opinions are split between 'for' and 'against' camps" (Nalick et al., 2016, p. 386).

Thus, sociopolitical matters are some of the most controversial issues and sensitive topics of the day that threaten the social, religious, economic, ethnic, partisan, or some historical sociocultural or geopolitical order (Haider-Markel & Meier, 1996). Second, sociopolitical issues are characterized by low information rationality, as information asymmetry and low information structures tend to curtail credible information and reasoning about the positionalities of the contesting camps, relative to the issue (Nalick et al., 2016). Finally, sociopolitical issues are marked by evolving viewpoints and issue salience.

CEOs on a Mission, 87–106

Copyright © 2023 Eric Kwame Adae

Published under exclusive licence by Emerald Publishing Limited

doi:10.1108/978-1-80382-215-020231005

## 5.2 Kotler and Sarkar's Brand Activism Clusters

Kotler and Sarkar (2017) place the evolution of brand activism on a continuum, arguing that brand activism developed out of: (1) market-driven goals (cause-related marketing and corporate social marketing); (2) corporate-driven (CSR/sustainability and PCSR); and (3) values/corporate purpose-driven (brand activism, often occasioned by social, political, economic, legal, environmental, and business concerns).

These scholars also observe that brand activism is reflective of rising environmental, social, and governance (ESG) concerns (Kotler & Sarkar, 2017). It has further been suggested that the rise in brand activism stems from widespread disappointment in CSR (Kotler & Sarkar, 2019), as illustrated by the afore-stated marketing and cognate censures of CSR. Brand activism runs counter to the profit-maximization philosophy of corporations for investors and embraces a values-driven multistakeholder agenda for brands' concerns for society's future, the planet's sustainability, and justice for all (Lirtsman, 2017). Brand activism is unique in being driven by corporations' concerns for the biggest and most pressing problems that remain unresolved by CSR (Kotler & Sarkar, 2017, 2018a, 2018b).

## 5.3 Corporate Social Advocacy and CEO Activism Issues

Dodd and Supa (2014) observed that "public stances regarding controversial social-political issues by executive leaders of major organizations (termed corporate social advocacy...) seem to be increasingly commonplace" (p. 1), situating the phenomenon at the intersection of two important areas of scholarship and practice, namely strategic issues management and corporate social responsibility.

CEO activism involves CEOs publicly speaking up on sociopolitical and environmental issues that are not directly related to corporate profitability, including such issues as climate change, same-sex marriage, social injustice and inequality, gun control, etc. (Chatterji & Toffel, 2018). CEO activism is spurred by such notions as serving the triple bottom line, CSR, brand activism, brand responsibility, and multistakeholder perspectives.

Once motivated to undertake CEO activism, the literature on CEO activism suggests that the next course of action would be for the socially minded activist CEO to select a range of sociopolitical issues that would serve as the fulcrum for their activism. In their hexagonal typology, Kotler and Sarkar (2017) argue that the main domains of brand activism include: (1) social brand activism (including brand concerns regarding equality, LGBTQ, race, age, gender, education, etc.); (2) political brand activism (including brand concerns for lobbying, campaign financing, etc.); and (3) legal brand activism (including brand concerns for taxation issues and employment laws, etc.). The rest of the categories comprise (4) economic brand activism (including brand concerns for minimum wage and related tax policies); (5) business/workplace activism (including corporate governance and corporate organization, CEO pay, worker compensation, labor and union relations, supply chain management, governance, etc.); and (vi) environmental brand activism (including brand concerns for climate change, land use, air quality, conservations, etc.).

The sociopolitical issue classes postulated by Kotler and Sarkar (2017, 2018b) were invoked to help organize the range of issue clusters that informants in this study disclosed. This chapter focuses on presenting findings on the range of sociopolitical issues pursued by the activist CEOs who participated in this study, based on the Research Question: *What range of sociopolitical issues do CEO activists in Ghana focus on?* Thus, the focus of this chapter is the investigation of the extent to which the range of issues that activist CEOs selected for this study in Ghana could fit these brand activism categories/clusters postulated by Kotler and Sarkar (2017, 2018b).

### 5.3.1 Pursuing Multiple Issues Simultaneously

Generally, it was found that rarely did the study participants focus on single issues. Many of the informants said they had advocated multiple issues simultaneously, such as gender diversity in Ghana, women's empowerment, national economic management policy and issues, African leadership concerns, corruption, and the environment. For instance, Participant #1 described the breadth of issues that have engaged the attention of some activist CEOs in Ghana:

> Most CEOs talk about gender diversity, women's empowerment, gender rights, economy, corruption, leadership in Africa, and environmental challenges. We haven't been too vocal on climate change, it is just the issue of illegal mining, water pollution, filth, and sanitation.

Some of the activist CEOs in this study had seen the need to create or belong to permanent special-purpose vehicles through which they undertook their social resistance actions. For Participant #14, such a formal special-purpose resistance organization was the One Ghana Movement (OGM), which they said they co-founded. Using the OGM as a pressure group, they revealed the broad range of issues or causes they had advocated, including demanding greater public accountability, the prioritization of Ghana's national interest over personal and party-political ones, and the promotion of civic responsibility:

> I have also taken stances for or against many issues. The One Ghana Movement stands for good citizenship; public policy accountability, prioritization of the national interest over partisan interest, and citizens' responsibility.

It became evident that activist CEOs such as Participant #8 had also spoken on a myriad of issues in Ghana. They disclosed that since January 2016, they had publicly pursued well over 77 separate issues or causes in Ghana:

> I was doing a count about two days ago, because some people have
> tried to attack us, saying we are currently not as active as we used
> to be during the previous National Democratic Congress (NDC)
> government. I am not done yet with counting, but between
> January 2016 and now [mid-November 2019], we have tackled
> 77 issues, ranging from relatively simple matters to more
> complicated ones.

Indeed, many participants in this research project discussed some of the specific sociopolitical and environmental issues they had advocated since adopting
the activist stance. While generally, most of the CEOs in this study tended to
pursue a cocktail of causes, some specific issues emerged as illustrating the causes
that the participants advocated. Although some of the issues identified were
cross-cutting and defied neat compartmentalization, they were placed in the six
clusters postulated by Kotler and Sarkar (2017, 2018b).

### 5.3.2 Environmental Activism

Several types of issues were identified that involved environmental activism
undertaken by the CEOs in this study. A handful of participants had made
environmental causes the mainstay of their work as activist CEOs. Within the
broad field of environmental concerns in Ghana, CEO activism causes were found
to include addressing problems associated with climate change, sanitation, and
pollution.

One of the chief environmental concerns that some of the informants in this
study had been working hard to tackle was the issue of *Galamsey*, a *Ghanaianism*
for illegal small-scale (typically gold) mining operations that occurred in all
manner of mineral-rich locations across the country (sadly, even within forest
reserves). Owing to the unregulated processes and procedures employed, such
illegal mining activities have been responsible for environmental degradation in
Ghana, including the pollution of rivers and water bodies.

Participant #6 testified that they had spearheaded consistent fights against
*Galamsey* in Ghana. They added that, for them, such a fight had a broader and
wider significance than those of being a business leader, asserting that pursuing
such a cause was more about being a responsible elder of an African community:

> I took on issues to do with the environment and causes to
> transform society. These have included working against illegal
> mining activities and the adverse impact of such irresponsible
> operations on the environment. I consider myself an elder. I
> can't look on when things go wrong in society. That'd be
> irresponsible of me.

Participant #6 had been working with various partners such as the Occupy
Ghana Movement and the Media Coalition Against Galamsey, to press against

the continued operations of *Galamsey* activities in Ghana. Similarly, other study participants reported working in the area of environment and sanitation matters, including advocating against poor waste management culture, poor sanitation standards and practices, and bad plastic waste disposal practices in the country. Some participants disclosed that they advocate for a cleaner environment and society, pushing for the mainstreaming of national discussions on plastic littering, banning single-use plastics, and promoting a culture of recycling and sustainable manufacturing and consumption practices in Ghana.

### 5.3.3 Business/Workplace Activism

Several issues that could be considered as business/workplace activism engaged the attention of some of the participants in this study. A consistent issue that had been of concern for virtually all the women CEO activists who took part in this study generally was the woeful underrepresentation of women in management positions and on the boards of most Ghanaian companies. Thus, the issue of breaking the proverbial ceiling ran through the activities of many of the women CEOs in Ghana.

Several of the women CEOs, especially those promoters and members of the Executive Women Network (EWN) who participated in this study indicated that providing effective avenues for more women to climb the corporate ladder in Ghana served not only as an impetus for the establishment of the EWN but also that it was a major fulcrum for their resistance activities. Noting that many institutional barriers worked against the progress of women across many fields in Ghana, Participant #1 indicated that helping more women in Ghana to break the glass ceiling had been a major issue for them:

> Here, few women rise the corporate world ... we're poorly represented in management and on the boards. I thought it was important that having gone through that process and risen to the top, it was essential to help others to also get them up there. The EWN is focused on addressing this.

One of the causes that had engaged the attention of some activist CEOs in Ghana was the need to promote a more vibrant and robust service culture in Ghana. For Participant #8, Ghana needed to focus on enhancing its service sector because that sector provided some of the glowing opportunities for the country to leapfrog in its developmental aspirations. They noted that Ghana's service sector held the keys to rapid socioeconomic development:

> I advocated very strongly that the government should prioritize the service sector because it presented brilliant prospects for Ghana. People didn't see my point and criticized because most they were thinking of industrialization, while I was looking at the service sector.

It turned out that Participant #15 had also been keen to promote a higher standard of customer service in Ghana. They expressed the belief that Ghana could enjoy competitive advantages if it improved the overall service culture while earning more foreign exchange through the promotion of tourism:

> I spoke about customer service in Ghana. Although we are a hospitable people, many tourists don't leave with that impression. If we say we want to be a destination of hospitality and history, it must transcend every fabric of our tourism. Service excellence is important to achieve that.

### 5.3.4 Sociocultural Activism

In a predominantly patriarchal society such as Ghana, a sticking issue for most of the activist CEOs who participated in this study involved diverse forms of gender-based injustices. Several participants indicated that they had been taking steps to promote the empowerment of women. The main thrust of Participant #3, CEO of the television production company, such social resistance actions had included some attention to a plethora of cultural and institutional barriers in Ghana, militating against the advancement of women and children. These have included tackling issues related to sexual harassment, employment conditions of working women, and the representation and work of women in Ghana's party-political spaces:

> I speak on issues that concern women and children. My purpose is to empower women holistically, while I speak truth to power; I advocate and make noise; I agitate, and I push for the right policies to be developed and implemented in Ghana that would advance the rights and position of women and children. Yes, my target is always the woman – the Ghanaian woman and her emancipation, empowerment, and advancement.

Other participants had been promoting women's empowerment, with advocacy campaigns based on the belief that empowering women was strongly linked with building a nation. For instance, Participant #23, CEO of a major bank deposit protection corporation:

> If you empower the woman, you are building a nation. I created a platform in 2014 to encourage like-minded women to aspire to greatness, provide useful information to each other and help them network and share ideas that would make them more impactful and successful in society.

Participant #13's activism started around 2007 and revolved around a range of issues connected with the empowerment of girls and women in Ghana, including economic empowerment through livelihood support, and prevention of teenage pregnancy by educating young girls about teenage pregnancy. During their interview, they reacted to some statements made by Ghana's President Nana Akufo-Addo at an international women's conference held in Canada in June 2019 that suggested that Ghanaian women were not availing themselves of opportunities to serve in decision-making positions. This informant indicated that the hydra-headed issues facing Ghanaian women meant that women could not be active enough and hoped that their activism would empower more women in Ghana to put their voices to the numerous serious issues facing the country:

> You may remember our president spoke at a women's conference in Canada and created the impression that women in Ghana were not active or amplified enough. Well, there are still a lot of issues in contemporary Ghana that women could stand up against or put a voice to. I hope my activities would encourage more women to come out and speak.

While being active within the area of the empowerment of women and girls in Ghana, Participant #19 had been focusing on boosting the involvement of women and girls in coding and the creation of technology. They disclosed that serving as an advocate for the economic empowerment of women and girls in Ghana would unlock numerous social outcomes for women and girls in the country, including greater levels of respectability, independence, and recognition:

> I've been speaking about getting more women and girls to create technology … creating opportunities for bridging the digital gender gap. I've been an advocate for getting more women and girls to create technology, and for them to cease from being only consumers of technologies. I've also been a very big advocate of economic empowerment for women and girls.

In January 2018, the Births and Deaths Registry in Ghana announced that it was planning to forbid the registration of certain names in Ghana it claimed were "title names." Under the proposed policy, people wishing to register indigenous Ghanaian names such as *Nana, Naa, Junior, Torgbui, Nii,* and *Maame* among others had been stopped by the Registry because it deemed such names as titles, rather than name-names.

Citing the law governing its operations (Act 301 of 1965), the Births and Deaths Registry claimed that it had the power to do so. However, Participant #10 disagreed and saw the need to confront the Births and Deaths Registry on behalf of many Ghanaians who perceived the proposed policy as an attack against their desire to adopt such indigenous names. Seeing the proposed policy not only as backward but also lacking legal basis, Participant #10 testified that their action involved writing a heavily worded letter to the Attorney-General's office, threatening to sue the Births and Deaths Registry of Ghana, if it went ahead to implement such an action:

> You might remember that the Births and Deaths Registry of Ghana decided that they were not going to register some popular and generic Ghanaian names such as "Naa," "Nii," and "Nana," etc. I realized there was no legal basis, so, we wrote to the Attorney-General, praying that office to instruct the Births and Deaths Registry to withdraw this or face legal action. Within two days, not only was this baseless action withdrawn, but the official who has sought to implement this was removed from that office.

It was learned that the actions of many CEOs who took part in this study also revolved around issues of empowering the youth of Ghana into becoming more entrepreneurial. As some of the informants in this study indicated, too many of Ghana's youth had closed their minds to opportunities existing outside of the formal employment sphere in Ghana. Participant #7 was one of the participants who made youth empowerment the pivot of their activism. This study collaborator disclosed that it was time for the youth of Ghana to take their destinies into their own hands in focusing on being business owners and employers, rather than limiting their options to becoming employees within the country's formal system:

> My activism comprises a mindset transformation for the African youth to go into entrepreneurship since Africa faces a high rate of youth unemployment. This is not because we lack the abilities, but more because I believe we have the wrong educational orientation that seeks to leverage us on training us to more of academicians, rather than performers or doers.

Again, on the theme of youth empowerment – not only in Ghana – but also across West Africa, it emerged that Participant #16 had been focusing on youth investment and personal development, entrepreneurship, and talent development. They indicated that they had been targeting Millennials since 2007, with an annual roadshow series and a weekly television program:

> What I've done is engaged 18 to 35-year-olds over 12 years so far, principally with a roadshow that travels nationwide … a radio broadcast every Sunday evening, on diverse developmental themes, including personal development, career development, grooming, character formation, ethics, and values, and laying the foundations that will produce out of emerging leaders, people who are ethical, and who are also very purpose-driven.

For a few participants in this study, the issue of concern was the dearth of financial literacy among huge sections of the Ghanaian population. Some of the informants in this study identified this lack of competence of commonsense

financial issues as a huge problem that had led to untold hardship, bad investments, and financial choices, and wrong life decisions among the population.

According to Participant #20, one of the major problems they had seen in
Ghana, which they had been acting on, was the prevalence of ignorance among
Ghanaians regarding everyday financial matters. They disclosed that since 2008,
they had been leading the charge to ensure that the average Ghanaian became
more competent in such life skills that involved personal financial management:

> I have been involved in such activism for over 10 years now, since
> 2008 ... promoting financial literacy in Ghana. I have a radio
> program that seeks to deepen financial literacy among the
> population of Ghana.

For some of the informants, an important issue that engaged their attention
was the need to confront the culture of silence in Ghana that had been a part of
the society since the 1980s. Some analysts believe that starting from the 1979
military takeover by Jerry Rawlings, most Ghanaians feared speaking out. For
Participant #12, the culture of silence in Ghana was anathema to the new
republican constitution of the country. They disclosed that they had noticed some
differences between the level of free speech and the democratic culture that they
saw during their student days in the United Kingdom and what pertained in
Ghana. They observed that they had a hypothesis for building a sound democratic culture in Ghana at the very beginning of Ghana's fourth republic in 1992:

> I hypothesized that unless you had a free and vibrant media,
> democracy would not thrive. I looked at the fact that we have
> had about three very short-lived republican constitutions in
> Ghana: The first lasted about six years; the second, about two
> years; and the third also lasted about two years. I could see this
> same danger on the fourth republic, where there was a very clear
> expression that you can establish a private media organization
> without licensing, yet any time anybody tried to apply that the
> bureaucracy would kick in and say that we're reviewing your
> application and we would get back to you, but they never did so.

Thus, this threat signaled the very genesis of this participant's life as an activist,
which saw them taking the view that the extant law must be enforced. Participant
#12 contended that Ghana's constitution was very unequivocal in promoting
media pluralism and free speech in the country:

> I took the view that the constitutional intent was very clear, so let's
> set it up and have a public fight ... to force the government to
> allow plural broadcasting .... So, I set up a pirate radio station,
> called Radio XXX [not the real station identity]. It was a lot about
> educating the public and bringing them along that the government
> eventually was forced to say they were also for media pluralism

.... The point is that you don't need a license to operate a radio station in Ghana. This is guaranteed in the Constitution of Ghana in Chapter 12, Article 1263 which says there shall be no need for a license.

Falling on their vast experience as an activist with some knowledge about how to engage in public campaigns based on agitation and propaganda *(Agitprop)* tactics, they said they knew exactly what to do to force the hands of the relevant authorities in Ghana to act in ways that would help their cause and to free the media landscape in Ghana:

You had all this background that says if you had just set up a radio station and just sat back and watched and the government would just send in the goons to come and shut it down. In this case, we set up a radio station, and in just over a couple of weeks, it was heard all over metropolitan Accra and national security raided it. But the interesting thing was that this was the beginning of the campaign; it was raided on a Sunday and Monday, we went to court and argued that by the Constitution of Ghana, you are not allowed to do what you have done.

Participant #8 disclosed that their activities had included fighting the government to provide essential services for Ghanaians. They disclosed that this struggle had led to the One Ghana-led #OccupyFlagstaffHouse protests in 2016:

We had the *Occupy Flagstaff House*, a march organized to stage a protest to the seat of Ghana's presidency. Generally, too many things were not going well in the country; *Dumsor* was at its peak, and we believed the standard of governance was just too low. This was why we decided to keep the pressure on the government to improve things in the country. These were why I called some of my friends and I formed Occupy Ghana.

Thus, they revealed that the main impetus for the formation of Occupy Ghana was the myriad of dysfunctions and failures in the country, in the run-up to the 2016 presidential and parliamentary polls. What had become popularly known as *Dumsor*, a *Twi/Akan* term for *electricity power frequently coming on, but then going off*, a reference to the erratic electric power situation in Ghana at the time, was the chief trigger for the formation of Occupy Ghana and its various protest actions. Besides, the group was also dissatisfied with the general standard of governance in Ghana. Participant #8 explained what Occupy Ghana did to help end *Dumsor*, and the circumstances surrounding his decision to part company with this activist group:

One of the biggest demonstrations ever held in Ghana has been the *"Dumsor Must Stop,"* held in May 2015 to press the then NDC government to take steps to end the power crisis that had plagued the country. We thought the government needed to address the situation, as a matter of priority. *Dumsor Must Stop* kicked the government into the overdrive action that culminated in the resolution of the power crisis facing the Ghanaian society.

It was found that some activist CEOs in Ghana had been instrumental in the passage of Ghana's Right to Information Bill into law in the middle of 2019. Participant #8 talked about how this bill was kept on the back burner for well over a decade. However, through the mounting of consistently stronger resistance action, the hand of the NPP administration of President Addo-Dankwa and the current Parliament of Ghana had no option but to take the bold action to pass the bill into law:

> The most is the Right to Information Law, passed in the middle of 2019. We had the Right to Information Bill for well over 10 years. We kept pressing and blowing the matter open. We now have the Right to Information passed into law partly because of our activism.

### 5.3.5 Political Activism

Among the range of measures that some activist CEOs in Ghana had advocated in their bid to fight endemic corruption in Ghana was the need to promote greater transparency by compelling politicians and public officeholders in the country to declare their assets. Some informants revealed that under the laws of the Republic of Ghana, the Auditor-General was mandated to ensure that all public institutions complied with the provisions of Article 286 of the Constitution and Public Office Holders (Declaration of Assets and Disqualification) Act, 1998 (Act 550).

According to Participant #10, as at the time of their interview for this study in the middle of November 2019, no public office holder had complied with this legal provision, neither had the Auditor-General of Ghana nor the Attorney-General actively enforced the law. They stressed that they were working with their colleagues at Occupy Ghana to right this perceived wrong:

> Occupy Ghana is working on compelling asset declaration in Ghana because currently, nobody is complying with the law that requires public officers to declare their assets. Tomorrow (November 15, 2019), we will write to the Attorney-General of Ghana, drawing attention to this blatant contravention of the laws of the land. We are going to invite the Attorney-General to agree with us that there is this contravention of the laws and that the Attorney-General's Department would take urgent steps to

enforce this law on the declaration of assets, failing which we are
going to drag the Attorney-General to court.

It was found that a CEO had engaged in a resistance action, designed to raise
the awareness of the Ghanaian public to the emergence of militia-style political
vigilantes who have been meting out various forms of violence against perceived
political enemies, particularly during various elections in Ghana. An instance of
the activities of political vigilantes occurred on January 31, 2019, during a parliamentary by-election at Accra's Ayawaso West Wuogon constituency to elect a
new member of parliament, following the demise of the NPP's Emmanuel
Agyarko (Amoah, 2019).

Despite having candidates from other political parties in the race, pollsters saw
the election as a direct contest between Lydia Alhassan (one of the late MP's
widows) and the NDC's Delali Kwesi Brempong. In the lead to the Ayawaso
bye-elections of January 2019, it was an open secret that the two main political
parties had organized and funded the operations of various vigilantes, with the
*Invincible Forces* and *Delta Force* associated with the NPP, while their counter-
parts at the NDC included *The Hawks* and *The Azorka Boys.*

Within hours of the opening of the polls, media reports had it that masked
men, dressed in National Security-branded uniforms besieged the home of the
opposition NDC's candidate in the elections, located around the La Bawaleshie
polling center, shooting and wounding some 18 civilians. Finger-pointing and
accusations abound, following the incident. The opposition NDC accused the
ruling NPP of masterminding the attack.

Media reports had it that many persons were injured, with some suffering
gunshot wounds. In a Facebook post, Sam George, the Member of Parliament for
Ningo-Prampram, reported that he had been assaulted by some macho men he
described as members of the NPP's Invincible Forces:

> I have just been assaulted by several members of the NPP
> Invincible Forces attired in National Security Council shirts and
> vests. They fired several rounds of ammunition at me simply
> because I was doing my legal job of monitoring the Ayawaso
> West Wuogon by-election.

Based on their experience with the Liberian civil war, Participant #13 revealed
that they became concerned about the growing pattern of electoral violence in
Ghana that was generally attributed to political vigilantes. They decided to
embark on a protest march #WHYIWALK FOR GHANA on February 26,
2019. In a petition presented to the leadership of parliament in Ghana, Participant
#13 gave the Government of Ghana one month within which all political vigi-
lantes should be disbanded in the country, failing which they threatened to keep
the pressure mounting by continuing to protest:

> The violence was at the Ayawaso West Wuogon by-election in
> 2019 ... In my statement, I said we would keep protesting until

things changed. I could not imagine living at peace within myself, with that explosive situation that such political vigilantes and electoral violence could bring to Ghana. If I don't act and something happens, can I live with myself? Can I look at my children in the face, knowing I could have taken steps to neutralize the situation?

Across Africa, elections are considered among the most contentious events on the calendar of many nations. The declaration of results of virtually every presidential and parliamentary election has been met with bitter protests from losing camps, with charges of the rigging of the election. Ghana has had its unfair share of such disputed election results. The declaration by the National Electoral Commission of the NPP's Nana Akufo-Addo as President of Ghana after the December 2016 polls in Ghana generated a heated protest in Ghana by the losing NDC, whose incumbent President John Dramani Mahama had lost the presidency. This culminated in a long-drawn election petition process that involved some eight months of disputations in the law courts of Ghana.

The Electoral Commission of Ghana had indicated that it was no longer going to supply political parties in the country the pink sheets, which were receipts from the various polling stations about what exactly happened at each station during the elections. This was because the Electoral Commission of Ghana had perceived these pink sheets as the main cause of electoral disputes in Ghana in the past. This development did not agree with the activist mindset of Kofi Bentil who saw the need to take some actions to help reform Ghana's electoral system:

> It was clear that it was wrong. I decided to rally around some lawyers for us to challenge this in the courts before any new election was held in Ghana. Lawyer Akoto Ampaw led us to go to court. The Supreme Court was surprised, and it was surprising to me that they were surprised because they had not noticed the anomaly. The Supreme Court ruled in our favor, stating that the Electoral Commissioner should provide all parties with the pink sheets from every polling station to the political parties. Looking at Ghana's electoral history, I think that was a significant development.

According to Participant #8, this landmark achievement concerning the pink sheets was not an isolated event. They described several factors that led to the culmination of this development, which was activist in nature. For instance, this study participant saw themselves as one of the first people who stood against the call for the country to compile a new electoral register. They explained that they felt the need to kick against this new electoral roll because doing so was going to entail too much financial outlay for a struggling economy like Ghana's.

Participant #8 asserted that their opposition to the planned program to have a new electoral roll called for them to speak at many forums. They added that this move on their part had attracted many attacks against them:

I was heckled, and there were instances of personal attacks and
people insulting me, but I stuck to my position because I believed I
was right. It is difficult to fight against the tide.

### 5.3.6 *Legal Activism*

Through legal activism, a few of the CEOs in this study reported resistance to the
pattern of state capture that had taken hold in Ghana. These participants were
disheartened to note that individuals who had a significant influence – including
those in government and others in policymaking positions – used such connections and privileges to change the rules of engagement, for the benefit of private
individuals, very much against the state interest.

Participant 22, former CEO of a huge petroleum company, observed that
resisting state capture had been the main thrust of their activism. For them,
everything must be done to preserve the interest of the country, over those of
private persons:

> Resisting state capture in Ghana is my advocacy now. My
> advocacy is that the state is paramount and that the state needs
> to benefit the most from any transaction we do, rather players -
> players, either in government or sitting in government, or players
> sitting outside of government, influencing players sitting in
> government to change the rules so that the private sector can
> benefit against the state. Whether it is a procurement bid;
> whether it is road projects; whether it is an oil transaction;
> whatever it is, they are always trying to influence the process to
> their advantage, rather than Ghana's. That is my Number One
> project in activism right now.

Participant #8 and some close friends decided to form Occupy Ghana to serve
as a pressure group to highlight some of the failures of the John Mahama-led
government and to hold the government to account by speaking truth to power,
through diverse resistance activities. One of the chief activities of Occupy Ghana
had become a test case in legal activism in Ghana, involving a case the group
brought against the state to compel the Auditor-General of Ghana to crack the
whip in the direction of checking endemic corruption in Ghana. Participant #8
offered some glimpses into the nature of Occupy Ghana's anticorruption drive:

> We sued the Auditor-General in the Supreme Court, asking for an
> order to compel him to do his job well. His job was to surcharge
> and disallow it when people have corruptly or improperly used
> government funds. The current Auditor General (Dominic
> Domelevo) is using that law, ... last week (early October 2019),
> he surcharged the Senior Minister (Hon. Osafo Marfo) for some

expenditure that the Auditor-General disallowed. That was historic in Ghana. That was a big win and I am happy that I was a part of that pressure.

Explaining aspects of their role in this matter, Participant #10 described it in terms of seeking to protect the public purse by activating sections of Ghana's 1992 Constitution that empowered the Auditor-General to work to recover funds that the nation lost through negligence or the misconduct of individuals, groups, companies, and other institutions:

> Our greatest issue has been the Auditor-General issue. We went to the Supreme Court of Ghana at a great expense to us, for a determination of the matter. The Supreme Court wondered why an existing law was not being enforced and instructed the Auditor-General to enforce the law.

Another action to probe and question the propriety of bilateral and related state agreements was the 2018 deal between the Government of Ghana and Haitian ICT firm Kelni-GVG. The agreement was aimed at developing and implementing a common platform for the monitoring of mobile phone traffic and the revenues accruing to the state thereof. Some described this as a controversial multimillion-dollar agreement in which Imani Africa, accused the Ministry of Communication of Ghana, acting in concert with its technical agency, the National Communications Authority (NCA), to award a 10-year contract worth nearly US $180 million to Kelni GVG, describing the contract as a "rape" of Ghana.

In June of the same year, a principal of Imani, Kofi Bentil, acting as a public interest lawyer, commenced multiple lawsuits, on behalf of one Maximus Amertogoh and one Sara Asafu-Adjaye against the Ministry of Communications on grounds of financial maladministration and privacy threats. The lawsuits brought by Kofi Bentil met significant delays, subterfuge, and resistance by the Ministry of Communications, making it clear that a legal course of action was not the best way out. Participant #8 offered the following reflections on this saga:

> Take the Kelni-GVG scandal in 2018 that exposed the controversial US$ 89 million deal, signed between the Government of Ghana and the Haitian firm, Kelni-GVG. We saw so many irregularities and decided to take the State to court, to compel them to account to the people of Ghana.

### 5.3.7 Economic Activism

It was found that some of the CEOs who participated in this study had been focusing on issues concerning ensuring better economic management in Ghana.

Some of them such as Participant #18 had been resisting the government for more effective management of the Ghanaian currency, the *Cedi* which had for many years, unfortunately, become accustomed to a pattern of huge depreciation against some of the major trading currencies across the globe, such as the US Dollar, the Euro, the British Pound Sterling, and the Japanese Yen.

Since the year 2013, Participant #5 appears to have taken on the persona of an unofficial shadow finance minister of Ghana, speaking up and questioning the soundness of some of the economic policies of the Government of Ghana under both the Mahama-led NDC administration and the Akufo Addo-led NPP. While observing that they had been concerned with the proper economic and financial management of the resources of Ghana, they also revealed that activism had been embedded in the corporate strategy of their company, with the view to achieving some corporate ends, including branding, marketing, and reputational goals:

> I've been speaking on economic issues since 2013. I have been talking about economic and financial management issues in Ghana, breaking them out and highlighting the failures in some of our national economic matters in ways that the ordinary Ghanaian would understand.

According to Participant #5, they had been deliberate in highlighting a range of economic and financial matters, including the weak competitiveness of Ghanaian companies, high rates of unemployment in Ghana, and huge import bills facing Ghana. They indicated that their activism had been propelled by their desire to ensure a business-friendly operating environment while exercising their social responsibility:

> I've spoken on generally on economic issues in Ghana; things that have got to do with the economy and their impact; I've spoken about Ghanaian companies not being productive enough; why companies in Ghana are not competitive, and the reasons why that is the case. One of my pet peeves has been about the Ghanaian currency, the Cedi.

For Participant #20, the specific issue of concern had been uncontrolled government expenditures by governments in Ghana and across Africa. They disclosed that they had lately taken up issue with the huge amounts that governments in Africa had been incurring for attending various bilateral summits of African countries and some of their partners, including the United States of America, the United Kingdom, India, and Russia.

Describing such expenditures as not going in the interest of Africa, Participant #20 disclosed that they had been advocating for such summits to be held in Africa on a rotational basis among the countries on the continent, rather than the current order that amounted to huge sums being drained out of Africa. They also noted that attending such summits in Africa would afford Africa's development partners the chance to have a first-hand experience of the issues they were seeking to address in Africa through such meetings:

> I took a public stance not too long ago about Africa's leaders' tendency to frequently travel for various summits. We have the US-Africa Summit; the UK-Africa Summit; the India-Africa Summit; Russia-Africa Summit, etc. Whenever it is time for any of these summits, you find every African leader and his/her team traveling to the venue, usually outside of Africa. This creates so much touristic value and benefits for these foreign host countries of these conferences, but nothing for Africa.

It became evident that those economy-focused CEO activists had also been interested in pursuing related causes such as selected programs and policies of the government of Ghana, such as the 1D1F, and cognate issues including food and hunger. Participant #18, who was one of the participants who appeared to focus on economic matters described the issues that had engaged their attention:

> I have spoken out about economic management in Ghana, currency management, or the depreciation of the Ghana Cedi, and I have spoken for the 1D1F. I have advocated for ending world hunger and feeding the needy all over the world. I have also spoken out against the poor waste management culture or poor sanitation in Ghana, the bad plastic waste disposal practices in Ghana.

Some activist CEOs in Ghana have been engaged in intellectual debates with the Government of Ghana on diverse public procurement deals and agreements with some international institutions. Such public debates have been based on the perception that these public procurements and agreements did not meet the value-for-money criterion and did not serve the best interest of the generality of Ghanaians.

One of these agreements was the STX Housing agreement. In 2009, a 12-member delegation of the Government of Ghana, led by Alban Bagbin, the then Minister of Works and Housing signed a housing project deal with STX Corporation of South Korea. The project would have seen the construction of 200,000 houses in Ghana for over five years, at an estimated project cost of $10 billion (Adu-Gyamerah, 2010).

In August 2010, Ghana's Parliament approved an initial off-take agreement for 30,000 housing units for the security agencies at a $1.5 billion, amid protests from the opposition New Patriotic Party (NPP) and several pressure groups and civil society organizations that were dissatisfied with some aspects of this agreement (Adu-Gyamerah, 2010). However, on December 30, 2011, Ghanaians received news that the Professor John Evans Atta Mills-led National Democratic Congress (NDC) government had decided to abrogate the controversial multi-billion housing deal (Kpodo, 2012).

Some observers also attributed the project's collapse to the ineffective and haphazard manner in which the Ghanaian government handled the agreement, including some murkiness surrounding the sovereign guarantee issued by the Ghana Government to STX to enable the joint venture to source for funding in the world's financial markets for the project. Participant #8 also criticized Minister Bagbin who disregarded all the objections raised by various stakeholders. They provided some details about their role in the protests:

> Intellectually, we have debated a project such as the $10 billion 200,000-unit housing project with South Korea's STX Corporation. We evaluated the project closely and realized that it was not going to work out well for the country. We agitated for well over one year, but the Government did not want to listen to us. Ultimately, this project crushed, right in their faces. If they had listened to us, they would have avoided a lot of the consequences of this failed deal.

The Komenda Sugar Factory is another flawed government project that had engaged the attention of Participant #8. According to them, this project had also failed because the government did not appreciate the intellectual activism that they and Imani Africa did to warn the government about why the project would not succeed as planned. The failure of such a huge project, they disclosed had led to significant financial losses to the country:

> I expressed the view that the Komenda Sugar Factory was going to produce more propaganda than sugar! We broke it down and explained it in very simple terms. The Government of Ghana did not listen to us, and at the end of the day, more than US $36 million of Ghana's money is down the drain, with totally nothing to show for all that investment. Everything we had said had come true.

One of the issues that had been the subject of Participant #8's actions has been a proposed 40-year development plan for Ghana. Without much attention to detail, the Government of Ghana tabled this long-term plan of development for the country. A group of activists and CEO activists in Ghana saw this move by the government as yet another ploy to pay lip service to the developmental challenges facing the country.

While failing to address some of the most pressing immediate needs and challenges facing the populace, the government was planning for a 40-year timescale. Noting that this supposed program of development was not only ill-conceived but would also entail some serious financial losses to the country, activists such as Participant #8 engaged to protest the proposed development plan:

We interrogated a proposed 40-year development plan for Ghana ... a very ill-thought-through plan. It was just nice and sexy for people to think that we were going to have a plan to deal with the development of the nation over the next 40 years. However, there was nothing to show that the Government of Ghana really knew what they were talking about. There were more immediate development challenges confronting us, such as water, health, energy, and education, about which nothing had been done. Yet, they were purporting to be planning for the next 40 years. Ghana was going to spend over US$ 2.5 million on education and sensitization. They had planned to spend Ghs 1 million (about US$ 250,000) for each of the 16 regions in Ghana to try to get people's views or reactions to the proposed plan. We objected to the approach, saying it was not the right thing to do.

## 5.4 Discussion

This chapter investigated the broad classes of issues that the study participants advocated. Currently, there is a preponderance of Western CEO activism cases, which has spawned numerous issues and examples of specific causes, most of which do not reflect the realities in non-Western societies. Some examples of CEO activism campaign issues have included gender rights, same-sex marriage, race relations, and immigration concerns – issues that may not necessarily feature as important matters in non-Western societies.

This chapter sought to address this gap in the literature on CEO activism by contributing specific examples of CEO activism issues, from a non-Western perspective. The chapter thus presents the various types of issues and causes that study participants disclosed to be the focus of their campaigns. While many of the participants typically took on a plethora of issues and causes simultaneously, it was possible to organize the various issues discussed, based on the six clusters of brand activism postulated by Kotler and Sarkar (2017, 2018b).

Thus, although Kotler and Sarkar's typology of brand activism clusters – comprising environmental activism, social(cultural) activism, legal activism, economic activism, business/workplace activism, and political activism – was developed specifically for brand activism, it was found that they were largely applicable to CEO activism, as the interview data showed that the wide diversity of issues advocated by the activist CEOs in Ghana could be placed under the various categories in Kotler and Sarkar's (2017, 2018b) typology. However, for this study, various cultural issues needed to be melded with social issues.

The findings make a useful addition to the literature, by introducing specific examples of issues advocated by CEOs within African society. The literature on CEOs, activism, and CEO activism had so far lacked insights regarding the general and specific forms of issues and causes that CEOs within the emerging markets context of Ghana and Africa. The findings could set the stage for studies comparing CEO activism issues in Africa with those elsewhere, such as American CEOs. These findings also provide some indications for future research in the area of the pathways through which gender dynamics shape CEO cause selection, as well as differences in issues chosen by men CEO activists in Africa, relative to those selected by women CEO activists.

Within the context of the working model for this research project, it is suggested that issue selection is made after CEOs have become motivated to become activists. The range of issues however determines the sort of actions the CEO activists take. Based on whether the actions are deemed to be pro-development or not, such resistance actions are termed as either progressive activism or regressive activism (Kotler & Sarkar, 2018a).

These findings further aid the evolution of the CEO Activism Development Model with the incorporation of the major clusters of issues that the participants in this study revealed. Evolution Two of the working model, as depicted in Fig. 4 (below), indicates the broad areas of sociopolitical issues/causes advocated by the study participants.

In implementing or giving force to their resistance actions, a range of tactics are deployed. The next chapter presents the research findings regarding the wide variety of tactics employed by the participants in this study, as part of their social resistance actions.

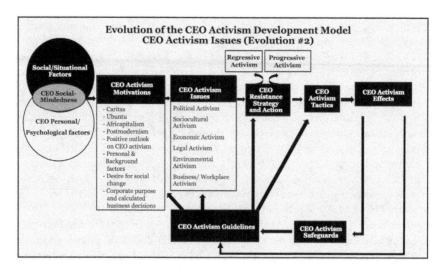

Fig. 4.   Evolution #2 of the CEO Activism Development Model (Indicating the Range of Motivations and CEO Activism Issues/Causes). *Source:* Author (2023).

# Chapter 6

# This Is How We Do It: Examining CEO Activism Tactics

## 6.1 Introduction

Casadesus-Masanelli and Ricart (2010) suggest that although on the face of it, the notions of business models, strategies, and tactics appear similar, there are important distinctions among these concepts. In a conceptual framework to highlight some of the distinctions among these oft-confused terms, these scholars state that "... business model refers to the logic of the firm, the way it operates and how it creates value for its stakeholders. Strategy refers to the choice of the business model through which the firm will compete in the marketplace. Tactics refer to the residual choices open to a firm by virtue of the business model that it employs" (p. 196).

This framework presents an acceptable hierarchy of the relationships among the three concepts. While strategies set up the business model, strategy refers to a higher-order of choices, designed to create a distinctive and value-laded position, through a set of tactical activities (Casadesus-Masanelli & Ricart, 2010). Strategy entails the overall plan or broad range of goals. It comprises a series of plans, methods, and activities, aimed at producing or achieving a given objective. Tactics are the specific actions that are taken as part of the broader strategy/game plan to achieve the overall plan or strategy. Thus, while strategy involves forward-looking and long-term plans, designed to achieve set corporate objectives, tactics are the lower order of actions taken on the road to achieving the strategic ends.

Nalick et al. (2016) distinguish between market or corporate strategy and nonmarket strategy. Generally, while market or corporate strategy focuses on how a company strategically relates to its direct business-defining stakeholders such as suppliers, customers, the labor market, and competitors, nonmarket strategies are concerned with interacting and relating to a wide range of noncommercial stakeholders, such as employees, activists, lawmakers, government agencies, the law courts, and the mass media.

Market strategies are concerned with ensuring that companies play to win in the marketplace, while nonmarket strategies focus on creating and managing relationships with nonmarket stakeholders. The general approach in the management literature is the adoption of the modernist view that focuses on the role of business in nonmarket issues with the presumption of some economic gains or

CEOs on a Mission, 107–126
Copyright © 2023 Eric Kwame Adae
Published under exclusive licence by Emerald Publishing Limited
doi:10.1108/978-1-80382-215-020231006

some competitive advantages for the firm (Hillman et al., 204), with such strategies as corporate political activity, corporate social responsibility, and corporate sociopolitical involvement (Nalick et al., 2016).

## 6.2 Extant CEO Activism Tactics

CEO activism is deemed to be "a fairly unique" (Baur & Wettstein, 2016, p. 171) nonmarket strategy (Livonen, 2018; Nalick et al., 2016) that employs several social movement tactics. It has been suggested that social movements usually employ a rich tactical repertoire (King & Pearce, 2010) to achieve the goals of their campaigns and to deliver the changes desired in society (Livonen, 2018). Such social media tactics include boycotts, letter-writing, demonstrations, marches, sit-ins, and strikes.

The tactics employed by social movements have been described as "culturally inscribed and socially communicated" (Livonen, 2018, p. 9), with new activists being capable of adopting and adapting from the tactical toolkits of existing social movements (Tarrow, 2011; Taylor & Van Dyke, 2004). Thus, it has been suggested that CEO activists could effectively employ existing tried and tested social movement tactics (Livonen, 2018). Livonen (2018) presented a taxonomy of CEO activist tactics, especially directed at three stakeholder groups, namely the government, employees, and the cause and the social movement, following a strategic review of the social movement literature, but also based on an analysis of some contemporary actions of CEOs.

Livonen (2018) however notes that although most of the tactics in CEO activism were culturally borrowed from the standard tactical repertoire of social movements, owing to the higher social statuses of CEOs, relative to the usual social movement actors, but also concerning their stakeholder groups, some of the tactics employed appeared significantly transformed in terms of both reach and impact. Thus, some of the tactics employed by and/or available to CEO activists are not available to the usual social movement actors.

Livonen (2018) presents a framework of the actions taken by CEO activists through their effects on selected organizational stakeholder groups, to the consequences of selected stakeholder reactions for CEOs and their firms, as well as for the focal cause and social movements. In her model, she notes that social movement activism tactics include boycotts, letter-writing, demonstrations, marches, sit-ins, and strikes. Generally, activism campaign tactics have included carnivalesque demonstrations and occupations of buildings to influence public opinion and to garner earned media coverage (Weaver, 2010), and to expose negative environmental impacts of corporations (Murphy & Dee, 1992).

Other activists have employed extreme action to build identity inside the group's constituency (Derville, 2005) and to share information among people who are informed about planned events (Jahng et al., 2014). Some activists also use the Internet and social media (especially Facebook and Twitter (Rodriguez, 2016), media coverage (Saffer et al., 2013), and websites and microsites (Valencia & Jones, 2018).

Chatterji and Toffel (2018) suggest that CEO activists generally employed two distinct classes of tactics in their toolkit. These are (1) *raising awareness* and (2) *leveraging economic power*. The tactic of *raising awareness* entails the employment of communication strategies and tactics designed to raise awareness, garner support for social movements and brand activism, and help drive change in the desired direction. An example of this tactical deployment is Lloyd Blankfein, CEO of Goldman Sachs, and Biogen's former CEO George Scangos publicly pitching in on government policies that affect the LGBTQ rights of individuals. On the social conservative side, Dan Cathy of Chick-fil-A publicly denounced gay marriage (Chatterji & Toffel, 2018).

The tactic of *leveraging economic power* revolves around the activist CEO tactic of putting economic pressure on states to either reject or overturn specific legislation, by threatening some economic or investment repercussions. These authors suggest that some of the most defining examples of CEO activism have involved activist CEOs mounting economic pressure on governments and states to reject or repeal some laws. For instance, Bill Oesterle, CEO of Angie's List canceled his company's planned expansion in Indianapolis, while Benioff threatened to halt Salesforce's employee travel to the state (Chatterji & Toffel, 2018).

The tactic of *leveraging economic power* could be undertaken as a solo effort or in concert with other CEO activists. Companies and their CEOs could thus exercise their economic power by donating to civil society organizations or some social movement groups that favored the interests or causes of the companies and their leaders.

In a related classificatory scheme of CEO activists' tactical repertoire, Livonen (2018) outlined two main classes of tactics, namely (1) *persuasive tactics* and (2) *disruptive/coercive tactics*. *Persuasive tactics* are generally directed at a specific target audience to get the audience to alter its behavior or practices. Such tactics may also be directed at some other stakeholders, to disseminate specific messages about the need to change the target's unacceptable behavior, relative to a wider audience, to engender public support, and press the target into changing behavior in a given direction (King & Pearce, 2010).

*Disruptive tactics*, on the other hand, are aimed at a target, with the view to neutralizing the target's capacity to achieve its goals, while imposing significant costs on it, if possible (King & Pearce, 2010). These two forms of tactics reinforce each other, with disrupting tactics tending to generate media publicity, while persuasive tactics seek to zoom in on the unpalatable facets of the target, such as inflicting reputational damage (King & Pearce, 2010). Livonen (2018) also identified (3) *supportive* tactics, seen as tactics employed by "elite allies" (p. 9), including issuing pro-movement statements/solidarity messages, providing financial support to activists, and giving face and name to the cause (Hutchinson, 2015; King, 2011).

Livonen (2018) notes that CEO activists could employ both persuasive and disruptive tactics in targeting governments. She identifies persuasive tactics as including making personal appeals to the target government, with sub-tactics including private appeals such as letters, phone calls, and meetings; public personal appeals such as open letters; and public appeals such as social media posts and ads. CEO activists also join collective appeals to the target government, in which case sub-tactics could include letter-writing campaigns and advocacy ads.

Livonen (2018) identified four main forms of disruptive tactics that CEO activism could use in targeting governments, with each main tactic spawning several sub-tactics. These disruptive/protest tactics include (1) supporting legal actions against the government (sub-tactics including joining or filing amicus briefs; and testifying at public hearings); (2) boycotting the target government (sub-tactics as canceling events, canceling/withholding investments, withdrawing business activities, and withdrawing services); (3) attending demonstrations against the target government (sub-tactics including joining demonstrations and joining employee-led demonstrations); and (4) broadcasting disapproval of the target government (sub-tactics including giving statements through the traditional media; and sending messages via social media).

The main tactics targeted at employees are *persuasion* and *support* (rather than *disruption*). These typically find expression in encouraging and supporting employee activism. Here, Livonen (2018) asserts that sub-tactics included encouraging donations, providing paid time off for activism, offering material support for activism, and supporting demonstrations by employees.

The main tactic that CEO activists could target at social movements is one of support (Livonen, 2018). This could include demonstrating support for social movements or the issue (sub-tactics including making donations, attending marches, broadcasting support for movement or the issue through the media, and giving a name to the cause). Supporting social movements could also entail offering support for the oppressed or the affected (sub-tactics including providing material aid, continuing existing practices/disregarding the target's decisions).

Livonen (2018) and Chatterji and Toffel (2018) have suggested some approaches (strategies and tactics) employed by CEO activists in their social resistance actions, based mainly on their observations of the works of CEO activists. The research question for this chapter concerns providing an empirical outlining of the tactics employed by CEO activists, presented from the "inside-out" perspective of activist CEOs in Ghana.

To what extent do the CEO activism tactics fit into the extant postulations, such as those of Chatterji and Toffel (2018) and Livonen (2018)? Given that these postulations were derived from the Western sociocultural context, it is expected that the extant tactics would be insufficient in fully describing the tactical repertoire of a non-Western society such as Ghana. Thus, the study sought to ascertain the wide variety of tactics employed by the study participants, based on the research question: *What tactics do CEO activists in Ghana employ in their resistance actions?*

## 6.3 The Activist CEO Tactical Repertoire

This chapter presents the results of the in-depth interviews conducted as part of this research project. The findings presented herewith are in response to the research question: What tactics do CEO activists in Ghana employ in their resistance actions? The analysis presented in this chapter seeks to combine both afore-stated taxonomies. Thus, an attempt would be made to analyze the findings under the following extant tactics: (1) leveraging economic power; (2) awareness creation and persuasion tactics; (3) support tactics; and (4) disruptive and protest tactics. However, some new tactics emerged that could not fit under these labels.

### 6.3.1 Leveraging Economic Power

Given certain situational factors in Ghana, most of the CEOs who participated in this study did not feel empowered to leverage their economic power. However, some themes emerged concerning how CEOs felt the tactic of leveraging economic power was manifesting itself in the practice of CEO activism in Ghana.

Participant #9 expressed views that were reflective of the general sentiment of most participants in this study in pursuing a path of awareness creation in their activities, rather than one of flexing their economic muscles, with threats of withdrawing their investments. They explained that most CEOs in Ghana did not feel that it was prudent to leverage their economic power as a tactic in CEO activism for several reasons.

Where the government was the target, there was usually the fear that such a course of action would result in some antipathy of the government toward the CEOs and their organizations. Another participant also believed that there was power dissymmetry, weighing in favor of the government in such cases. Thus, CEOs and their organizations in Ghana generally felt less powerful, relative to the Government of Ghana:

> Everything I've done is more of awareness, lobbying, and influencing rather than exercising economic power. I don't see CEO activists in Ghana leveraging economic power during their activism campaigns.

Owing to such factors, this participant expressed the feeling that she and other CEO activists in Ghana would rather tread cautiously when engaging in activism by avoiding the tactic of leveraging economic power. They took their time to illustrate their point by using a recent situation in which the Ghana Association of Bankers (GAB) found itself having to confront the Government of Ghana concerning negotiations to settle huge long-standing energy sector debts that the state-owned Volta River Authority owed to several banks in Ghana. A participant noted that matter, the members of the GAB felt powerless and hardly contemplated taking any adversarial actions:

> A lot of us feel we can't afford to be in the government's bad books since that could harm our businesses. Companies in Ghana are not too powerful to be able to force the government to take certain actions by threatening some economic actions. We aren't yet in a

position of power where the private sector or CEOs can start
calling shots and using their economic power to force the hand
of policymakers to do the right thing.

They observed that the tactic of leveraging economic power, investment protest, or economic protest ought not to be seen only in terms of threats to withdraw
investments. According to a participant, such an approach could have a flip side
where CEOs and companies could show the government how with more cooperation from the state, the relationship with the private sector could work to
benefit the country as a whole:

> Leveraging of economic power should not only entail threatening
> to withdraw your investments but also showing the government
> how much you can help by investing more in the system if they
> cooperated with you.

Participant #19 revealed their way of leveraging economic power, as a CEO
activist in Ghana. They indicated that rather than threatening the government or
some state institution, they had been leveraging their economic power by making
targeted investments that would lead to the production of some of the changes
they desired in the Ghanaian society of the future. They suggested that they had
mainly been employing strategies of awareness creation, although they sometimes
leveraged whatever economic power they could muster:

> With the economic power side, I do it differently by empowering
> certain groups ... and putting my investment in a certain space
> that I would bring some change in especially the women and girls
> ... where I figure would create a domino effect that would affect a
> greater number of people.

Unlike what some scholars had suggested regarding some activist CEOs in
America leveraging their economic power during their activism, it emerged that
activist CEOs in Ghana did not feel so empowered, so far, to use or threaten the
flexing of their economic muscles in their activism.

While accepting that companies in Ghana may not have the financial where-
withal to leverage their economic power in their resistance actions, some participants believed that a group of companies could join forces in employing such a
tactic to great effect. On the same issue, some participants were of the view that
some companies in Ghana may have employed such tactics, albeit covertly.
Participant #6 shared the belief in CEOs coming together to apply economic
pressure in Ghana:

> We can do that through a coalition of fair-minded, big-thinking,
> and big-picture kind of leaders where we decide to withdraw our
> monies or investments from some part of the system if we don't see
> the change we desire. We could threaten to abort a project or

investment we had planned to do if some change or some action is not effected on the part of the government.

Although they saw more prospects for coalitions of CEOs and companies uniting to flex their economic muscles, they noted that Vodafone Ghana had done so as singlehandedly, by promising to match investments by the Government of Ghana in empowering the youth of the country with skills in coding, artificial intelligence, machine learning, etc.:

> Vodafone Ghana launched a coding program, promising to invest in it if the government also invests in it. The idea is that corporations and brands are wielding both the carrot and the stick. Vodafone is in effect adopting the carrot approach, telling the government that it if invests in a specific program, the company would match the government's stake in it. This is positive activism; it is saying that the company wants this action done by the government and that if it is done, the company would support it with a given amount of private investment.

While being cognizant of the possibility or viability of employing tactics related to leveraging economic power, the study showed that some CEO activists found themselves caught up in a catch-22 situation. While some genuinely felt a lack of economic strength to take on the government by threatening some economic sanctions, others felt that doing so could end up turning back the very clock of social progress they had been seeking to advance.

### 6.3.2 Awareness-Creation and Persuasion Tactics

Many participants shared that they employed diverse awareness-creation and persuasion tactics, including various forms of media advocacy, special events, and diverse high-powered meetings.

It was found that CEO activists in Ghana had found a rich vein of the most popular traditional media houses in Ghana. Knowing the strong command they wielded over many media houses, the activist CEOs who participated in this study were very aware that the media in Ghana listened attentively to them as credible sources of news. This was not only because of the celebrity statuses they occupied as CEOs but also because of the economic influences of their companies over the media organizations who depended on the companies ran by the CEO activists for advertising billings and related promotional purposes.

Some activist CEOs in Ghana employ the powers of various channels of mass communication in their activism. This approach entailed making public pronouncements on diverse issues on radio, television, print news media, and other media vehicles. According to Participant #8, the use of relevant media platforms was vital in his activism because of the high levels of illiteracy in Ghana. They explained that employing strategically selected media vehicles in Ghana was not only a powerful way of reaching relevant sections of the public but also a significant way of countervailing the dominant metanarratives of politicians in Ghana. They revealed how they used media advocacy as part of their brand of intellectual activism:

> Radio program producers would invite the ministers and government appointees, and we would debate them vigorously, and the public would see who was making the soundest arguments. That's intellectual activism – confronting the leaders on-air, based on deep policy analysis and the objective dissection of policy alternatives.

For others, media activism included weekly columns in up to five newspapers in Ghana at some point, especially at the start of Ghana's current Fourth Republican era. He stressed that the focus of his media commentary had always been on national developmental issues.

It came up strongly that one of the most enduring platforms in Ghana for women to discuss issues concerning women and their development and empowerment was a television program created, hosted, and produced by Participant #3. This television program had been running for well over a decade on some of the television channels with the most coverage in Ghana, including the widest-reaching *Ghana Television (GTV)*. Participant #3 spent some time explaining the philosophy of the program as an advocacy and activist tactic in the fight against patriarchal institutional structures in Ghana:

> In Ghana, women have been kept down by unfair social processes and institutions. There're many spaces where women are denied opportunities. The program is a voice for the voiceless ... for women's voices; a platform for women to share their experiences ... to tell their stories, both exciting and sad news. A safe space for women to know despite the challenges they can still get somewhere great in life. For our 10th anniversary, our theme is, 'The Woman on the Move' ... a clarion call for women of Ghana to always be on the move and strive to be the very best they can be.

Other CEO activists indicated their preference for radio, the medium with the widest penetration across Ghana. Participant #20's medium of choice in their financial literacy advocacy campaigns since 2008 had been a popular purposely designed radio program. However, radio only served as the lead medium in his arsenal:

> I have created a radio program to articulate my views; I speak at special events, such as at churches; and I am quite active on social media, especially on Facebook. I partner with like-minded groups; I speak at programs by other activists, and I volunteer for others. I offer technical support behind the scenes. I take advantage of TV

programs. Whenever the opportunity presents itself, I speak out; I say it, I write it, I do it, and do it convincingly.

Participant #5's eclectic use of media vehicles was found to include press articles and features, media publicity, staging special events, and appearing on various news analysis and media discussion programs:

> Since we started in 2013, we've used the print media ... done print news stories; press articles, and features; the media has covered our programs; ... whenever there's a controversial economic or financial matter I speak. We've done print, and radio, and we have started to get active in the digital space and on social media. I use a lot of advocacies, but I'm beginning to think about using some economic power, but I like to say that in a very humble manner because I'm not wealthy.

Other participants in this study indicated their belief that their role was partly that of a watchdog, shining the light on the actions of the Government of Ghana, speaking truth to power, and ensuring that the public officeholders were constantly kept on their toes. They explained their through-the-line media approach of mixing social media, print media, radio, and television in calling out corrupt and ineffective leaders, and in proposing alternative solutions to some of the country's challenges.

As part of his youth empowerment campaigns, Participant #16 disclosed that they employed a bouquet of tactics to reach the youth of Ghana and West Africa, including a youth empowerment roadshow series, school clubs, curricula development for tertiary educational institutions, online mentoring programs, bulk SMSs, and radio show produced as a "virtual university":

> We have clubs that meet weekly in universities to follow a 52-chapter curriculum on career development, leadership, excellence, public speaking, etc. ... online mentoring programs ... daily bulk SMS messages ... social media posts ... over these past 12 years, our Springboard Roadshows have produced 200,000 alumni ... that means 200,000 virtual graduates.

Some of the participants reported leveraging some of their core competencies in their approaches to activism. For instance, besides employing digital and social media, and building a coalition of like-minded activists, Participant #13 leveraged their skills as a filmmaker in shining the light on issues that mattered to her. In a feature movie they produced, they highlighted aspects of women empowerment in Ghana, focusing on the plights of *Kayayei* (women head porters who operate in the open markets in Ghana):

> As a filmmaker, the film medium is one of my biggest tools. For instance, I did a film that focused on women empowerment in the

market and *Kayaye* five years ago. We did a campaign for two years on this. Most of the issues we advocated for have since received some action from various institutions, including a provision in the 2020 national budget to build quarters for *Kayayei.*

Some of the CEOs who participated in this study invested in the production of various advocacy videos as a tactic for getting their word out. Such videos were of various durations and placed on televisions stations and various social media platforms. Participant #3 revealed that they had recently used such a video in getting the President of Ghana to act decisively in a recent child molestation case:

I released an advocacy video, calling on the President to speak for the girl-child and to save the girl-child. A four-year-old girl had been abused, but nobody taking any action. That video clip went viral and the President was compelled to act, ordering the Inspector General of Police to bring the offender to book. The molester has since been jailed.

Despite the general employment of all forms of media channels, some of the activist CEOs indicated a preference for new media platforms such as Facebook and WhatsApp. A wide array of social and digital media vehicles is featured in the various promotional mixes. The social media tools *LinkedIn, Twitter, Facebook*, and *WhatsApp* featured prominently in this regard. These were sometimes used as support media to amplify protest marches, leading to greater national and global publicity of such events. Participant #8 shared some thoughts on how *Twitter* and *Facebook* were particularly instrumental in the *Occupy Flagstaff House* march:

Social media is the most impactful. I employ all manner of social media platforms, especially *Twitter, WhatsApp, and Facebook.* When we did Occupy Flagstaff House, the number of people on the street was between 500 and 1000, but we reached so many more people on social media because the protesters were mostly professionals who all had smartphones and were tweeting and posting about the demonstration. The event became a global phenomenon.

During the conceptualization and planning of protest marches and well before the staging of such events, social media messages were used to engage protesters and to whip up public support for upcoming marches. Participant #8 explained the extent to which *Facebook* and *Twitter* were employed in the planning and concept phases of the *Occupy Flagstaff House* protest march to engage protesters:

During the planning of the event, I had posted about it on Facebook, reaching well over 30,000 primary followers of mine on that platform. It went far, and most of my social media friends and followers were present on the day, to join the action. *Twitter* and *Facebook* have been most effective for my activities.

Unlike, most people who employed their social media handles to share posts about themselves, Participant #2 said they decided to take a diametrically different route to the use to which she put social media:

> My social media is not about me. I make it more about weightier matters. I don't tell stories about what a wonderful day I had. It's always relevant to a story. I realized that social media is such a wonderful tool to actively reach a large number of young people.

Thus, the focus of using social media for some of the participants was to express their stances on their chosen causes and get more members of the audience to adopt the positions advocated by these CEO activists.

Some participants indicated that following the pronouncements of Ghana's President Nana Akufo-Addo during the June 2019 conference of Women Deliver in Canada, they had taken some steps to engage the president on some of his assertions. At this widely publicized event, Nana Akufo-Addo had said that women in Ghana were not active enough and they were not amplified in making themselves available for selection when it came to big-ticket positions at tables of power and decision-making.

The membership of the EWN held a closed-door meeting with the first gentleman of Ghana to present their reaction to what he had said in Canada. Participant #21 spoke of their significant role in this encounter with the Ghanaian president:

> What I wrote on the EWN platform about the president's speech led to a closed-door meeting with the president and some of his women ministers and about 10 members of the EWN. We presented what I wrote and the President. We said he could have said it better. Women are not standing up for politics for many reasons. We explained the social and cultural barriers facing women in Ghana.

Some of the activist CEOs in this study reported using special events in their campaigns. Using a high-traction hashtag, Participant #5 organized a special event in partnership with the Chartered Institute of Marketing (Ghana) on the theme of "Ghana's Economy in 2018." This had been part of his perennial actions to expose ill-advised national economic management policies in Ghana. In a Facebook post, Participant #5 had written:

> I'm honoured to be speaking on 'Ghana's Economy in 2018' in partnership with the CIMG, this Tuesday, the 27th of March at the Alisa Swiss Spirit Hotel. Join me …

During this special event, Participant #5 spoke candidly about numerous failures in the nation's economic management that made the cost of living very harsh for most Ghanaians. Contrary to statements by the Ministry of Finance that the country's economy was doing well, at the event, Participant #5 declared that the country was broke and was "heading for a disaster" because of over-borrowing and bad economic and financial policies. They urged the managers of the economy to "face up to the realities" and to take bold measures to set the economy right. The event was transmitted live on several digital media channels, including Facebook and YouTube, and widely reported across various media platforms.

Some of the CEOs said they employed several types of special events and speaking engagements to get their word out. These included local and international events such as TedX Talks, hosting media receptions, and making publicized presentations. For instance, Participant #2 revealed that in 2016, they were approached by TedxEuston to speak at one of their events. They saw this as an opportunity of a lifetime to lay out their ideas on ethical leadership, STEM, and the development of Africa in general:

> I was approached by TedxEuston to speak. It was as though I was always prepared for that ... I called it "The New Normal." That's how the idea of the *Bold New Normal* was born, in which I laid out how to create the Africa where everyone prospers.

However, it became obvious that some of these special events and speaking opportunities served to kick off some of the campaigns, as videos and publicity materials from the events usually became the content for several digital media platforms such as videos on YouTube.

Some study participants disclosed that they had undertaken book projects as a means of crystallizing and promoting their views. Participant #2 expressed confidence in their ideas to create and promote their vision of a bold new normal for Africa that challenged and change the paradigm of successful developmental outcomes for the continent.

Participant #2 disclosed that their 2019 book presented ideas about how to transform Africa at various levels into a place where its citizens had real options in exploiting genuine opportunities to prosper, rather than merely subsisting. They indicated that their ideas for Africa's transformation were based on some proven approaches:

> The first mass tool I used to share the message was social media, but the second mass tool that I'm using is a book on the subject of The Bold New Normal. I believe in it and I'm passionate about it. I want them to have the ideas in the book in their hands.

### 6.3.3 Disruptive Tactics

The study participants disclosed some tactics that could be described as disruptive in seeking to neutralize the ability of the target of the activities of CEOs to achieve its goals. Such tactics also tended to court negative publicity for the perceived target. A participant described it as *Agitation and Provocation*. At the start of the current Fourth Republic in Ghana in 1992, one participant disclosed that they were dissatisfied with the prevalence of a culture of silence in Ghana, made worse by limitations placed on the media landscape. While free speech and vibrant media were enshrined in Ghana's constitution, strong barriers were placed in the citizens' bid to exercise those rights.

Based on more than two decades of personal experience in activism in Europe, Participant #12 shared that they decided to take some action to help lift barriers to free speech in Ghana. They established a pirate radio station in Accra, to force the political establishment into a legal determination of the constitutional provisions regarding a free media landscape. Some 25 years since his actions, Ghana now boasts a relatively buoyant media landscape:

> I took the view that the constitutional intent, so I decided to do some agitation and provocation. I decided to set it [Radio XXX (not the real station identity)] up and have a public fight – even including the international system – to force the government to allow plural broadcasting, which is precisely what happened. But it wasn't the radio station that brought media pluralism; it was the agitation after the station had been established, getting public support and international involvement in the issue of democracy and the role of the free media.

Some of the informants in this study revealed that sometimes what was required for effective activism was the mobilization of mass public action to engage in street protests. Participant #8, however, explained that intellectual activism was sometimes inadequate on its own to drive the needed change, especially when it was necessary to put significant pressure on politicians in Ghana. They explained how protest marches could be impactful:

> We realized that intellectual activism was not enough, which was why we escalated our activities to now include street demonstrations, several of which I convened and led. When you go on marches in the streets, you put pressure on the politicians.

One of the issues that caused Participant #8 to engage in some protest actions was a popular public procurement nightmare that confronted the John Dramani Mahama-led NDC administration. This involved the award of a contract to Smartty's Management and Production Limited for the branding of a fleet of public transit buses belonging to the state-owned Metro Mass Transit (MMT) Limited in 2016. Some commentators described this contract as not only dubious and corrupt but also involving many infractions of Ghana's public procurement laws. Participant #8 was one of the key actors that exposed and censured the deal:

> There was this very corrupt deal that caused public outrage, involving the branding of some buses of the Metro Mass Transit. It ended up costing the nation hundreds of times what should have been reasonably charged. We found that Smarttys was awarded and signed even before the commencement of the formal procurement process, a blatant violation of Ghana's public procurement laws. I led an action to demand information to expose this act of corruption.

For some CEOs, engaging in activism also involved some mass media shouting matches with politicians and public office holders in Ghana. According to some of the informants in this study, such raw shouting matches usually took place on live radio or during television discussion programs. For instance, in discussing details of his action against the planned rollout of a new policy for the registration of all cellular SIM cards in Ghana in 2010, Participant #10 revealed that they had to engage the Director of Ghana's National Security in a not-so-merry war of words on one of the most popular radio stations in Ghana, although it may not have been a safe thing to do because of the risks it exposed him to:

> At the time, I was younger and probably more reckless. I had a shouting match on live radio with the then Head of National Security. It must have been on Peace FM or Joy FM. This action may have been probably ill-advised.

Quite unlike the typical Ghanaian approach that tended toward ambivalence, diplomacy, tact, and circumlocution, some of the participants chose a pathway of activism that involved being forthright and straightforward. According to Participant #14, *I do my things straightforwardly. I would stand in front of you and tell you my mind and walk away. I'm a straight shooter.*

Similarly, describing his approach in martial terms as one of an army general, Participant #6 disclosed that they also had a direct and front approach to their social resistance actions. They described this aggressive approach as involving the manner of speaking with authority, being bold and courageous, and being forthright, when necessary:

> Mine is a frontal type of activism ... I don't shy away from taking an issue head-on if that's what's needed to neutralize the opponent. Most people who know me describe me as *"The General"* because of my combatant style.

Even for those activist CEOs who expressed a preference for a direct, adversarial, and confrontational approach to activism, campaign and communication effectiveness remained the primary goal. Given that, they observed the need to vary approaches according to various target audiences. In doing so, Participant #6 expressed the importance of being emotionally and culturally intelligent in varying methods according to different cultural situations and communication contexts.

The interviews showed that some situational factors facing CEO activists in Ghana have led to variations in strategies and tactical approaches adopted. For instance, the bloodiness and fatalities of the *Kumepreko* protests that took place in the mid-1990s, and the violent responses of elements within the Ghana Police Service and the Ghana Army to some more recent protest marches had led CEO activists such as Participant #10 and activist groups such as Occupy Ghana to rethink their tactics.

### 6.3.4 Intellectual Activism

As part of his tactical repertoire, Participant #10 appeared to favor a brand of intellectual activism they described *as A battle of minds*, designed to set the tone for issues, shape the media agenda, forcefully raise the issues and drive the debate, stopping the opponents in their tracks, while offering effective protection against brutalities by the nation's security services:

> We realized that if we went marching in the streets, we wouldn't win any argument. If feet-on-street all the time, they have the police and the army to deal ruthlessly with us. We decided to have a different kind of protest movement – a battle of minds. Let's have a fight where you won't meet me physically to assault me, but we would be "assaulting" you where the mind is concerned. We would be forcing you to respond to the issues we hold dear.

Besides safety concerns, it turned out that such intellectual activism was also driven by practical, logistical, and cost-management factors. Participant #10 provided more explanations and justifications for choosing his *Battle of the mind* approach to activism as comprising significant financial outlays involved in organizing media coverage, venue rental, equipment rental, and the procurement of other events management logistics. Thus, some of the tools employed in his *battle of the mind* approach include issuing press statements, position statements, and taking legal action:

> Our arsenal includes press statements, private and open letters, and position statements to the government. If we push long and hard enough, without achieving any results, we take legal action.

### 6.3.5 Legal Activism

Beyond the virtual fights or battles of ideas in the public sphere that Ace Ankomah described, others believed in a tactic that went beyond the court of public opinion and into the courts of law in Ghana. Here, Participant #8 described their actions as entailing a mixture of intellectual activism and legal activism, where Ghana's legal system engaged. They described their idea of intellectual activism as involving incisive research and the analysis of relevant issues, with the view to unpacking the various ingredients in ways that help to shed light on otherwise complicated public policy issues.

Participant #8 indicated that they also employed a good deal of legal activism that involved the courage of taking on and fighting various governmental bodies in Ghana in various courts of competent jurisdiction, intending to obtain court rulings that would serve the general public's interest. Participant #8 commented on their concept of intellectual and legal activism:

> My approach is a mixture of intellectual activism - calling things out and advocating for them – and legal activism. That is part of the distinctiveness of my activism. My activism is not only about raising awareness about issues. I like to use all legal means, including resorting to the use of the courts to push for legal reforms that would help make our society better. I am a lawyer, so I find that I can go to the courts to ensure that justice is served the good people of Ghana. The law is my forte, so I try to use it to great effect.

### 6.3.6 Naming and Shaming

Several participants also spoke of the inadequacy of awareness-creation strategies in producing the desired levels of social change sought. For Participant #6, what was sometimes required was an approach that involved calling out and ridiculing government officials for their inactions and lack of accountability to the people of Ghana. Participant #6 revealed that such naming and shaming approaches could include efforts at influencing voter behavior against those nonperforming politicians:

> I think I have gone beyond awareness creation because I have realized that it is not enough. It is now about exposing those who are doing wrong. Naming and shaming is the name of the game. Politicians and public officeholders in Ghana do not react to your awareness creation; they only react to voting behaviors. So, as an activist, you need to find ways of influencing the voting behaviors of the public toward erring politicians by naming and shaming public officers.

### 6.3.7 Activism by Industry Group Representatives

CEO activism was not entirely for altruistic reasons. Interviews revealed that at least three of the participants in this study worked for one trade association or the other. For instance, while Participant #8 led an association of telecommunication firms, Participant #14 worked for some bulk oil distributors, and Participant #15 served the tourism interest group. It is noteworthy that while they led a strategic communication firm at the time of their interview, Participant #4 in March 2020 accepted an offer to serve as the CEO of a group of upstream petroleum firms in Gnana.

Naturally, these are all industry advocacy roles for the CEOs who are serving in those positions. While most of their actions were directed at altruistic common-good ends, there was reason to believe also that some of their actions were aimed at achieving the interests of the companies that made up the membership of the respective chambers headed by some of these CEOs in the study.

For instance, it was found that Participant #6 had engaged in at least one activist campaign to sway public opinion and pressure the government to rescind a decision to implement a proposed communication services tax policy, which policy would have made telephony services offered by the companies who make up the membership of the chamber headed by Participant #6 more expensive to Ghanaians. They reflected on the instrumentality of CEO activism in shaping public opinion and ensuring that some policies of the Government of Ghana aligned better with the expectations of sections of industry and society:

> We learned that the government was planning to slap taxes on mobile money transactions. I was on air and kicked against the planned policy. The government heard us, and the proposed tax policy was withdrawn.

### 6.3.8 Activism by Living by Example

For several of the study participants, activism ought to really start with the activist. Taking the environment as an example, if one believed in it and was passionate about it, then it behooves the CEO activist to lead by example by changing or aligning his/her corporate policies to ways that reflected the desired public policy.

Essentially, for Participant #14, an imperative strategic route for CEO activism is for CEOs daring to show exemplary leadership, live by example, and demonstrate the sort of positive change they want to see by serving as strong insider activists, working for desirable changes within their organizations:

> If you believe in something, be that example, live by example by changing your own corporate policies to reflect the change you want to see in the wider scheme of things. Let your light shine within your own organization. If you want society to go green, show that example by going green within your own organization. Just do it, make a statement in that direction and let everyone know why you have done so. Live the example and be the change you want to see.

Similarly, other participants disclosed their preference for green and responsible management practices, such as demonstrating their abhorrence for plastics by deliberately excluding such materials in their production processes. Participant #14 disclosed that this was essential because the public tends to share corporate values, even as they interact with corporations, but also in the corporate advocacy outlook and the extent to which companies live those ideals:

> For instance, I can't stand littering. I have a farm, and when I arrive there and see any form of littering, the managers are in big trouble. As managers, they'd have to pick up the rubbish themselves because they have allowed it on the farm.

### 6.3.9 Support Tactics

The participants reported employing some support tactics in Ghana, including serving as elite allies and having mentoring programs and workshops, aimed at supporting specific populations and other social movements.

One of the major issues that engaged some of the informants in this study was the deep-rooted culture of patriarchy in Ghana. It was the view of some participants that for the country to leapfrog on the path of rapid socioeconomic development, the patriarchal system that some saw as crippling most women and girls in the society ought to be toppled. Thus, it was found that some of the resistance and tactics employed by some of the participants in this study targeted some of the pillars that supported patriarchy in Ghana.

For instance, as part of her resistance activities, Participant #24 had seen the need to run various mentoring and workshops aimed at liberating women in Ghana from the shackles placed on them by the culture of patriarchy in the country. It emerged that Participant #24's nonprofit group that focuses on mentoring women in Ghana through positive modeling had been running an intensive four-day workshop series called *Imagine* that sought to chip away at the hold that patriarchy placed on Ghanaian women, by empowering women to become vocal through mechanisms such as positive modeling and sensitization:

> I have supported some women to be vocal. Through my activism, my mentoring programs, and my non-profit activities, I run different workshops in empowerment … to help build women's agency and self-esteem. I empower them to do what they want or desire.

A similar supportive approach was adopted by the EWN. However, the approach adopted by this organization entailed what Participant #9 described as *direct community engagement*. In explaining this approach in action at the severely underprivileged Chorkor fishing community (a suburb of Ghana's capital city of Accra), Participant #9 noted that the fulcrum of the strategy was the *Family*

*Strengthening Program*, which was undertaken by the EWN, in partnership with the SOS Children's Village in Ghana. According to Participant #1, these included special events such as media-publicized talk series and conferences that featured local and international speakers:

> If there is an issue with women, we take a position. But the main thing is to empower professional women through mentoring sessions, coaching sessions, and our monthly talk series. The approach is getting people who have made it to come in there and talk to the gathering. It is a powerful modelling opportunity that shows members that if others have made it, then they can also succeed.

Other CEO activists had been undertaking diverse fundraising drives, designed to support various groups in Ghana who had been affected by disasters. Participant #10 described some of their roles in such initiatives within Ghana and the West African subregion:

> There are many other things we do on the quiet. Whenever there is a disaster, somewhere in Ghana, we lead a fundraising drive to mobilize donations for the victims. We have even undertaken such efforts outside the shores of Ghana.

## 6.4 Discussion

This chapter set out to investigate the tactical repertoire of activist CEOs in Ghana. It presented the findings from the interviews of the 24 CEO activists who participated in this study, relating to the tactics employed as part of their social resistance campaigns. Interviews suggest that the tactics employed by CEO activists are influenced by some situational tonic and toxic factors. Although a few CEO activists in Ghana employed the tactic of leveraging economic power, most study participants tended to favor awareness-creation tactics, comprising various media strategies and tactics in their resistance actions.

The findings suggested that neither the taxonomy of CEO activist tactics suggested by Chatterji and Toffel (2018) nor Livonen's (2018) postulation was adequate to categorize the full gamut of the tactical repertoire of CEO activists in Ghana. While Chatterji and Toffel's (2018) schema lacked the category of support tactics and disruptive tactics, Livonen's (2018) lacked the essential character of tactics of leveraging economic power.

It was necessary to meld the two systems of categorization in order to adequately capture the rich variety of tactics deployed in Ghana. In this regard, the findings of this study make the case for an eclectic taxonomy of strategies and tactics, including (1) leveraging economic power; (2) awareness creation and persuasion tactics; (3) disruption and protest tactics; and (4) support tactics.

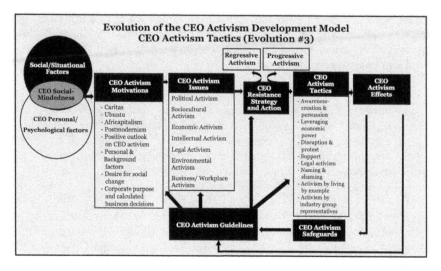

Fig. 5.    Evolution #3 of the CEO Activism Development Model (Indicating the Range of Motivations, Clusters of Issues/Causes, and CEO Activism Tactics). *Source:* Author (2023).

However, the findings further suggest that, based on the intended goals, there could be other classes of tactics that have so far not been reflected in literature on CEO activism, including *activism by living by example, intellectual activism, activism by industry group representatives, naming and shaming, legal activism*, and marked extensions of the notion of leveraging economic power that added to the meaning posited by Chatterji and Toffel (2018), such as the positive use of economic power in which CEO activists undertake to match government investments.

These findings facilitate the further development of the working model for this research project. In Evolution #3 of the CEO Activism Development Model (see Fig. 5 above), the findings regarding the tactical repertoire of participants in this study are incorporated. Within the framework of the working model for this research project, the tactics employed in a CEO activist campaign are expected to have some effects, outcomes, and consequences. The next chapter lays out the findings concerning the effects of engaging in CEO activism in Ghana, as described by the participants in this study.

Chapter 7

# Counting the Costs and Reaping the Dividends: Examining CEO Activism Effects

## 7.1 Introduction

Generally, there appears to be a relative lack of scientific investigation into the outcomes produced by CEO activists (Adae, 2020). The thin literature currently available on the consequences of CEO activism has focused on Western contexts and dwelled on the phenomenon's impact on organizational outcomes, including consumer purchase intents (see e.g., Dodd & Supa, 2015) and impacts on public opinion (Chatterji & Toffel, 2019a).

Given the mixed blessings that are associated with CEO activism, Larcker et al. (2018) described CEO activism as a "double-edged sword," and Chatterji and Toffel (2018) similarly argue that CEO activism could produce both risks and rewards for CEOs and their companies. The risks include criticisms against the CEO activist, and negative consequences for companies, charges of hypocrisy, double standards, and bad press (Chatterji & Toffel, 2017).

For instance, shortly after President Donald Trump became president, Under Armor CEO Kevin Plank was widely criticized for praising the president. This culminated in a Twitter hashtag #BoycottUnderArmor. Following this avalanche of criticism and threats of a boycott of the brand, although the company placed a full-page ad to clarify what its CEO had said, it still had undesirable effects on the company's stocks. Other risks of CEO activism include charges of hypocrisy, double standards, and bad press (Chatterji & Toffel, 2018).

Despite the risks, there could also be rewards for CEO activism (Chatterji & Toffel, 2018), with some scholars suggesting that there might be a business case for CEOs speaking up on social issues. CEO activism has been shown to have the potential to sway public opinion and increase customers' interest in purchasing a brand (Chatterji & Toffel, 2016). While it may not be the motivation of CEO activists, consumers appear to respond favorably to a company's products when they agree with the public stances taken by CEO activists. For example, Weber Shandwick (2017) found that Millennials' buying decisions are influenced by CEO

CEOs on a Mission, 127–157
Copyright © 2023 Eric Kwame Adae
Published under exclusive licence by Emerald Publishing Limited
doi:10.1108/978-1-80382-215-020231007

activism, with 51% of this section of the American population indicating that they will buy a brand whose CEO speaks up on an issue they agree with.

Dodd and Supa (2014) sought to illuminate current understandings of organizational stances on sociopolitical issues (which they termed *Corporate Social Advocacy* or CSA) as well as explore its impacts on consumer purchase intention. Drawing on sections of the theory of planned behavior, their online survey experiment explored the impact of organizational stances on selected sociopolitical issues – particularly, gay marriage, health care reform, and emergency contraception – on organizational financial goals. It was found that organizational engagement in social advocacy has the potential of having tangible outcomes for organizations. Overall, greater public congruency/agreement with the corporate stance results in greater intentions to purchase, while lesser congruency/ agreement by the public with a stance has been found to be associated with lesser intention to purchase (Dodd & Supa, 2014).

In a field experiment, Chatterji and Toffel (2017) investigated whether CEO activists make any difference to the corporate bottom line. It was found that CEO activism is associated with some impacts on public opinion and some consumer attitudes. Specifically, these scholars examined the impact of Apple CEO, Tim Cook's public statements opposing a pending religious freedom law that critics warned could promote discrimination against same-sex couples. Chatterji and Toffel (2017) found support for the influence of issue framing on public opinion, potentially to the same extent as politicians. Besides, it emerged that Cook's activism led to increased consumer intentions to buy Apple products, particularly among the consumer segment of proponents of same-sex marriage.

It has also been suggested that CEO activism has some influence on employee retention and the retention of top talent. Forty-four percent (44%) of Millennials indicate that their loyalty to organizations if its CEO took a position on a hot-button issue, especially when such advocacy campaign aligned with those of Millennials (Weber Shandwick, 2017). Public perceptions of not engaging in activism include criticism from media (30%), customers (26%), employees (21%), and government (9%).

Evidence from the developing world is neatly absent from all of these findings. What tonic and toxic effects are associated with CEO activism in non-Western societies? Thus, this study addresses the relatively thin literature on CEO activism in non-Western sociocultural contexts by focusing on an examination of the diverse effects/outcomes produced by the social resistance campaigns of a group of self-identified men and women activist CEOs in Ghana, based on the research question: "What effects have been produced by the resistance actions of CEO activists in Ghana?"

## 7.2 The Bitter-Sweet Effects of CEO Activism

The findings presented in this chapter are based on the analysis of the in-depth interviews with the 24 CEO informants in this study. Generally, the participants described a hierarchy of three-tiered effects of their actions in terms of (i) positive greater-good socioeconomic and environmental outcomes produced, including specific achievements realized for the benefit of the entire Ghanaian society; (ii) tonic effects (positive outcomes) for individual activist CEOs and their organizations, but also (iii) toxic effects (negative/undesirable outcomes) for the activist CEO and their organizations.

The following sections describe this hierarchy of effects of CEO activism in Ghana.

## 7.3 Positive Effects Greater-Good Outcomes of CEO Activism for the Ghanaian Society

The study participants described various effects of their social resistance actions in terms of some achievements produced within Ghanaian society. It was found that the perceived social improvements produced by CEO activists in Ghana included advancing the gender agenda, environmental stewardship, democracy, legal and policy reforms, citizens' empowerment, economic and public financial management, and shaping public opinion.

### 7.3.1 Advancing the Gender Equality Agenda

Within the context of patriarchal norms in the country, many study participants disclosed that their actions had positively impacted efforts to empower women in Ghana. According to some of the study informants, their campaigns had helped more women to find their voices in a predominantly patriarchal Ghanaian society. Participant #24 described some ways in which their actions had enabled more women to develop self-confidence and become more liberated:

> I've influenced women to be vocal. As part of my activism, I run workshops to help build women's self-esteem and agency. My "Imagine" workshops empower women to create the lives that they want, rather than being dictated to by the culture.

Some participants said they had targeted the issue of the lack of gender diversity among corporations in Ghana. Especially, they were dissatisfied with the underrepresentation of women in senior management positions and on the various boards of directors of companies operating in Ghana. Although many of the CEOs in this study saw more room for improvement, they spoke of some victories in this regard.

For instance, Participant #9 believed that their previous stellar performance as managing director of the Ghanaian subsidiary of a leading global bank had increased confidence in the ability of women to manage some of Ghana's highest-flying corporations. Describing themselves as a trailblazer, they claimed that they paved the way for more women to be appointed as heads of several blue-chip companies in the country:

> Although there's still more to do, we've chalked successes. Before I became the managing director for XXX Bank (not the real name of the institution), no Ghanaian woman had led a bank in Ghana. I was the only woman managing director for a long time. Since then, a few women have been appointed to the helm, so there's progress. My performance and the advocacy work of the Executive Women Network have encouraged more women to believe in themselves. You can say I broke the glass ceiling in Ghana's banking sector.

It was found that improvements in gender diversity in Ghana were not limited to the banking sector. For instance, Participant #11, former CEO of an independent private electric power producer in Ghana, also described some of their achievements as helping to mainstream the notion of gender parity within the country's energy sector. Here, they described the role of such interest groups as *Women in Energy*, which has been pivotal in agitating and pushing for women's advancement within the men-dominated oil and gas sectors in Ghana.

Similarly, Participant #19 saw their achievements as including the increased participation of women and girls in coding and the digital spaces, noting that since 2012, their actions have helped promote the broader participation of women and girls in software engineering and cognate digital spaces in Ghana:

> I started advocating for women and girls in technology and coding since 2012. This was even when the world movement in this direction was hardly underway. Now, everybody is talking about women and girls coding and computer science.

It emerged that Participant #13's efforts at mainstreaming the housing challenges facing *Kayayei* (a local term for women head porters who operate in the open markets of Ghana) had led to some provisions in Ghana's 2020 national budget, for the construction of some residential quarters to house these workers at selected markets across the country:

> I produced a film that focused on women empowerment and *Kayayei* and did a campaign on the issue. There is a scene where someone said the government should provide housing for the *Kayayei*. Many of the issues I highlighted have been addressed. In the 2020 budget, the government announced some provisions for housing them. That brought me a lot of satisfaction.

### 7.3.2 Environmental Stewardship

It was found that the actions by some of the activists in this study had produced some effects in the fight against illegal small-scale gold mining in Ghana. For instance, Participant #6 expressed the belief that their consistent resistance actions since 2013 against illegal small-scale mining in Ghana, popularly called

*Galamsey*, had galvanized the current president of Ghana, Nana Akufo-Addo to clamp down on such deleterious mining operations in the country.

Participant #6 explained that in March 2017, the government announced a six-month ban on *Galamsey* and set up the multisectoral group called Operation Vanguard to enforce the ban. The ban saw the seizure of excavators and mining equipment. As explained by Participant #6, their actions created public awareness about the environmental effects of *Galamsey*:

> The work of the Media Coalition against Galamsey gave the President the platform to show political courage regarding illegal mining operations in Ghana and to call the bluff of political blackmailers in saying that, even without their votes, he was going to stop Galamsey. The President formed Operation Vanguard to enforce the ban on such mining operations.

### 7.3.3 Deepening Democratic Dividends

Some of the collaborators in this study indicated that their actions have led to improvements in Ghana's democratic culture. For instance, the works of some CEO activists had led to the measures being taken to address disputed national elections in Ghana. Hitherto, most presidential and parliamentary election results had sparked disputes and posed significant threats to the peace and security of Ghana. This has been because of the lack of transparency in some facets of the electoral processes in the country.

It was found that through legal activism, activist CEOs such as Participant #8 had been able to win landmark legal judgments against the Electoral Commission of Ghana that had required the Electoral Commission to provide greater transparency over the conduct of elections in Ghana. For instance, such legal reforms now required the Electoral Commission of Ghana to be more transparent in providing pink sheets to the various political parties, as evidence of the pattern of voting at various polling stations during elections in Ghana. These pink sheets serve as audit trails and vouchers provided to the various political parties, to enable them to have parallel collations and tabulations of polls. As explained by Participant #8, their legal activism produced some victories for democracy in Ghana:

> The Supreme Court ruled in our favor, stating that the Electoral Commissioner should provide all parties with the pink sheets from every polling station, to the extent that as soon as an election was over, it was possible for each political party to independently determine the results, even before the declaration by the Electoral Commission.

Participant #13 disclosed that their #WHYIWALKFORGHANA protest had created more awareness about the danger that political vigilantes posed to

Ghana's stability and democracy. They disclosed that their protest march had led to some commitments being made by the government to address the issue:

> When I did my walk, I themed it *The Power of One: Why I Walk for Ghana.* From feedback, I know it was discussed in powerful political quarters. At least, some promise has been made that my concerns are being resolved.

It was found that Participant #13's protests produced more than promises from the political establishment in Ghana. A special commission of inquiry was established by the President of Ghana to probe the Ayawaso West Wuogon by-elections that triggered the latest violence (Seneadza, 2019). After an incisive investigation, this three-member commission presented its report to the President of Ghana. On April 12, 2019, President Nana Akufo-Addo announced the placement of a bill before Parliament, to help disband political vigilante groups in Ghana. In July 2019, the Vigilantism and Related Offenses Bill of 2019 was passed, proscribing political militias and vigilantism in Ghana.

Some participants traced the unfortunately high spate of corruption in the country to state capture and crony capitalism resulting from the prevailing system of political party financing and the so-called winner-takes-all culture of politicking in Ghana. According to several informants, the cloaked sources of electoral financing left Ghana worse off, as politicians pillaged the nation's resources in the bid to reward their campaign financiers.

Thus, the social resistance campaigns of some of the informants focused on pushing for reforms to political party financing in Ghana. Some participants indicated that their protests were bearing fruit, as the Electoral Commission of Ghana was requiring political parties to submit their financial statements, together with notes revealing the sources of their funding and the flows of such funds. Participant #8 shed some light on his work in this regard:

> We believe that political party financing and the present *"winner takes all"* imperative is a major source of corruption in Ghana. The courts ruled in our favor, instructing the Electoral Commission to demand the political parties to submit their financial statements, with notes of the sources of their funding. The Commission is to make these submissions public for us to see.

Another area in which CEO activists in this study said they had positively impacted Ghana's democracy was related to a proposal for political parties to participate in provincial/district and municipal-level elections in Ghana. During his interview on November 15, 2019, Participant #14 indicated that they and the *One Ghana Movement* were planning a campaign to push for a "No Vote" or even a cancellation of the referendum by the Electoral Commission of Ghana for the Ghanaian public to agree for the district and local-level elections to be held along political party lines:

The Electoral Commission has scheduled December 17, 2019, to conduct a referendum to approve a bill to amend Ghana's 1992 Constitution. The One Ghana Movement's position is that the proposal wouldn't work in the nation's interest, so we are promoting a "No vote," or a cancellation of the referendum. The climate in Ghana is too politically polarized and we believe that this proposal, politicizing local-level elections in Ghana would worsen things. We must put Ghana first, rather than parochial political party considerations.

The protests against the planned referendum proved to be hugely successful. At a national briefing on December 1, 2019, Ghana's President Akufo-Addo announced the cancellation of the referendum, to decide on an amendment of Clause 3 Article 55 (3) of the Constitution that would enable political parties to sponsor candidates during local-level elections (Citi Newsroom, 2019). The President cited the absence of national consensus on the matter and directed Hajia Alima Mahama, Ghana's Local Government and Rural Development Minister to withdraw the Bills seeking to amend Articles 55 (3) and 243 (1).

### 7.3.4 Legal and Public Policy Reforms

Several participants described their social achievements as coming by way of some legal reforms and changes in public policy. After remaining as a bill for over a decade before Parliament without being considered, various activists pressured for the Right to Information Bill to be passed into law (Shaban, 2019a). In March 2018, the Right to Information Bill was approved by the Parliament of Ghana. On May 21, 2018, Ghana's President Akufo-Addo signed the bill into law (Shaban, 2019b). Ghana's Right to Information Law provides for the actualization and operationalization of the constitutional right to information from key public and selected private institutions, subject to exemptions consistent with the safeguarding of the public interest. Participant #8 saw themselves as contributing to this achievement:

We have successfully got the passage of the Right to Information Law in Ghana. Now, anyone can demand any kind of information from any government agency in Ghana.

Other participants described their achievements in terms of improvements in getting the political establishment to listen to dissenting voices on public policy matters. For instance, during the planned implementation of cellular SIM card registration in Ghana at the start of 2010, citing threats to the privacy of citizens, Participant #10 revealed that they had become a one-(wo)man army, kicking against the planned policy. They spoke of having to engage the then Director of Ghana's National Security in a shouting match on live radio:

> Whenever you've stared long and hard enough at politicians, they'd blinked first. They called me for a quiet meeting one night and requested the law I was referring to ... I drafted the law and sent it to them. In Parliament, they amended the law to say that the equipment they were acquiring would not be used to monitor conversations. It was a quiet victory that emboldened me to find my voice. We would put stuff out there, but the initial reaction of the government was to ignore us. But as we kept mounting pressure, we started achieving some results.

Some participants described community outcomes such as improvements in Ghana's economy, changes in government policies, reforms in defense and internal security, and better sanitation and environmental conservation. Participant #8's testimony during their interview at the end of November 2019 was instructive:

> My actions have led to changes in government policies. The outcomes have been on different fronts, including economic improvements for Ghana, changes to unbudgeted subsidies, and their implication on the economy... We are currently pursuing reforms in the security sector because of some credible torture allegations we have received.

### 7.3.5 Empowerment and Liberation

Several themes emerged that indicated a pattern of community achievements in the area of the empowerment of the generality of Ghanaians. For instance, it emerged that Participant #20 referred to his decade-long campaign to promote a financially literate population:

> My actions on financial literacy have shaped individual income levels and promoted economic empowerment. My advocacy on multiple streams of income has led many Ghanaians to consider several other things they could do to supplement their primary income sources.

Among the effects of the actions of CEOs was the empowerment and building of the agency of members of Ghana's middle class. During the late 1970s and the 1980s, there had been what many have described as a "culture of silence" in Ghana, which had been characterized by the disempowerment of the middle class and the generality of Ghanaians, especially during the Rawlings era between 1979 and 1992.

However, with the liberalization of the media landscape in Ghana, the promotion of democracy, increased roles of civil society groups, and the works of activists, political actors, and public office holders were beginning to be held accountable. Politicians were said to be especially becoming increasingly aware of the power of the middle class to demand greater transparency and accountability. Participant #8 described this sense of awakening:

> The idea that today, Ghanaian politicians know that the middle class would not sit aloof and watch them mismanage this country is important. Now, everybody in public office knows that if it gets beyond a point, they're going to get some of us confronting them and mobilizing people against them. Our actions make public office holders in Ghana more accountable and uncomfortable in knowing that their actions would be scrutinized. It's important if we're to develop that they don't see themselves as the be-all and end-all.

Participant #13 observed that her #WHYIWALKFORGHANA and other campaigns continued to encourage and embolden Ghanaians from all walks of life, who continued to express their ability to now speak out on issues that mattered to them:

> People reach out to me every day, speaking about being emboldened by my actions ... that I've encouraged them to find their voices. I get these messages from all manner of people, telling me about what huge impacts I am having on their empowerment.

Those CEO activists who focused on youth empowerment saw their achievements largely in terms of developing a corps of ethically minded future leaders for Ghana. For instance, Participant #16 spoke about the futility of social development, devoid of an ethical base for the youth:

> I keep emphasizing ethics because achievement without ethics can build a problematic society. The biggest achievement is not just building entrepreneurs and people who're rising the corporate ladder, but people who're trying to do so ethically.

### 7.3.6 Economic and Public Financial Management

It was learned that some CEO activists have worked to produce overall improvements in Ghana's economy and enhancements in the general quality of public financial management. For example, it was found some of their actions, aimed at getting the Auditor-General of Ghana to flex its muscles for the first-time during Ghana's fourth republican constitution regarding surcharging individuals, groups, companies, and other institutions had led to the recovery of huge sums of money by the state.

As recalled by Participant #10, legal activism jointly staged with the pressure group Occupy Ghana got the Supreme Court to instruct the Auditor-General impose some surcharges:

> The Supreme Court agreed with our position and ordered the Auditor-General to exercise constitutional power. The current Auditor-General (Daniel Yao Domelovo) for the first time, saved Ghana Ghs 5.4 billion (about US$ 1 billion, at the prevailing exchange rate of GHs 5.4 to US$ 1 at the time). Some people had plotted to take that amount from the Government of Ghana and the Auditor-General was asked to vet the transaction. As we speak (as of November 30, 2019), the Auditor-General has recovered GHs 67 million (about US$ 12.4 million) from people who had taken the nation's money and were forced to refund the same because of the judgments Ghana had got in court. If I am unable to achieve any other thing for Ghana, I would still be satisfied.

Some participants expressed some of their achievements in terms of contributing to better economic and public financial management in Ghana. Here, a few informants said they had contributed to some positive transformation in the implementation of a new regime of Tax Identification Numbers (TIN). For Participant #20, seeing that their recommendations for refining the original plans for TIN in Ghana had been a welcomed development:

> I wrote about the implementation of Tax Identification Numbers (TIN). I advocated for the promotion of the benefits of having a TIN, rather than threatening people. I was happy when I realized the Ghana Revenue Authority and the Ministry of Information did just that.

Other participants said their pressures against the government and other state actors involved in negotiations of some petroleum deals between some oil exploration companies and Ghana had led to changes in some of those contract terms. Participant #22 had been agitating against what they saw as an unfair petroleum contract between Ghana and Aker Energy. During their interview, they expressed joy in noting that this contract was being revised, so that the interests of Ghana would be better served in the deal that had granted a lucrative oil concession to Aker Energy:

> Aker Energy had brought a plan to develop the oilfield. My advocacy has changed that. They've taken back their plan of development that they presented to the minister, and they are going to revise it ... because of the holes I had punched in the initial plan. Their actions would have kicked against our local content laws until I spoke up and exposed their actions.

### 7.3.7 Shaping Public Opinion

Many of the CEO activists who participated in this study said they felt that their actions shaped public opinion in Ghana. Most of the study participants believed that the impact they had on public opinion had galvanized the many Ghanaians who hitherto had felt helpless and fatalistic. For example, through increased public engagement generated by their actions, some participants observed that many Ghanaians now felt some sense of enablement that had led to increased active citizenship. In Participant #8's words:

> When we started these actions, going on the streets, we attracted so many people who came out to support our actions. The effect on the general populace is that now there is a resurgence in active citizenship. People feel that if something goes wrong, they have a potent voice. The citizens feel they have a voice, and that when they speak, something will happen.

Some participants observed that speaking out on some issues had helped to place the limelight on those issues. In the specific case of the One District One Factory (1D1F) program, Participant #18 believed that their actions helped to publicize and legitimize this government program:

> I think it [1D1F] received a lot more visibility because banks came behind it to give it legitimacy. Because I spoke and other banks came out visibly to support in words and by financial investments, it gave the program a high level of legitimacy.

As indicated by Participant #19, their activism in seeking to effect changes within the Ghanaian social structure that kept women and girls out of the computer software and digital professions had required her to make her actions impactful in shaping public opinion. They observed that among happenings that convinced her about the influence of her actions on affecting public opinion had included basic changes concerning the place of women and girls in the digital spaces, to the extent that more parents had become positively predisposed to their daughters pursuing such professions:

> Previously, parents didn't believe in their daughters' education. Fathers were cynical about educating daughters, saying, "She has to be in the house; she belongs to the kitchen." Now, we're seeing a change in attitudes and more women and girls enrolling in technology programs. Husbands are enrolling their wives, and men are leading in getting more women and girls in these programs. Husbands joining in the action, and we have more positive men voices supporting our cause. That's a positive shift that's happening now.

Some of the informants had called for some changes in the educational sector in Ghana. Among those participants who had expressed dismay at the perceived sinking standards of Ghana's educational system, especially at the tertiary level, had been Participant #14. While attending an event to mark the 70th anniversary,

Participant #14 could not bottle up their frustration at the failures of Ghana's educational sector:

> I attended the 70th anniversary of the University of Ghana. I took frankly drew the attention to their mediocrity. I challenged them to start thinking more creatively in producing people with relevant and employable skills ... I called for a transformation of the school ....

They revealed that they were quite impressed with the public reaction to their calls. Although the public reaction was mixed, they were pleased to see more support for their position.

It is however noteworthy that while some of these CEO activists may have contributed to some positive changes in Ghanaian society, some big problems persist. For instance, *Galamsey* is still prevalent, and more remains to be done in terms of the gender agenda.

## 7.4 Effects of CEO Activism on Companies

Not all achievements or effects of CEO activism in Ghana pertained to the environment or the wider Ghanaian society. It was found that the practice of CEO activism in Ghana had produced some distinctive outcomes for the companies led by the respective activist CEOs that participated in this study. It emerged that these effects of CEO activism included both positive and negative consequences for the companies.

### 7.4.1 Tonic Consequences for Companies

Several participants noted that CEO activism had the potential of producing some business advantages for the CEO's company. For instance, Participant #18 recalled that when they started expressing open support for the government's 1D1F program in 2017, although the Board of Directors of the bank they led was apprehensive because of possible business disadvantages and reputational dents because of the polarized political clime in Ghana, their activism rather proved fortuitous:

> We're a financial institution and this is a political issue ... the board was probably concerned about potential business losses it may bring. Since this happened in 2017, I can say with all facts on the ground that the business of the bank was rather aided by my pronouncements ... it propelled the business. Our image was improved, and other CEOs recognized that it was good, leading to four other bank CEOs joining us to sign an M.O.U. with the government.

The Government of Ghana, under the presidency of H.E. Nana Akufo-Addo, envisioned an ambitious industrialization program throughout Ghana. Under the One District, One Factory (1D1F) program, the government aims to build at least one factory in each of the country's administrative districts. Since its launch in 2016, this policy has been polarizing in Ghana, depending on which side of the political divide one belonged to.

While supporters of the ruling NPP saw it as a positive policy, members of the opposition saw it in a largely negative light. It is the perception of the divisive nature of the subject matter, coupled with the fact that it had become a hot-button issue in Ghana that may have made the members of the board of directors of the XXX Bank (not the real name of bank) apprehensive to find Participant #18 (the bank's managing director at the time), publicly expressing their support for the policy.

Participant #4 saw some positive consequences of CEO activism in Ghana and across Africa in terms of business opportunities for strategic communication firms. They observed that the nascence of CEO activism presented opportunities for their public relations firm to create a corporate practice(s) to advice current and future activist CEOs about effectively engaging in such resistance actions:

> There's an opportunity to position a communication firm along these lines. We're considering a practice to advise CEOs who want to become activists. Because we understand business, public policy, political action, and advocacy, we can guide them on this journey.

Some participants drew more direct correlations between CEO activism and the financial performance of their companies. Participant #5 described how their role as an activist CEO had enabled their wealth management and leasing company to mobilize cheaper-than-average funds from the marketplace. They explained that this was a development that had a strong, direct, and positive impact on the company's profitability:

> On the organizational level, it [CEO activism] has a direct relationship with our profitability. As a financial institution, we trade in money. My actions make people have confidence in the brand, and we borrow money at least two percent less than the market. If you take our profit of US$ 2 million, that translates straight into the bottom line.

Others described some benefits for companies in terms of improved corporate images. Participant #6 indicated that his actions against *Galamsey* and transparent elections in Ghana in 2016 had led to an improved corporate reputation for the Graphic Communications Group, the biggest newspaper group in Ghana:

> There have been positive outcomes for the organizations I have led. When I was Managing Director of the major newspaper

publishing company, my actions on *Galamsey* and free and fair elections strengthened the brand equity to the point where people realized and accepted that the newspapers within our stables are the national mouthpiece and that they say the things that are important to Ghanaians ... they set the national agenda and communicate facts about things that we hold dear as a people.

Indeed, most of the participants described some of the reputational dividends of CEO activism as emanating from the generally positive media reportage and good publicity enjoyed whenever the CEO made pronouncements that were carried out and discussed in the mass media. Some saw the corporate profiling benefits as emanating from being seen in good company, such as when Participant #18 recalled being invited by the President of Ghana to the commissioning of one of the flagship projects under the 1D1F program:

It wasn't by accident that when the President was cutting the sod for the Ekumfi Fruits and Juice Factory, XXX Bank (not the real name of the entity) was the only bank that was invited and given prominence during the event and in media reports. Those are some of the positive linkages you get – the acceptance and the positive light in which you are viewed as being part of the progressive forces in society.

Although other participants such as Participant #6 did not initially envision some of the positive consequences of their work as CEO activists, they indicated that it was not long before such positive outcomes became glaring to them, especially in terms of corporate benefits such as better employee loyalty, driving customer brand preference, and as a means of gaining some competitive advantages:

I realized that it is one of the best ways of branding yourself, without paying for it. Immediately, you stand out as a unique CEO. I go to places, and people spontaneously identify me as "*The Galamsey Man.*" It helps a company's competitive positioning. CEO activism could be a point of differentiation for your customers. If it's well-aligned with your team, then they would believe that you would take a bullet for them so they would also take one for you.

Indeed, some of the informants disclosed that some of the positive consequences of CEO activism were felt internally within the companies. Such positive effects were said to include a feeling of pride and respect felt by employees. As recounted by Participant #1, their activities boosted the morale of their employees:

My people feel more respected because the notion is that you're fighting for the rights of women in organizations. I wouldn't limit this feeling of respect to only my women employees. I think it applies to men and women employees alike because they know you are fighting for the general good. Your social actions as a CEO make your people more committed and engaged.

### 7.4.2 Toxic Consequences for Companies

A recurrent theme of the consequence of engaging in CEO activism in Ghana was some perceived negative effects on business opportunities. It emerged that the business disadvantages arising out of CEO activism in Ghana were multifaceted. For some participants, there was a general loss of business opportunity, such as when contracts or business deals eluded the activist CEO's firm because of his/her resistance actions. Participant #8 described a general pattern of business disadvantages they had suffered because of a feeling of being conflicted as a result of his public pronouncements on various issues:

There's a downside to doing CEO activism. I'm aware that sometimes, the business hasn't come in simply because of my public stances. Often, a matter or client comes up that I can't accept because I have publicly said something, and there're times when I see that I am conflicted in a matter because of my activist stance. Activism entails great sacrifices and losses for my business.

Several CEOs in this study felt scared to weigh in on what they perceived as contentious matters of a political nature in Ghana. Participant #7 disclosed that their trepidation about speaking on political issues stemmed from the fear of jeopardizing the fortunes of their businesses:

Although we seem to have freedom of speech, you are restrained because it is scary in Ghana if you have to say something that does not go down well with a political party. It's scary because your business can easily be victimized. You could lose a business contract, and as an entrepreneur, you find yourself not wanting to contribute to political issues.

For Participant #13, although their activism caused some business deals that were under negotiation to disappear, they were not concerned about such losses because they were smaller prices to pay, compared to the risk of political instability in Ghana:

People had their reservations about working with me or my businesses, just because of my activism. Some pushbacks I experienced included losing business deals. A few talks that were on the table went away because I'd brought unnecessary attention to myself. If you're going to take away your business because of this, be my guest. If I have to weigh the outcome of me not being able to live with myself vis-a-vis losing some businesses or money, I think it was a risk I was willing to take.

It was not only prospective contracts that could be undermined by CEO activism. Participant #22 testified that businesses in Ghana risked having contracts that had already been signed, sealed, and delivered to be revoked if the activism of their CEO was not seen favorably by political officeholders. They noted that while some companies had suffered such misfortunes because of CEO activism, they believed that some of the companies had been able to push back and enforced the sanctity of their contracts:

Tenders have been canceled, and some lost things that were already signed. However, some of these companies also tend to have some political strength, so they can push back somehow.

Participant #3, whose media production company depended on corporate sponsorship, disclosed that such support for her television productions and special events had been hard hit because of their activist stance against patriarchal forces in Ghana. They revealed that most men CEOs in Ghana viewed their work in liberating women and strengthening the forces in the direction of shattering the proverbial corporate glass ceiling with a disdain:

The negative aspect is that we struggle for sponsorship. I do it out of passion and conviction, and not for money, so I decided that I wouldn't accept a sponsor or brand that is harmful to women. Such a decision limits sponsorship options for the company. The few avenues left for me are companies ... led by men who don't agree with my fight against patriarchy in Ghana and are reluctant to approve sponsorship packages ... for my company's projects.

According to Participant #18, historically there had been a strong "gagging mechanism" in Ghana, where eminent businesspeople such as B.A. Mensah, Appiah-Menkah, and Kwabena Darko had been victimized by past military rulers for speaking about some of the big issues during their days. Participant #4 observed that within the Ghanaian context, CEO activists tended to encounter many difficulties, including being treated as a pariah:

It [CEO activism] is a difficult thing to do, especially in our sociocultural setting here in Ghana. Although they may not openly admit it, some companies may blacklist you and choose not to have any business to do with your company because they consider you to be some sort of risk.

According to Participant #8, their role as an activist CEO had made other CEOs who could have given their firm some business deals become fearful of openly associating with them and their business because of their public stances, usually against the political establishment in Ghana:

> I've had situations where even people who would've done some business with me have told me they're afraid of doing so because of my activism. They're apprehensive because they don't want to be associated with my activist stances. That's why a business associate asked me to give up activism and focus on being a businessman.

Some participants revealed that engaging in CEO activism took too much time, effort, and precious resources from the core business. Participant #16 counted the cost of their perennial CEO activism to their company:

> The negative consequences of CEO activism included getting caught up and getting carried away; For me, it was the sacrifice of time and time and time. Especially, when you are away during the critical first quarter of the year, the cost to me was the sacrifice of time, resources, effort, and the adverse effects of these on my business.

It emerged that an activist CEO who negatively spoke publicly against the Government of Ghana ended up not only being personally targeted but also having his or her business become the focus of numerous attacks. A few informants in this study revealed that although such negative profiling and targeting took various forms, generally legitimate business compliance requirements and certifications by diverse government departments and requirements served as the basis of harassment. In describing such political name-calling, harassment, and attacks, Participant #24 said that such scrutiny tended to keep the CEO activist and their company on top of their game:

> They will go and look to see whether you have paid your taxes. You must ensure that you comply with all rules and regulations, including certification by the Food and Drug Board, the Ghana Revenue Authority, etc. When you choose to be an activist in Ghana, you must expect a lot of harassment from the powers that be who can ruin the business.

They described other reactions of various government agencies and departments to their comments about the exclusion of budgetary allocations for the construction of roads in the Volta Region in Ghana's 2020 national budget, including orchestrated attempts to incite their out-growers not to supply them raw materials.

## 7.5 Effects of CEO Activism on Individual Activist CEOs

Besides some strategic corporate dividends, almost all participants in this study described some personal rewards for engaging in CEO activism. It was found that CEO activism had some positive and negative consequences for the CEO activists.

### 7.5.1 Tonic Consequences for Individual Activist CEOs

Generally, participants spoke of some tonic personal outcomes – positive effects – of engaging in CEO activism. Such benefits were in terms of stronger personal brands and public recognition. However, for others, the perks of engaging in CEO activism extended beyond building a public profile.

All the CEOs who participated in this study observed that they derived some personal satisfaction from engaging in CEO activism. It emerged that personal reactions arising out of CEO activism included various reactions that related to the enjoyment of a beneficial state of mind for the activist CEOs. These reactions were expressed in several terms. For instance, Participant #8 spoke of having some peace of mind, a better quality of sleep, and the confidence of knowing that they had lived a good life because of their work to transform society positively:

> I sleep better at night. If I die now, I'd have lived a good life. For me, that's what counts the most – the internal satisfaction in knowing that you've done the right thing in fighting for society.

For other participants, when the actions of the CEO received positive media publicity, there was a sense of pride and a generally good feeling that the CEO experienced. According to Participant #7, such feelings tended to be so strong that they were also felt by employees and other corporate stakeholders:

> There's a feel-good factor when you and your organization are in the news for the right reasons. You don't have much control over the nature of media reportage about you and your organization, but if you're in the news for a cause about which you have spoken, that places you in a positive light and you've got a deep sense of pride.

It was learned that engaging in CEO activism tended to positively profile the personas of some of the activist CEOs who participated in this study, as observed by Participant #8:

> I have not benefitted financially or materially from my activism. I have made more sacrifices than I have benefitted, but the benefit shouldn't just be in money terms. There are lawyers in Ghana who are richer than me, just as there're richer consultants. But I think I am viewed publicly more favorably than most. A strong personal brand is one of the benefits of my activism.

Some positive consequences of engaging in CEO activism included being accorded great respect and recognition from various sections of Ghanaian society. Many study participants disclosed that their current social recognition was more attributable to their work as CEO activists than to their core business operations. Participant #16 intimated that they owed a great deal of their social standing to their social advocacy over the years:

> My social standing has been impacted significantly not by my work as a business leader, but more by my role as a social activist. For some years, I've been voted in the top 100 of the most influential individuals in Ghana, won awards, and been spotlighted in publications. These were not because of my profit-making activities, but mainly because of my social advocacy. Interestingly, that translates into business opportunities … people like people who do good, and good business follows doing good. CEO activism favorably impacts my business prospecting activities because people see you as one who has given your all for the greater good.

Several participants indicated that engaging in CEO activism had enhanced their personal profiles and offered them career benefits. For instance, while Participant #6 expressed the belief that their new role as head of an association of telecommunication companies in the country may likely have stemmed from their long-standing track record as an activist CEO, Participant #17 indicated that they had been offered a board position because of their activism:

> I know for sure that, after we went to speak at a session at Joy FM on an important social issue relating to women's rights and liberation, somebody said I had to sit on their board. Right away, my name came up and I am now a board member of that company.

Thus, most of the CEOs in this study regarded the stature and overall public profile of the CEO both as an important determinant and outcome of CEO activism. Many of the participants shared the view that activism built them up as CEOs, just as their perceived public profile or CEO celebrity statuses determined the success of their actions. For Participant #18, this status-conferral ability of their activism campaigns could never be downplayed:

> My activism builds me up as a CEO and there is an unintended benefit that you derive as a CEO activist. Your social profile or personal brand is elevated in ways that enhance your public recognition and also feed into my activism, as it enables me to command more public attention.

Several of the participants mentioned some enhancements in their social consciousness since embarking on the activist journey. For Participant #18, since speaking out in support of the government's 1D1F program, they had started thinking more about what else they could add their voice to developmental issues within the society. They noted that becoming a CEO activist had broadened their outlook on life in ways that had seen them thinking less about themselves only, but more about others. Thus, they described a heightened sense of social-mindedness as an effect that CEO activism had had on their overall outlook on life:

> Once you start engaging in activism, you are boxed into a certain kind of thinking beyond just yourself and thinking less about bread-and-butter issues, and more about others, society, and what else you can do to support the empowerment and development of others.

Some CEOs in this study shared the view that their actions had generated positive reactions from their families. For Participant #18, the feedback from their spouse and their close associates had been all plaudits:

> Where my family is concerned, I think it has been more on the positive side. My wife, for instance, kept telling me that her friends kept praising me and telling her that I am doing very well in the various activities I have been engaged in. Because of the positive feedback, she was getting, she encouraged me to do more in supporting that kind of initiative.

### 7.5.2 Toxic Consequences for Individual Activist CEOs

It emerged that although CEO activism in Ghana may be associated with some desirable consequences for the activist CEO, this is not always the case. For many of the informants who participated in this study, CEO activism also came with a baggage of negative ramifications.

#### 7.5.2.1 Physical, Verbal, and Media Attacks

Many informants mentioned some specific dangers of a physical nature they had faced for engaging in CEO activism. Such physical attacks or dangers included assaults, robberies, and various acts of arson. Participant #24 described some of these physical attacks:

> There are physical dangers or attacks ... CEO activists have been robbed and their phones, laptops, and personal possessions were taken away. Your home gets broken into, basically to put fear in you and prevent you from continuing to speak. Others had their car tires deflated and vehicle brakes tampered with. Another had

parked somewhere, and when he next moved his car, his tires were coming off because the wheel lugs had been loosened by arsonists, just because of his campaigns.

For Participant #10, such attacks came in battalions that he termed "concerted," including rapid fires of name-calling as hypocrites; smear campaigns and defamation across various media; cyberbullying on Facebook; arson attacks such as tampering with the car tires of CEO activists; and fabricated stories in sections of the media:

> There have been concerted attacks directed at me and Occupy Ghana. Despite all that we've done to hold the current NPP government to account, some people still attack us and call us hypocrites because they claim we are not speaking up against the ruling government. My reaction is that I can point to some 77 issues we have raised in less than three years that the current government has been in office.

It was found that such attacks could come from shocking sources, including one's kinsfolk. Participant #6 recounted their experience of being attacked on social media by a relative who felt disappointed in them. They also described a physical attack against them, where an assailant had tried to run them over:

> There have been backlashes … they would rain insults, threats, and attacks on you and call you names. People have tried to bully me and attacked me on social media over this *galamsey* matter. Somebody tried running me off the street some time ago during my early morning walks. A cousin of mine attacked me on social media ….

Some participants indicated that such physical attacks were becoming more commonplace. During their #WHYIWALKFORGHANA protest, Participant #13 had to face the reality of physical attacks, and the scary prospect of risking their safety meant that they had to undertake their protest march with a sizeable police contingent:

> What I did had its security concerns in many ways. It was a bit scary for me, my family, and my friends, for me to put a voice to such a high-tension issue and expose myself on the street of Accra. Attacks come in many ways – physical, verbal, social, etc. The police were concerned, and I ended up walking with a contingent of more than 30 police personnel following me.

It emerged that powerful women were especially targeted in such attacks. Participant #1 shared several accounts of unpleasant attacks on several social media platforms. They found it shocking that as an eminent member of Ghanaian society, they could be attacked and called bad names on social media. They described such name-calling as part of bad attacks against powerful women in Ghana:

> I have been attacked and called all manner of terrible names, especially on social media. Yes, even I, an empowered, moving, and shaking corporate executive face net-bullying ... because of my activism.

According to some informants, mores of Ghanaian culture where people of relatively higher social statuses such as CEOs were exempted from verbal attacks did not extend to CEO activists. Thus, engaging in CEO activism exposed some participants in this study to insults and attacks, despite their eminence in Ghanaian society. Besides being a CEO, Participant #3 is married to a powerful traditional Ghanaian chief. However, they disclosed that they had not been spared:

> I have been called a witch and so many unprintable names, just because of my social advocacy campaigns. If you are an independent and strong woman in Ghana, you are hated and called all manner of names. I have my fair share of innuendos and insinuations.

It turned out that it is not only the women CEO activists who suffered such attacks. Some men CEOs in this study recounted experiences of being bashed on social media, but also in the traditional media spaces. Participant #10 shared their testimony about suffering smear campaigns and bad press:

> There are smear campaigns. I have been defamed. I sued this guy, sitting in New York, who decided to insult me regarding issues that completely have nothing to do with me. Yesterday, a friend of mine set us up to be insulted on his Facebook wall.

While both men and women CEOs in Ghana suffered unpleasant attacks, some participants suggested that such name-calling and card-stacking were especially institutionalized and set heavily against women. Some of the women CEOs in this study spoke of several negative terms, labels, and tags used in Ghana against outspoken women. For Participant #1, many cultural and social institutional structures and systems existed in Ghana for demonizing, scandalizing, and vilifying women in general, but especially very liberated women. They expressed their suspicion that the Ghanaian society had something against womenfolk, including being called "too known":

> Ghanaian society also has something against women who are activist CEOs. Vocal women are branded in a way; they term you as "too known."

According to Participant #19, seeking to advocate for improved rights for women and girls in the technology space had caused them to encounter a great deal of resistance and accusations, including those that alleged that empowering women would make women disrespectful of men, feelings that women would overtake men, and a general feeling of insecurity and discomfort among many men in Ghana:

> I face a lot of resistance. Some say that now men will be disadvantaged, or women are getting too many special privileges … that these gender agendas would be a license for women to be disrespectful of men. Many men feel some intimidation and fear that women will take over. Also, men feel that they must protect their position, so they are uncomfortable when women are arising, and when women are asserting themselves.

A distinct form of verbal attacks against CEO activists in Ghana related to fabrication and false accusations. For a participant, such attacks had targeted her marriage. Describing the consequences of engaging in CEO activism as "very big," Participant #23 revealed that some of their verbal assailants had gone to the extent of calling their spouses on the phone to report all manner of falsities to them:

> I remember my husband would get phone calls from people who thought they were doing him a favor, who would seek to report to him, or wonder why he would allow me to go on business trips with my bosses and meet all manner of people. Thankfully, that marriage has been strong, and we have survived these things.

Participant #2 described some of the attacks they had experienced, including questioning their marital statuses and whether they had any children:

> I've had on occasion a few business leaders – not just men, but typically men – who feel that it's a lot of hot air; that you're making too much noise and you should forget about it all. They try to discourage you; saying it is not the place for a woman to be doing this. They want to find major minuses and the major minus is not being married and not having children.

Among the major negative tags that women CEO activists in Ghana faced was being labeled as "a feminist." It turned out that in Ghana, such a label carried many negative connotations, borne out of a poor appreciation of the meaning of the concept. Participant #19 indicated that the "feminist" label had been many times hurled at her, in hopes of stopping her from speaking up against the patriarchal norms and institutions in Ghana:

> When they say you're a *feminist*, they mean you hate men, and
> that you don't want men to progress. With such a tag in Ghana,
> you always have that immediate negative reaction, even without
> having your thoughts heard.                                    .

Participant #19 mentioned that some of the opposition to the gender diversity agenda in Ghana had been from other women. They explained that such a tendency by the few successful women in Ghana to break the glass ceiling to feel the need to protect their turfs had something to do with the pattern of tokenism in the appointment of women to senior positions in the country.

Other participants indicated various forms of name-calling, as arising from their activism. A participant disclosed that she and her colleagues belonging to the Executive Women Network (EWN) had been referred to in unsavory terms as "The Diva Club," or "The women doing their thing," indicating some condescending and patronizing attitudes that reflect the fact that those making these comments do not take the EWN seriously.

Several participants disclosed that such attacks had caused them to feel concerned about their safety and the security of their families. Participant #19 indicated that, as they were becoming increasingly strident in their activism, such voices in their heads kept urging them to become more restrained in their utterances:

> Another resistance I face involves the security of my loved ones.
> I'm getting increasingly vocal as I'm getting older and as I am
> having more opportunities to speak. When I was younger, I was a
> little more controlled in my pronouncements. Now, I'm unhinged;
> I'm fully liberated, and I have found my voice. I worry that will get
> me into trouble.

Some participants indicated that many media attacks had been politically motivated by members of the sitting government who may perceive the pronouncements of the CEO activist as making the government unpopular. For Participant #22, some "rottweilers" and serial callers to radio and television call-in programs had been unleashed on them:

> Most of the negative outcomes have been from political people.
> They unleash their *rottweilers* on you. Instead of exposing
> themselves by coming directly, they have these serial callers or
> serial social media guys who try to pounce on you.

Participant #9 described a range of problems that came the way of CEO activists in Ghana because of their desire to drive positive social changes. They disclosed that such negative consequences included being perceived as an enemy; others picking personal fights with you due to your activism; name-calling; and several other forms of attacks:

... always personal attacks on you. You encounter many enemies and politicians see it as a personal fight with you because you're targeted as an enemy of the establishment. The environment for democratic encounters and accountability is not well-developed in developing countries. It's a bigger risk to be a CEO activist where debates, reasonableness, and tolerance are not appreciated. That's why we have fewer CEO activists here.

Participant #24 described a series of attacks she had to endure. Soon after participating prominently in the Occupy Flagstaff House protest in 2014 and engaging a member of the-then National Democratic Congress (NDC) government in a heated confrontation on live radio, they were attacked in a biting publication in a popular tabloid that was sympathetic to the NDC party. They recounted how their images were splashed on the front page of this tabloid, together with a press feature that was designed to put them in a negative light. According to them, they were not so much concerned about the content of the press feature in the tabloid as they were about the motivations and capabilities of those that masterminded the bad press attacks against them for their role in the Occupy Flagstaff House protest of 2014:

> Whatever the story contained was no news at all. What bothered me was that if they were so desperate to write such a story about me, then I figured that they were capable of physically harming me too.

Thus, they expressed feelings of fear and insecurity because of the extent to which their attackers went into maligning and ridiculing them in the media. This experience left them feeling fearful about their safety and the security of their family members.

### 7.5.2.2 Arrests and Detentions

A direct effect of engaging in CEO activism in Ghana was the risk of being arrested or detained by the Ghana Police. According to serial activist Participant #8, during the Occupy Flagstaff House protest march, they were arrested by the Ghana Police for being the convener of the protest.

In Africa, when your actions deprived politicians and their favored business cronies of lucrative, but ill-deserved financial resources, you are putting yourself in very clear and present danger. For Participant #8, the threats had come in many forms, including beatings and death threats. These have made their family and close associates concerned for their health and safety. However, they disclosed that they were not deterred and that their father's advice had kept them going:

> I've been threatened many times ... all manner of threats, from beatings to many others. I don't dwell on that because you could walk out of here and get run over by a car. I am not reckless, but

it's clear to me that we all have one life to live, and we must choose how we want to live it. Live every day like it's a special gift. When it's all said and done, I want to be part of the solution. As my father said, even if you don't get the results you desire, just play your part.

Several study collaborators intimated that their families had expressed grave concern and worry about their continued role as activist CEOs. Participant #6 shared that their immediate family had been telling them about their unease:

There are times when your close family members feel concerned. Family members remind you that you are the breadwinner and that you ought to be mindful of the repercussion of your activism. Should something bad happen to you, and the impact on your dependents could be telling.

Participant #8 disclosed that although their family members appreciated and celebrated their role as an activist, such feelings of support were interlaced with a strong sense of foreboding:

It's not a comfortable thing ... it's not something that my family jumps up and down about in excitement. Things happen, and you'll never know how it's going to turn out. I thank God that nothing serious has happened to me so far, but anytime I put myself in harm's way, my family wonders how it is going to end. They're uncomfortable because they bear the brunt of it all. If my business is not going well, my family will be the first to suffer. I am always in the forefront ... I was attacked by the police ... I was arrested ... everybody worries about what could happen to you when you keep on challenging politicians.

### 7.5.2.3 Removal From Office and Suffering Exclusion

Some CEOs suffered attempts to bring them down, using false allegations and anonymous letters, written to various investigative and oversight organizations in Ghana. Participant #6 disclosed that several such letters had been sent about them to Ghana's Economic and Organized Crime Office (EOCO), falsely alleging that they had misappropriated funds of the company. They indicated that these were schemes designed to intimidate them or have them removed from office:

People wrote letters to the EOCO and the National Media Commission (NMC), alleging that I was using corporate funds and resources at the company to fight *Galamsey*. They write anonymous letters to powerful people and regulators to try to intimidate you.

Many informants indicated that engaging in CEO activism could lead to the removal of the CEO from office. While such a risk confronted most CEOs, it was felt that it was more so for other CEO activists. It emerged that in firms that were regulated or influenced by the government, CEO activism was significantly curtailed, especially when the action was against some workings or policy of the Government of Ghana.

Thus, one notable consequence of CEO activism in Ghana was the risk of job losses by CEOs of firms regulated by the government, as described by Participant #8:

> In Ghana, if you work in an industry, a sector, or a firm where the government influence is strong, you can't be an activist. They will get rid of you ... you will surely lose your job. In Ghana where the government controls virtually everything – including finance, oil, and gas, etc. – if you work in any of those sectors, activism puts you at great risk.

Some participants disclosed that their actions had not been without collateral damage, especially in terms of exclusion from the political establishment. For instance, although being an important part of the New Patriotic Party (NPP) in power in Ghana at the time of data collection, Participant #12 revealed that their activist stances over the years had led to their alienation from the inner circle of the party.

They explained that they had marched the streets of Ghana alongside some of the current bigwigs of the NPP during the early days of Ghana's Fourth Republican constitution, including joining the current president Nana Akufo-Addo during the *Kumepreko* demonstration against the introduction of a regime of value-added taxes in Ghana in the mid-1990s. During their interview for this study, they expressed the conviction that the very people they marched with, who were now in political leadership in Ghana had excluded them from the core, simply because of their divergent opinions:

> Those who were very active with me 20 to 25 years ago are now in government. We were together when we were doing all the major activities such as the *Kumepreko* demonstrations. Our current president was the chief legal advisor for *Radio XXX (not real station ID)*. Most people would've thought that I would be his Chief of Staff ... it doesn't matter because, at the end of the day, it is what is best for Ghana that matters. CEO activism has its pitfalls.

In talking about some of the negative consequences of engaging in CEO activism, some informants discussed differences between CEO activism in Ghana and elsewhere. According to a participant, despite attacks against CEO activists, they must persist because of the prevalence of the pursuit of private interests, corruption, and state capture. They stressed that the stage of an activist CEO's lifecycle has a strong influence on the sort of pronouncements they could make. This participant explained that being advanced in years, they had nothing to fear and that they had the boldness and courage to ask the hardest of questions with less to lose than the relatively younger activist CEOs:

> I'm in a very comfortable position at the end of my life to be able to put out those questions ... now the activism I do is mainly asking the questions that people who are more active in their professions will like to ask but dare not do so. It is not exactly a question of some people being scared, but it is more because they have families to take care of. CEO activism can jeopardize your livelihood.

A few participants expressed the view that others may seek to engage in activism when they knew that they had nothing to lose. Referring to this as an "Odjwain funu" (*Dead Goat Syndrome*), a participant disclosed that some CEOs may engage in activism, knowing that they were well on the way out:

> I'll take Mr. XXX [name withheld], he was never an activist, until he knew he was about to leave XXX Company Limited [corporate brand name withheld] because he had been pushed out. In his case, it was more like *Odjwain funu (Dead Goat Syndrome)*. So, in his case, at the time, there was less danger to his position.

The *Twil/Akan* expression "Odjwain funu" literally means "the corpse of a goat." In Ghana, it is generally said that a dead goat cannot be frightened with a knife, since it is already lifeless. The expression was made popular in March 2015 when former President John Mahama was reported to have told a group of Ghanaian expatriates in Botswana that:

> I have seen more demonstrations and strikes in my first two years. I don't think it can get worse. It is said that when you kill a goat and you frighten it with a knife, it doesn't fear the knife, because it is dead already ... I have dead goat syndrome.
>
> (Quist-Arcton, 2015)

Akin to the English epigram "He that is down needs fear no fall," which is attributed to John Bunyan, it is a metaphorical reference to the feeling of fearlessness and nonchalance because of a battalion of problems, runs of bad luck, and similar chains of challenges that may confront an individual.

It was found that the litany of negative consequences suffered by activist CEOs appeared to be affecting their appetite to pursue social actions in Ghana. According to a participant, such negative consequences were gradually rendering many corporate executives in Ghana jelly-boned and risk-averse. They observed that most corporate chieftains who would have taken up activist stances have instead chosen to belong to the "mimp3 mihu as3m" (*meaning* "I don't want trouble for myself" or "I need to save my skin" in the *Akan/Twi* language in Ghana) camp. Participant #12 also noted some negative branding of activists in Ghana:

> If you stuck out as an activist, others would label you as *controversial* – a term that gets used in this environment for people who are exceptional and who push against the grain, and a reference to trouble seekers who needlessly provoke or destabilize the social fabric with their social resistance activities.

Similarly, Participant #17 revealed that many CEOs they knew (especially women CEOs in Ghana), who would have taken on activist stances in Ghana, had been cowered by the fear of such attacks into choosing instead to mind their own businesses. They indicated that they had personally suffered such negative consequences and spoke of some collateral damages against the person of the CEO activist and their organizations:

> Such threats are real because I know a lot of CEOs are in that capacity – especially the women – who are not coming out to speak. They have chosen to rather focus on managing their companies because they don't want to be tagged and attacked. If you are a woman and you speak out in Ghana, they tag you a bitch, meaning that you are trying to be masculine. I have felt like recoiling because of such attacks.

## 7.6 Discussion

This chapter discussed the effects/outcomes of CEO activism within the non-Western sociocultural context in Ghana. It was found that the role of CEO activists was associated with some improvements in society, but also positive, as well as negative consequences for companies and individual CEO activists.

It emerged that within the Ghanaian context, numerous negative consequences were occasioned by the resistance actions undertaken by CEOs. While both men and women activist CEOs suffered their share of such repercussions, it appeared that women activist CEOs faced some special challenges and attacks. It could be possible that the relentless attacks and negative effects of CEO activism in Ghana could be working to discourage some CEOs from taking the activist path.

These findings are consistent with current literature on CEO activism that suggests some effects of CEO activism, including some impacts on CEOs and their organizations. For instance, Chatterji and Toffel (2018) paint the picture of several risks for CEOs, including charges of hypocrisy, double standards, and bad press; Chatterji and Toffel (2019a) speak of potential pitfalls of CEO activism, including such consequences for various stakeholders, including online protests, boycotts, viral social media protests, and CEO removals. Weber Shandwick (2017) found that CEO activism did not only have an influence on the buying decisions of Millennials but that it also had some implications for the retention of top talents in Millennial populations.

Several other organizational outcomes have also been found to be associated with the practice of CEO activism. For example, Chatterji and Toffel (2017) found that CEO activism had an impact on some consumer attitudes and public opinion on selected issues and causes; while Dodd and Supa (2014, 2015), Dodd (2016), and Chatterji and Toffel (2016) all found that CEO activism affected customers' purchase intents.

Despite these findings in the extant literature, the findings reported in this chapter build on the current literature in several ways. Besides generally introducing and contributing findings from the developing world into the literature, it is significant in also introducing the voices of women CEO activists, whose lived experiences as activist CEOs have been significantly elided from the literature.

The findings in this chapter could deepen our understanding of CEO activism by identifying various classes of effects of CEO activism on society, but also identifying company effects as well as effects on CEO activists. The effects of CEO activism identified for a developing country such as Ghana included gender rights promotion, environmental stewardship, promotion of democracy, and protection of economic and public financial management.

Several positive and negative consequences are reported for companies and CEO activists. These can serve as the basis for further investigation by scholars who may be interested in undertaking further studies in the developing world or comparing such a typology of impacts (on society; on companies; and on CEOs) between Western and non-Western societies.

The findings indicated that CEO activism performs some social functions, but also has tonic and toxic consequences for companies and activist CEOs. Again, these findings necessitate the further evolution of the working model. The next iteration saw the incorporation of the range and types of effects produced by the actions of CEO activists in Ghana, as shown in Fig. 6 (on next page). The findings relating to the effects of CEO activism called for some fundamental changes to be made to the original formulation of the model.

In the original (basic) formulation of the conceptual framework, it was expected that the effects produced by CEO activism would lead to (i) safeguards and (ii) influence guidelines for future CEO actions. However, the findings call for some rethinking of the working model. The expectation is that the dyadic patterns of outcomes – tonic and toxic – generate diverse pathways of action to trigger changes in the evolution of the working model.

Owing to their undesirable nature, it is expected that the negative effects of CEO activist campaigns would cause affected CEOs to actively put in place diverse safeguards to (i) insulate themselves from such effects and/or (ii) minimize any such unwanted effects of CEO activism. However, positive effects (because they are desirable outcomes) are expected to inform guidelines for future activist campaigns.

Thus, overall, within the context of the working model for this research study, the tactics deployed in CEO activism led to some effects. The effects produced could relate to improvements in society, but also positive (desirable) and negative

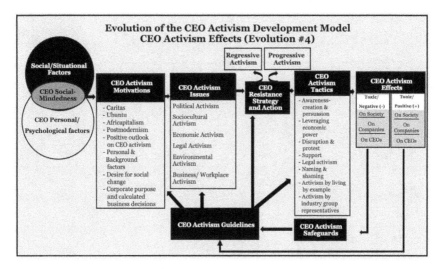

Fig. 6.   Evolution #4 of the CEO Activism Development Model (Indicating the Range of Motivations, Clusters of Issues/Causes, the Tactics, and the Effects/Outcomes of CEO Activism). *Source:* Author (2023).

(undesirable) consequences for (i) companies and (ii) individual CEO activists. While positive corporate and personal consequences are suggested to inform guidelines for future CEO activism, the negative consequences necessitate some safeguards, designed to shield the CEO activist from harm.

The next chapter presents the findings on the range of safeguards employed by the participants in this study to insulate themselves from the toxic consequences of engaging in CEO activism.

Chapter 8

# Taking Cover: Examining CEO Activism Safeguards

## 8.1 Introduction

While CEO activism is associated with positive functions and desirable outcomes for society, corporations, and activist CEOs, it also presents some negative repercussions for activist CEOs and their companies, among other stakeholders (Adae, 2020). Undesirable consequences of CEO activism on companies whose CEOs engage in activism include diverse business disadvantages, loss of business contracts, political victimization, harassment, physical attacks, verbal and media attacks, arrests and detentions, exclusion, and removal from office.

Despite mounting evidence of some toxic outcomes of engaging in CEO activism, scholars have not focused on researching the range of avenues open to activist CEOs to protect themselves. This study seeks to address the woeful dearth of scholarly work on CEO activism, by investigating how the phenomenon is evolving within the context of a non-Western developing society such as Ghana, by focusing on how activist CEOs protect themselves from the undesirable effects they faced as a result of their roles as CEO activists.

## 8.2 Why We Should Study CEO Activism Safeguards

Adae (2020), Chatterji and Toffel (2018), and Larcker and colleagues (2018) all argue that CEO activism could produce both risks and rewards for corporate leaders and their companies. The hazards of CEOs engaging in social resistance actions include media and public criticisms against the CEO activist, and negative consequences for companies.

Generally, the notion of CEO activism safeguards has been neatly absent from the corps of literature on the phenomenon. Although some scholars have reported several negative effects of engaging in CEO activism, the literature appears devoid of empirical examinations of measures that could be taken by activist CEOs to insulate themselves and their companies from the undesirable consequences of engaging in CEO activism. Adae (2020) made a case for "CEO activism safeguards" as a plausible site of research within the fledgling field of research in CEO activism.

CEOs on a Mission, 159–176

Copyright © 2023 Eric Kwame Adae

Published under exclusive licence by Emerald Publishing Limited

doi:10.1108/978-1-80382-215-020231008

CEO activism is a high-stakes nonmarket corporate strategy, and Chatterji and Toffel (2019b) advised that CEO activism be carefully considered and tactfully executed, bearing in mind some guidelines. These scholars offered two broad classes of what could be interpreted as communication-specific guidelines, each with three specific pointers for considerations. In offering their playbook for safer CEO activism, Chatterji and Toffel (2019b) offered some tips on: (i) when should you speak and (ii) how to speak effectively. In speaking out, CEOs are advised to gauge the level of support from their employees; speak in ways that reflect their corporate values; and to speak as close to when the issue is live as possible. These scholars also advocate for having the support of a rapid response team (a kitchen cabinet), anticipate and plan for any backlash, and work with professional communicators.

Chatterji and Toffel (2018) suggest additional safeguards, including the careful selection of issues; ensuring that the CEO's voice is seen by the public as appropriate for the chosen issue/cause; and undertaking joint actions with other activists, rather than solo campaigns. It is noteworthy that the prescriptions by these scholars could be seen as postulations/suppositions that were not based on any empirical data. With the growing incidence of CEO activism in all parts of the globe, there is a need to better understand the potpourri of measures that activist CEOs could adopt in protecting themselves, particularly within non-Western contexts where such corporate sociopolitical involvements could be hazardous because of the weak formal institutional structures.

This study, likely a pioneer investigation of the range of protective measures available to CEO activists, conceptualizes *CEO Activism Safeguards* as a slew of measures adopted by activist CEOs to help them identify, avoid, and minimize risks, harms, and pitfalls for engaging in sociopolitical and environmental activism as CEOs. These stratagems could serve to shield CEO activists and their families, businesses, allies, and the wider society from harm and any undesirable fallouts arising out of their social resistance actions. It is envisaged that these CEO activism safeguards pervade every web and tissue of the social resistance actions of the CEO, including the design, implementation, and operation of activism campaigns. It is further expected that with the growing incidence of CEO activism, a deeper understanding of CEO activism safeguards could energize the conceptualization and implementation of public relations campaigns that entail corporate social advocacy (CSA) as a strategy.

## 8.3 The Focus of the Study

Owing to the negative impacts that may be occasioned by CEO activism, it is likely that activist CEOs would employ a range of safeguards to insulate themselves and their companies from the undesirable effects of being CEO activists. Chatterji and Toffel (2019b) suggest that CEO activists could minimize some of the negative effects of their actions by paying heed to *when* they communicate and *how* they communicate. Are communication-related safeguards the only avenues open to CEO activists? Are the negative consequences of CEO activism only occasioned by communication challenges? What other safeguards are open to CEO activists? How does the sociocultural milieu in an emerging market context such as Ghana shape the safeguards employed by CEO activists in that country? Given these questions, the objective of our study is an exploration of CEO activism safeguard measures.

This study focuses on addressing an important gap in the literature by identifying and explicating the range of measures adopted by CEO activists in the Ghanaian emerging market context to protect themselves, their companies, and other stakeholders from the hazards of their resistance actions. The study revolves around addressing the following research question: *What safeguard measures do CEO activists in Ghana employ to insulate themselves from the pushbacks they face because of their resistance actions?*

## 8.4 How Activist CEOs Protect Themselves

Despite the risks and negative consequences of engaging in CEO activism in Ghana, most of the participants expressed the resolve to persist in their roles as activist CEOs. This was generally because they did not see engaging in CEO activism in Ghana as amounting to a zero-sum game. They indicated that they adopted some safeguard measures to shield themselves from some undesirable consequences of engaging in CEO activism. It was found that various combinations of safeguard measures were employed by the participants in this study, "social safeguards," "spiritual safeguards," "corporate safeguards," "personal safeguards," "CEO activism best-practice safeguards," and "communication-related safeguards."

### 8.4.1 Social Safeguards

A category of safeguards emerged from the conversations with the participants, which related to diverse forms of safety and protection found in various types of human social relations. Particularly, these described a hedge of protection that was provided to CEO activists because of various alliances and coalitions they created, led, or belonged to. Most participants stated that CEO activism ought not to be a solo activity. Thus, for many participants, an important safeguard involved finding safety and strength in joining forces with others.

It emerged that safe and successful CEO activism revolved around creating what some described as "a coalition of the willing." This referred to the need for the CEO activist to have a group of like-minded people and organizations who could help with various aspects of the campaign: from legwork, brain work, staying ahead of opponent strikes, and helping the activist to navigate any pitfalls.

Participant #6 shared their perspectives on forming such a coalition during their long-standing fight against illegal small-scale gold mining activities in Ghana:

> Form a coalition of the willing, comprising those who can help.
> You can't achieve much as a lone ranger. It's not safe for you to be
> a one-man army. Have people who'd ask hard questions of you
> and look out for your interests.

Others highlighted creating well-knit communities of people who shared the ideas and ideals of the campaign, and who also found each other within a defined locality or digital echo chamber such as followers on a social media platform. It emerged that such an alliance served to provide opportunities for community members to meet each other to plan actions within the community and provide needed support to achieve the campaign goals. For instance, Participant #2 described the importance of such groups:

> Create communities of people who share these ideas, but also find
> each other within their locality. Give them the channel to find each
> other, meet, plan actions, and support each other. They will shield
> you when bad things are in the offing.

Referring to traditional Ghanaian adages that highlight the importance of drawing in-depth strength from social ties, an overwhelming proportion of collaborators identified significant benefits of building coalitions, including the utility of profiting from diverse perspectives. These participants testified that such social groups offered protection from attrition and scuttled attacks on members. In this regard, Participant #15 testified:

> There's safety in numbers. A Ghanaian proverb says, 'a broom
> straw can be easily broken, but when the sticks are tied together
> into a broom, the broom may bend but cannot easily break.' Bring
> people together, not only because of numbers but also because of
> their diverse perspectives. Building a coalition brings resilience and
> insures against attrition.

Many of the informants saw the importance of activist CEOs supporting each other. For those that shared this viewpoint, the common spirit shared by all activist CEOs was the commitment to risk themselves in the fight for the common good. Participant #8 noted that CEO activists should support and provide a hedge of protection for each other:

> CEOs should support other CEO activists. There's something
> about people who are prepared to put themselves on the line. If
> you're a CEO, you must support others who decide to play activist
> roles.

Such cooperation could be in various respects, including funding and the provision of diverse forms of moral support and protection. We found that owing to the nascence of the phenomenon, activist CEOs in Ghana were in a minority. It was important for CEO activists to close their ranks and support each other in their actions. However, the need for partnerships and strategic alliances extended beyond working with other CEO activists. For Participant #5, it was essential to derive strength from many individuals, institutions, and groups that could comprise an activist CEO's "Kitchen Cabinet," including directors, employees, and family members:

> A critical thing is that you must find good people to work with, such as employees, other CEOs, your family, the community, civil society organizations, and directors. I could never have done this alone.

Participant #8 indicated that because their stances were open, the Ghanaian public had a good impression of their supporters as well as their adversaries. Thus, should they face any attack, the possible suspects would be obvious, and was confident in their supporters' protection:

> Your supporters look out for your interests. There've been many times when we've planned to engage in some actions and others have tipped us off regarding plans to attack us.

### 8.4.2 Spiritual Safeguards

It was found that most informants resorted to spiritual protection, including supernatural forces, the God factor, ancestors, spiritual symbols and ornaments, or similar metaphysical forces. Participant #8 disclosed that although they had personal security measures, there was only so much they could do. They described their reliance on God as their ultimate protector:

> My faith in God is ultimately the strongest source of strength for me. We do what we have to do to protect ourselves, but security is a myth. Those who find themselves with all the security in the world are not more protected than the rest of us who leave ourselves to outright exposure. Do what you can, but leave the rest to God.

In the same vein, Participant #24 explained how they feels protected by unseen and supernatural forces:

> People will try to harm you. I can't do much about that, except keep quiet. Yet, I can't keep quiet because of who I know I am. Pray about it, then head out and soldier on, knowing that you're acting in truth. Forgive all, and those that try to harm you would be piling coals of fire on their heads because God will deal with them.

Similarly, Participant #6 said they drew significant strength from spiritual sources. They disclosed that although they sometimes felt scared, they took refuge in the corporate prayers of significant others:

> As an activist, you have your fears ... you're afraid for yourself, but you think it's a price worth paying. I remind those who express concern for me that the best they can do is to support me with prayers. I believe many people I don't know have been praying for my safety and the protection of all who join me in my actions.

### 8.4.3 Corporate Safeguards

It emerged that some participants found safety in the protection offered by their companies, including hedges of protection offered by companies, boards of directors, individual board members, other members of the C-Suite, and employees.

An important safety measure emanated from some strong alignments between the CEO's actions and the corporate strategy. Such strategic linkages come in various forms and at diverse levels and contexts. For instance, Participant #5 disclosed that right from the incorporation of his corporation, activism was identified as a strategy for promoting and positioning the company, while driving social change. They descried several benefits and attributes of such an activism-embedded strategic focus, including working to provide some consistency, authenticity, and budgetary support for his actions. Beyond energizing they activist campaigns, they noted that these factors further supported and protected their social resistance action because of the corporate strategic intent involved.

It was found that many participants were protected by their organizations because their resistance actions were driven by elements within their companies such as connections with the corporate purpose, mission, vision, and goals. According to Participant #5, their activist stance had always enjoyed significant corporate support because it was grounded in the corporate strategy:

> The board has been supportive. I have a board chair, who doesn't interfere needlessly and the board hasn't prevented me from doing what I do as an activist CEO. From incorporation, we planned to build the brand by advocating for the greater good. Advocacy is a part of our strategy and everybody here knows why I speak out. I have a management team that's familiar with what I say, who can guide me, give me valuable feedback, and can shape my messages.

A few participants highlighted the utility of the so-called "Kitchen Cabinet" which comprised a carefully selected team of people who served as consultants, reviewers, and several other roles in guiding and assisting the CEO activist in their resistance actions.

Another theme that emerged regarding safe CEO activism was the need for corporate values and principles to drive CSA. Several participants noted that

CEO activism ought not to be a knee-jerk (re)action and that CEOs must ensure that their actions were underpinned by some higher-order corporate purposes, as explained by Participant #19:

> The purpose of being in business and showing concern for the greater good should precede activism. It's these corporate ideals that signal that something happening in the environment doesn't sit well and prompts the company or the CEO to take some action. When the CEO's actions are informed by corporate purpose, the company would be a solid shield of protection for the activist CEO.

Several benefits of deriving CEO activism from the corporate purpose included the safeguard it offered against being inauthentic and ill-prepared by making CEO activism a deliberate corporate action. Related to being purpose-driven and deliberate about activism, a great number of the informants underscored the importance of being consistent in their campaigns, including consistency in the causes pursued; messaging strategy and communication tactics; and the overall campaign approach. For Participant #2, the benefits of consistency included affording mastery over the issue advocated:

> Your consistency will pay off because you will understand what you are doing more. You will not have all the answers from Day One, but you become a greater expert in your activism if you keep doing it consistently. That will save you from so many issues.

Many participants underscored the need for CEO activists to select their issues properly, to assure some safety and the success of their campaigns. Participant #4 advocated for CEOs to have a "signature advocacy" that would help to define the CEO's actions:

> Select causes well because you can't solve every problem in society. Have a signature advocacy - issues that define who you are and what you stand for, and causes that can deliver the change you seek, but without much negativity or backlash.

Some participants mentioned that having such flagship advocacy is related to consistently sticking with an issue or a family of intersecting issues. For Participant #10, it was crucial to be known for a given cause or a range of causes:

> Don't set yourself up for attacks by flip-flopping; do this today and something else tomorrow. If that must be the case, it must be because you are adding on or naturally extending your initial cause. Be sure that the range of causes mutually reinforces each other.

Several study participants said it was therefore important to select issues or causes that reasonably fit in with the core business of the company. In this direction, Participant #4 noted that safer CEO activism involved ensuring that the range of causes pursued was not regarded by the public as far-fetched, given the CEO's track record or the reputation of the organization:

> First, identify something that lies within your area ... something that makes sense for you as a CEO activist to be doing, because it is not contrived or far-fetched, judging by the operations of your organization. Don't engage in an activity that would make people question why you are concerning yourself with such a matter. The cause must ring true and be in sync with what you or your organization stands for.

It was learned that consistency involved being principled and staying true to one's position(s) irrespective of which political party was in charge. When an activist CEO keeps fighting consistently, opponents do not only give up on resisting them, but that such consistency ensured the authenticity, neutrality, and issue-mindedness of the CEO activist, as recounted by Participant #14:

> When you keep fighting consistently, your opposers tend to give up on fighting you. If this political party does something and you can speak out against them, but you can't do so when that other political party does so, it means that you don't know who you are. You must be consistent in your activism for your own good.

### 8.4.4 Personal Safeguards

Most informants employed a range of personal safeguard measures. These were diverse measures that participants felt lay within their personal power to take in protecting themselves. Although effective activism required activist CEOs to engage with multiple stakeholders, many of our collaborators identified the importance of being careful and gauging the extent to which they exposed themselves.

Some participants stressed the need to be mindful of their personal security and the long-term viability of their companies and cautioned CEO activists to endeavor to limit the extent of exposure to attackers. As explained by Participant #8, these included investing in strong private security:

> Don't over-expose yourself to attackers. Invest in personal security, safety, and protection. Activism here can be dangerous, so you must safeguard yourself very well, including having security advisors.

Some participants believed that owning shares in businesses made it easier for them to be targeted. Thus, several informants said they steered clear of having investments in businesses in Ghana, choosing instead to invest in money market instruments, and in major foreign currencies, as stated by a participant who does not want to be named, as articulated by Participant #22:

> I don't own businesses. I just have investments in shares and financial instruments. Here, your opponents will try to harm your businesses, especially, if you do business with the state.

To make it difficult to be targeted by their detractors, some participants revealed that although they may be the main brains behind their campaigns, they sometimes delegated the task of speaking to others. For instance, Participant #5 sometimes allowed some board members to speak on his behalf, while Participant #20 testified to adopting a similar hedging strategy:

> I am beginning to play a background role. I try not to be the only face. I am beginning to stay back because if you are not careful and you are out there all the time, it might affect the business badly.

Sometimes, taking personal charge of their security meant constantly looking out for danger. Participant #13 disclosed that since their protest march against political vigilantes and electoral violence in Ghana, they had become extra vigilant with their personal, familial, and corporate security:

> I am very conscious of my physical security. After my protest march [against electoral violence], I was for a couple of months consciously aware, looking to see anything unusual.

Owing to the numerous attacks, some participants stated that despite their passion for driving social change, they had contemplated applying the brakes on their activism. Others said they would be careful about encouraging other CEOs to become activists. However, despite many sources of discouragement, many informants indicated that having a strong belief and personal conviction kept them going. For Participant #1, without a deep sense of belief in oneself and a strong passion for the cause, any CEO's attempts at activism would fail or be short-lived:

> Don't put your voice to an issue that you're not passionate about because it is usually a very long journey. Whatever the cause, be ready to commit to the struggle. Believe in your cause and have a personal conviction. Don't do it simply because you think it looks good on you or your business.

Others saw such personal safeguards in setting some limits beyond which they ought not to extend their actions. Participant #6 saw much safety in boundary-setting:

> There's a tendency to get carried away, so set boundaries for
> yourself. There's an extent beyond which activism shouldn't go.
> Everything has limits, so set limits and be governed by them.

Some participants expressed the idea that safety involved looking out for dishonest people, including being conscious of many forms of mistrust. Participant #10 described diverse shades of backstabbing that must be guarded against:

> When you fight corruption, it fights you back harder. Some who
> cheer you openly, jeer at you privately. That's the nature of many.
> It is not just hypocrite; it is duplicity.

Being prepared also meant activist CEOs immersing themselves in research material on the issue to ensure a good grasp of the matter, while remaining apolitical. This included relying on research insights in selecting cross-cutting issues and ensuring a broad appeal to a wide cross-section of the public. Thus, an unacceptable situation is to speak ignorantly, since that not only calls one's reputation into question but also exposed the activist CEO to ridicule and attacks.

While activism was regarded as an important role for the modern CEO, some saw the need for the CEO to first develop a credible personal brand before seeking to positively change society. For Participant #4, one's personal brand could prove protective:

> It is good for CEOs to get into this space because they are
> institutional leaders and they must inform and shape social
> change. CEOs must first build a personal brand that becomes
> attractive for others to listen to and want to associate with.
> Without this, you only open yourself up for attacks and failure.

A few informants said vital protection involves appearing to be authentic change agents, rather than unnecessary naggers. Some saw the acid test of a valuable CEO activist as one that had relevancy and authenticity in offering solutions to social problems.

### 8.4.5 CEO Activism Best Practice Safeguards

In referring to their means of protection from the negative effects of being CEO activists, some participants described what they saw as following some best practices. Several informants pointed to following the actions of other CEO activists. They encouraged CEO activists to read documented cases of the works of other CEO activists. Participant #6 called for the establishment of Afrocentric research-informed guidelines for successful CEO activism within the African context:

> CEOs should have access to rule books to find out how other CEO
> activists have done this; to learn what are the things that have
> negative repercussions; what are the boundaries; and what are the

needed resources. This is toolkit you should have in your arsenal before engaging in such battles. Our brand of CEO activism is beginning to shape up as a practice, and we must have standards that ought to be followed.

For some participants, safeguards involved the careful selection of one's tactical repertoire. Some of the participants revealed that there were various approaches to CEO activism, of which an adversarial or frontal approach was only a part. They indicated that alternative approaches could include influencing the position statements of pressure groups and similar civil society organizations and through funding or financing other activists in ways that assured the CEO opportunities to influence the causes of campaigns. Several informants underscored the adoption of an indirect path, rather than being needlessly vociferous. These include working behind the scenes with pressure groups, partnering with others, and issuing position statements through others.

Thus, safeguarding oneself as an activist CEO in Ghana often meant avoiding conflict by being somewhat inoffensive. In advocating against an adversarial stance, several informants noted that CEO activism should not always be offensive or entail a controversial posture, no matter how polarizing the issue may be. For Participant #14, an effective approach was a "kind" one:

> As an activist CEO, your approach should not be brash and offensive. Kill them with kindness by being deliberately tactful and diplomatic. Naturally, I am frontal in my approach, but that ought not always to be the way to go.

Some informants disclosed that they shielded themselves by grounding their actions on such values as truth, honesty, integrity, and authenticity. Thus, it emerged that the pursuit of truth ought to be a primary principle for CEO activism, just as authenticity was important in ensuring that a CEO's actions were not contrived. Here, Participant #4 found protection in such ideas:

> The key thing is to be true to oneself. You don't want to engage in whitewash stuff. CEOs who make this happen are those who work for meaningful social change, rather than only for their company's strategic ends. CEOs and their companies must identify causes and genuinely throw their weights behind, for the good of all. Ultimately, it is in you interest to do so.

For a few participants, the element of truth offered some protection because it was considered an enduring value that many people could identify with. Participant #2 indicated that genuineness ought to be the very foundation of CEO activism and that business executives should embark on activism that is derived from a true desire to change society for the better, and not for any other reason:

> Activism must start from what you can relate to authentically. The thing about being authentic is that it means your activism will be expressed in different ways. If you are authentic, then you will do what comes naturally to you, and what comes naturally to you will not be what comes naturally to another person. So, you will express your activism in different ways.

Others saw the role of consistency and authenticity in driving down the cost of activist campaigns while improving the effectiveness of the communication effort. Participant #5 noted that being consistent, speaking the truth, and being authentic had contributed to increasingly minimal activist campaign budgets:

> You don't need as many resources as you think because over time, if you are consistent and you speak the truth, and you are authentic, people start to listen to you; but you can't buy the public's loyalty. While I've been doing this, I suppose some CEOs have felt that I've been taking too much of the space and have tried to also do some activism of their own, but they have not quite had the same impact. For me, activism is a core part of my strategy, and I know exactly why I do it.

In staying true to their efforts, a few participants warned against blind copying of others. For Participant #4, it was important for CEO activists to stay true to themselves:

> I think CEO activists are potentially impactful in shaping public opinion because we have a significant public profile or influence as thought leaders who are now taking on a new role as social activists. The head of the organization in many respects represents the soul of the organization. Organizations that can leverage the CEO's profile tend to become more successful and are the forerunners in the world of work today, especially when truth and authenticity are the hallmarks of their activist effort.

Thus, a widespread sentiment among the participants was that acting in truth served to inform the selection of issues that resonated with a wide cross-section of people, minimized attacks, emboldened activist CEOs in rebutting attacks while engendering vocal support from allies whenever an activist CEO was under attack.

Some informants noted that an important safeguard for activist CEOs was to play by the book. In this effort, the overwhelming sentiment shared by the participants was for CEO activists to ensure that besides the propriety of their resistance actions, that every other aspect of their normal business operations and personal lives was blameless. The CEO activist must have the moral authority to be a vanguard of social change. This is because engaging in CEO activism necessarily brought activists into direct conflict with entrenched and powerful interests in the societal and political establishment who would use anything they could lay their hands on against the CEO activist's image. Ergo, playing by the book was seen as a significant hedge against such attacks, because it provided the needed moral foundation for the activist CEO while offering a safeguard against attacks.

A common attack against activist CEOs in Ghana comprised a multitude of harassments by government departments and agencies, swarming the offices and operational locales of the activist CEO. The modus operandi of these government agencies was to serve as an inescapable distraction for the activist CEO. We learned that many demands are then placed on CEO activist, as numerous requests are made for unwarranted audits, operational checks, and the verification of permits and certifications, among others. These placed a significant strain on the ability of the CEO activist to focus on the efficient running of their business.

Participant #24 demonstrated how operating above reproach should be a cornerstone for the activist CEO in Ghana:

> When you want to engage in CEO activism, make sure you are blameless; Your business, books, licenses, permits, etc. should all be in order, before you can start thinking of helping others. Otherwise, it would be used against you.

Other collaborators stressed the importance of running a transparent business that employees support. A few participants expressed the belief that although no organization could be completely above board, it was important to be open in gaining the support of one's employees. According to Participant #6, a key part of gaining the buy-in of employees entailed having a clear game plan:

> Nobody is perfect, but you must run a transparent business because the people who either carry you or crucify you are your employees. They are the first people who would either encourage people to do business with your company or not. So, get your employees aligned and believe in you and your cause.

Participant #5 further explained that it was worth engaging in CEO activism in a manner that carried employees along because, doing so could produce desired business outcomes, including deepening employee loyalty and building a company's customer base:

> As a leader, you sell a vision and you need the people to believe in that vision. Once you gain their buy-in, they would most probably help you to achieve that vision. However, if they don't believe in the vision, you can never achieve it. My activism gets my employees to become more loyal and has attracted more customers. My employees will take a bullet for me.

### 8.4.6 Communication-Related Safeguards

Some participants found safety in focusing on some aspects of the communication process, including approaches that tended to build support, cooperation, and understanding rather than dissensus for the sake of conflict. Many informants indicated that they had to reevaluate the messaging strategies employed in their resistance actions. It emerged that such revisions in messaging were varied, ranging from changes in tonality that tended toward solutions and conciliation, rather than criticism for its sake, to a greater focus on demonstrating the benefits to be derived from adopting the positions proposed by the activist CEOs.

Participant #20 shared some aspects of his survival tactics, including changing the tone of his utterances, and positioning himself as a genuine publicly spirited expert who was a problem-solving facilitator:

> I've altered my narrative, making it clear that I am focusing on the issues, rather than personalities. I also ensure that my audience realizes that I am suggesting and proffering solutions. I highlight the positive impact of implementing my suggestions. That counts!

Among the most popular safety measures was the importance of taking the middle line, being objective, and communicating clearly. Others included one's ability to defend one's position, based on facts while demonstrating neutrality by being apolitical. Here, Participant #18 urged their colleagues to be strategic and tactful in their public statements. Indeed, being strategic also meant having a media strategy that would not needlessly expose oneself to attacks:

> Speaking out tactfully; not always being on the radio and talking – that way, you only work yourself into becoming a political agent. You need to know when, where, and how you speak, and to whom you speak because your voice can easily be taken away. How you activate your activism, and how you roll it out is very important.

Some informants underscored the importance of separating the views of the activist CEO from those of the organization. It emerged however that this is not always an easy Gordian knot to untie. For instance, Participant #14 shared that they had many times found that their personal positions aligned with those of their organization, but do not necessarily reflect those of the individual petroleum distribution companies that comprised this business chamber they led:

> I make it clear that my activism is my personal opinion or based on my conviction. We issued an industry report and shared some strong opinions as a secretariat. My members may not agree with a lot of the things we shared. However, we issued a disclaimer that this is coming from my office and the Chamber, but that it does not necessarily represent the views of the members of the Chamber. That means that if anyone has any issues whatsoever

with the contents of such an industry report, they ought to contact the Chamber, rather than its members. This distinction is very important to make for the good of all.

## 8.5 Discussion

Considering that CEO activism presents "a double-edged sword" (Larcker et al., 2018) of positive, but also negative consequences for CEO activists and their companies (Adae, 2020), the main purpose of this study has been to investigate the range of safeguard mechanisms employed by activist CEOs in the Ghanaian emerging markets context to insulate themselves from the negative externalities of their resistance actions.

Scholars have not focused on empirical investigations into how activist CEOs protect themselves from some of the unpalatable effects produced by their social resistance actions. This pioneering study on CEO activism within the emerging market context of Ghana set out to address the dearth of literature on CEO activism by investigating the self-reported range of protective measures available to CEO activists. I conceptualize *CEO Activism Safeguards* as a whole range of protective measures taken by activist CEOs to identify, avoid, or neutralize the hazards of mixing business with politics and leveraging their corporate executive positions to engage in CEO activism.

It was found that activist CEOs in Ghana resorted to various forms of safeguards, hitherto unarticulated in the literature, designed to help insulate them from the pitfalls of their resistance activities. This study identified these six archetypal CEO activism safeguards as: (i) personal safeguards, (ii) social safeguards, (iii) spiritual safeguards, (iv) corporate safeguards, (v) communication-related safeguards, and (vi) CEO best practice safeguards.

Chatterji and Toffel (2018) posit that safer CEO activism involved careful cause selection; CEOs adopting an apt tone of voice; and micropolitical actions and the formation of alliances, rather than solo campaigns. Chatterji and Toffel (2019a) expressed two main communication-related CEO activism safeguards, namely (i) when to communicate and (ii) how to communicate effectively. They proposed three safeguards under each of these two main headings. "When to communicate" was associated with (i) when the nudge comes from employees; (ii) when your corporate/personal values – and your corporate practices – align with the issue at hand; and (iii) when the issue is live. On the other hand, "how to speak effectively" entailed (i) setting up a rapid response team to help the CEO activist plan for the unexpected; (ii) anticipating backlash from opponents as well as proponents; and (iii) working with your communicators.

Compared with the findings in this study, it is apparent that while Chatterji and Toffel's (2019a) and (2018) CEO activism postulations are reflected in some of the outcomes of this study, we argue that their postulations fairly intersect with the "communication-related safeguards" found in this study. While their postulates relate to "when" and "how" to communicate issues relating to CEO activism, our

174 CEOs on a Mission

findings suggest that CEO activism is emerging as a more cross-cutting phenomenon that requires more than communication-related safeguards.

The findings in this study offer a more comprehensive range of CEO activism safeguards. Rather than being regarded as an extension of the communication-specific CEO safeguards posited by Chatterji and Toffel (2019a) and (2018), the findings make a compelling case for the consideration of a wider gyre of safeguards available for CEO activists.

These findings are relevant to members of the upper echelons and related fields. For instance, the Public Relations Society of America's modern conception of public relations underscores the field's posture of mutual beneficence to organizations and their publics (Corbett, 2012a, 2012b). The usual approach is to discuss such relationships in terms of employees and external stakeholders as the beneficiaries of the organization's actions. The findings in this study tend to, for instance, reverse this usual focalization by positioning CEO activists as beneficiaries too, as companies could also work to offer some "corporate safeguards" for activist CEOs who sometimes work in the corporate interest by making companies more socially responsible and sustainable through their progressive social resistance actions.

These findings extend extant notions relating to some Afrocentric philosophies that align with sustainability, such as *Caritas, Ubuntu, Africapitalism* (see Adae, 2020, 2021a), and such cognate themes as *Consciencism, Ujamaa, Negritude, the Spirit of Harambee, Bantu philosophy, Akan philosophy, Igbo epistemology,* and the *Sankofa philosophy* (see Pompper & Adae, 2023), which stress the ideas of community and relationship building in ways that promote the genuine pursuit of the common good (Mbigi, 2007).

These findings reflect the ethical bedrock obligation of organizations (Tilson, 2014) to protect CEOs as members of an organizational constituency. The findings in this study mark a counterintuitive expression of the ideas of Tilson (2014) and Haviland (1978) in considering the responsibility of companies and the wider society in caring for CEO activists who work for the greater social and environmental good.

This study contributes to the emerging corps of literature on CSA (e.gs. Afego & Alagidede, 2021; Austin et al., 2019; Dodd & Supa, 2014, 2015; Waymer & Logan, 2021), Corporate Political Advocacy (Baur & Wettstein, 2016; Wettstein & Baur, 2016), Corporate Sociopolitical Involvement (Nalick et al., 2016), CEO activism (Adae, 2021a, 2021b, 2020; Chatterji & Toffel, 2015, 2016, 2017, 2018, 2019a, 2019b), and CEO Sociopolitical activism (Hambrick & Wowak, 2021). This study contributes to the literature by not only formally introducing the notion of "CEO activism safeguards" but also providing a model of six categories of safeguards, based on empirical evidence in Ghana. Thus, the findings in this study make a more realistic case for the multiplicity of *life jackets* that could help secure CEO activists in their resistance actions. We argue for a wider range of safeguard mechanisms available to CEO activists within a non-Western and emerging markets context.

This study intersects with studies that focus on the effect of CEOs' political attitudes on business strategies such as CSR practices (see e.g., Chin et al., 2013;

Di Giuli & Kostovetsky, 2014). It contributes to the literature on Upper Echelons Theory that examines how the personal preferences of C-level executives and board members influence firm behavior (see Hambrick & Mason, 1984; Finkelstein & Hambrick, 1996). The findings particularly contribute to the literature on how CEO preferences, characteristics, and beliefs impact organizational strategy (see e.g., Chen et al., 2014; Plambeck & Weber, 2009).

This study has various policy implications, notably corporate policy, communication policy, corporate governance, nonmarket strategies such as corporate social responsibility/sustainability, and business ethics. The literature points to a growing popularity of CEO activism, especially as an expression of brand responsibility (see Kim, 2018) and *sustainability transitions* (see Delmas et al., 2019). Within the context of this growing importance of CEO activism comes the need for companies to provide various measures to control the effects occasioned by CEO activism. The safeguards found in this study could provide signposts to companies and their leaders about how and what to think about when it comes to the subject of managing the ramifications of CEO activism, especially within non-Western contexts. With these findings, public relations practitioners and scholars now have a better understanding of how to build safety measures into CEO activism campaigns.

Indications are that most boards of directors are not very familiar with the practice of CEO activism and tend to resist CEOs who decide to undertake CEO activism (Larcker et al., 2018). Regarding corporate communication policy, these findings serve to shed some light on various risk management measures that companies and their leaders could consider when joining the CEO activism fray.

### 8.5.1 Limitations and Further Research

Some caution should be noted concerning the utility of this study. The findings presented relate only to the time and spatial context of the study. Its relevance is further limited to the lived experiences of the informants in this study. The findings are scarcely generalizable since this is not a quantitative study. Besides, purposive sampling methods were employed. Given that the data for this study were collected from a non-Western context, our findings may not be applicable to CEO activists in different sociocultural contexts.

The field of CEO activism safeguards research provides some interesting prospects for further research. This study is but an initial minuscule foray into the range of research possibilities. Future research could focus on explicating the safeguard measures adopted by activist CEOs in Western contexts. Scholars could undertake deeper comparative studies vis-a-vis non-Western contexts. Other research could consider the relative reliance that CEOs could place on various safeguard measures, with the view to gaining a significant understanding of the relative covers provided by the various safeguard measures. Still, scholars could investigate some associations between specific negative effects of CEO activism and specific safeguard measures.

### 8.5.2 Evolution of the CEO Activism Development Model

Again, the findings in this study provide further insights into the next evolution of the basic model. The next iteration saw the inclusion of the six CEO activism safeguards found in this study, as shown in Fig. 7 (below).

The next chapter presents the findings on guidelines for more effective CEO activism campaigns.

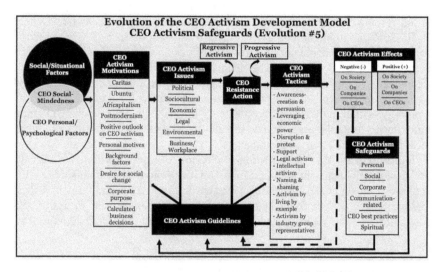

Fig. 7.   Evolution #5 of the CEO Activism Development Model (Indicating the Motivations, Issues/Causes, Tactics, Effects, and Types of CEO Activism Safeguards). *Source:* Author (2023).

Chapter 9

# Profiting From Experience: Examining CEO Activism Guidelines

## 9.1 Introduction

With the growing popularity of CEO activism, there is a need for a deeper examination of the phenomenon and the establishment of guidelines for safer and more effective implementation of activist CEO campaigns. While CEO activism is becoming commonplace as a nonmarket corporate strategy with significant outcomes for society, corporations, and CEOs, precious little has been investigated regarding guidelines for activist CEO campaign management. Extant postulations about CEO activism guidelines appear somewhat limited to the findings of Chatterji and Toffel (2019b, 2018) and their prescriptions for CEO activists. Importantly, we are yet to locate an empirical study on the CEO guidelines, based on evidence from non-Western sociocultural contexts.

Chatterji and Toffel (2018) offer what could be considered to be some CEO activism campaign guidelines. These include strategically choosing what issues to weigh in on; when to weigh in; how to weigh in; playing the inside game well by aligning the object of the activist CEO campaign with the ideals of internal stakeholders; effectively predicting the reactions of diverse stakeholders; and gauging the results of such campaigns. Further, Chatterji and Toffel (2019b) suggested two broad classes of what could be deemed to be some communication-specific rubrics, with each containing three considerations, covering (i) *when should you speak* and (ii) *how to speak effectively*. These guidelines offer some tips on listening to employees, connecting activism to the corporate purpose, staying on message, having a *Kitchen Cabinet*, performing issues management, having a crisis plan, and involving professional communicators such as public relations professionals.

In this regard, it is especially instructive to profit from the experiences of real-life CEO activists, rather than assumptions, suppositions, and conjectures by scholars and commentators. Thus, this study addresses the relatively thin literature on CEO activism in non-Western contexts by focusing on an empirical examination of guidelines, as disclosed by self-identified men and women activist CEOs in Ghana, governed by the research question: *Based on their lived experiences as CEO activists, what do participants say should be guidelines for more effective and safer activist CEO campaigns within the African context of Ghana?*

CEOs on a Mission, 177–200
Copyright © 2023 Eric Kwame Adae
Published under exclusive licence by Emerald Publishing Limited
doi:10.1108/978-1-80382-215-020231009

## 9.2 Guidelines for CEO Activists

Without a doubt, CEO activism is an emerging phenomenon that scholars are yet to fully scope out, conceptualize, and operationalize (Wettstein & Baur, 2016). While some scholars have contributed to the idea of having some guidelines that could guide the successful implementation of CEO activism in general, most of the current proposals quite clearly pertain to Western sociocultural contexts. This is because most scholarly studies on the phenomenon have been situated in Western/American contexts.

Countries in the developing world have unique political, cultural, social, and other situational factors that could make some of the extant guidelines of limited effect. Among the motives of this research study is the development of a playbook to guide the successful implementation of CEO activism, especially in the developing world. Indeed, it is the contention of this researcher that many CEOs in the developing world are yet to embrace their evolving role as activists, partly because they do not fully understand how to effectively perform such roles. It is hoped that with the development of such a playbook, the current mystique surrounding CEO activism would be stripped away while providing activist CEOs in the emerging markets of Africa with a powerful arsenal of situationally developed toolkits to enable them to better perform their role as activist CEOs.

Based on their experiences as activist CEOs, the participants in this study were asked to suggest some guidelines that other CEOs desiring to become activists could follow in order to assure more effective or successful actions. The following sections reflect the views of informants concerning the guidelines and some of the critical success factors for engaging in successful CEO activism, within the context of a developing society such as Ghana.

### 9.2.1 Be Certain It Is What You Really Want to Do

Typical of virtually every business decision, the participants in this study shared the view that a major guideline that any CEO who wants to become an activist ought to follow is to convince themselves that it is a course of action they really want to pursue. Many of the informants, therefore, spoke of the need for the activist CEO to be absolutely sure that they feel called to engage in activism.

The views of Participant #10 were not only striking but also extremely surprising. Despite being a long-standing activist, they would rather discourage others from joining the fray. The following perspectives they shared proved instructive:

> You have to sit down and take a deep look at yourself to see if it is something you really want to or have to do. How much of the Ghs5.4 billion and the Ghs 67 million I helped Ghana recover comes to me personally? None. But this sort of activism allows people to insult you. It exposes you to danger and to public criticism. You've raised a family. You have children who go on social media, only to find their father being insulted by everyone

because of things he has not done. No doubt, there is a personal price to be paid here ... Sometimes, it feels like it's not worth it at all... Yes, I want to see Ghana do well, but I am not sure Ghana wants to do well. I'm being honest and frank with you.

Thus, according to many of the study participants, CEO activism in Ghana is a horrible minefield that exposed the activist corporate executive to many risks and attacks, such that, anyone who wanted to serve in such an office ought to be candid with themselves in doing a lot of soul-searching. Ace Ankomah would like the neophyte activist CEO to know that it is not only a thankless and fruitless role but one that is also usually a lonely road to travel.

### 9.2.2 The Importance of Boundary-Setting

Several participants urged activist CEOs to set some boundaries, beyond which they ought not to extend their actions. Participant #6 observed that a useful guideline for CEO activists involved doing some boundary-setting, right at the outset, that would enable them to know the safe limits to which to take their struggles:

> In life, everything has boundaries or limits, beyond which we must not go. I would personally need to be guided by this guideline. Driven by their passion for the causes they pursue, there's the tendency to get carried away. However, you need to draw boundaries for yourself. There is an extent to which activism should not go.

Similarly, Participant #16 believed in setting some delimitations, right at the outset. While offering such words of caution, they expressed gratitude for the fortuitous manner in which their social advocacy had led them on a pleasurable journey of self-discovery, which has seen them redefining both their personal purpose and that of their business:

> Anyone going into activism must count the cost. They must also tell themselves exactly how far they are willing to take this; how far they would want to go with their activities. This is important because many people have out of this distraction have found themselves wrong-footed, and perhaps lost out on significant business opportunities. I'm not really complaining when say that it took away a lot of my time and resources. In my case, my activism redirected my path to a more meaningful purpose and set my feet on a more significant journey.

### *9.2.3 Being Guided by Patriotism and Having Genuine Care About the Wider Context*

Many participants observed that it is important for all activist CEOs to become very knowledgeable about what it means to be a citizen, rather than a spectator. This is because of their belief that the bedrock of any activism is a deeply true sense of patriotism and citizenship. Participant #8 believes that it would be naïve and self-defeating for CEOs to think that their organizations can thrive within a sociocultural context that does not support the growth of businesses. The deep and wide forward and backward linkages between a company and the environment in which it operates make it necessary for CEOs to concern themselves with the creation and maintenance of an external operating context that facilitates the realization of the objectives of the business. They describe this in terms that suggest some enlightened self-interest for being an activist CEO, a responsible brand, or for engaging in corporate advocacy:

> They must understand citizenship and become more knowledgeable about patriotism because you must be a patriot first. Your business is set in a country and you can't succeed in business if the operating context is failing. You need to make your environment conducive to successful business activity. That is the *selfish* reason why a business leader, a brand, or a company must be an activist. But the *unselfish* reason why you must be an activist is that you must be a patriot, with a passion for making the country a better place.

Some participants spoke about the importance of the modern CEO developing a keen sense of his/her social environment, based on the realization of a strong interconnectedness between the company and the wider operating context. Participant #13 expressed the importance of being socially conscious. For them, corporate leadership was synonymous with social leadership:

> You also have to be conscious of the fact that you live in an environment, so, cannot be cocooned or siloed in your own world, and unconcerned about happenings around you. You must be conscious of your environment, and be prepared to put your voice to things that matter to you ... because if you are a leader in business, you have to extend that leadership to your environment. Wherever you find yourself, you have to show strong leadership and be a positive influence on happenings around you.

Other participants shared the idea that it made business sense to think beyond the narrow confines of a company's profit motive. According to Participant #19, an integral part of the modern role of companies was caring about other stakeholders:

CEOs must understand that doing good can also mean doing good business. More CEOs must come to the point of realization that doing social good and doing good business are not necessarily mutually exclusive. If you do good or you impact society, or you are an activist, that doesn't take away from turning profits or making money ... so that should be the underlining factor. Now, pursuing social causes as a business or a business leader ultimately helps your company or your brand. You can find that sweet spot where by doing good, you can also set your company or brand apart and also make some good money too (laughs) ... when you find that special sweet spot, that is a privileged position; that is very positive and great for business.

Some CEOs said they owed it to themselves, their companies, and the society to leave a good legacy for the next generation. Those who shared such views added that it was inappropriate to limit the evaluation of the performances of CEOs and their companies only to the attainment of business results. For instance, Participant #7 called for CEOs not to limit the evaluation of their roles to the ability to deliver shareholder value. They advocated for broader criteria for measuring the performances of the private sector:

CEOs should realize that they have a responsibility toward society and that it is incumbent on them to ensure that they positively impact society and leave a good legacy.

### 9.2.4 Authenticity and Truth-Based Activism

A huge majority of the study participants shared the view that a supremely important guideline for successful CEO activism in Ghana or anywhere else is that such activities ought to be based on authenticity and truth. Many participants made the point that activism that is contrived would not be successful because members of an activist's strategic constituency would be discerning enough to see through any multiple layers of deceit and selfish motive.

However, some noted that, when truth and authenticity served as major pillars on which a CEO activist acted, greater success and effectiveness were assured. This was because these features had a powerful way of shaping the choice of more meaningful issues and causes, drove the deployment of relevant resistance strategies and tactics, and assured a greater success while offering an effective shield of protection against any pushbacks faced by the activist CEO. Participant #22 noted that a mantra that worked for them was:

Trust in God and do the right thing. You have nothing to fear if you know you have done everything right and in absolute truth. In saying so, I am not saying I have done everything right. For instance, if because of my activities, someone decides to come to check my books to see whether I have paid my taxes, I would have no fears about that because my books are straight. You'd have nothing on me. Yes. You'll find no wrongdoing at all on my part.

Weighing in on the need for authenticity, Participant #2 believed that genuineness ought to be the very foundation of a CEO's activism and that business executives should embark on activism that is borne out of a true desire to issues that matter to the activist, and not because activism is now a cool thing, the in-thing, or because it sounds or looks good. They noted that an important value of authenticity-based activism is the uniqueness of signature value it accords to campaigns:

> I think number one is authenticity. You must be true to yourself. It [activism] has to start from what you can relate to authentically. The great thing about being authentic is that it means your activism will be expressed in different ways. Because if you are authentic, then you will do what comes naturally to you. What comes naturally to you will not be what comes naturally to me. So, we will express it in different ways.

Some informants revealed that a part of being authentic and truthful in activism involved being candid. Candor emerged as an important element of authenticity because of its ability to serve as a strong defense or protection from attacks against perceptions of the lack of objectivity on the part of the activist CEO, as explained by Participant #14:

> In Ghana, when you're candid, you will always end up ruffling feathers all over the place. So, you have to let people realize that you're not necessarily attacking or going after their political party. Make them know that what you're doing is probably based on your personal conviction.

For others, being authentic was also about leading by example, and not merely in words. Activist CEOs such as Participant #18 were of the view that activism was really a doing word and stressed the importance of being the change that the activist wants to see in society. To illustrate his point, they referred to how they led the XXX Bank (name withheld) in supporting the government's 1D1F program:

> On the issue of One District One Factory (1D1F) program in Ghana, I made sure that it was not just by word of mouth. We were the first bank to disburse money under this initiative and it came out of the statement, or promise I made to the President of Ghana to the effect that I believed in it (the project), and that I would do the best I could to support its successful rollout.

While such a gesture may on the surface be regarded as completely altruistic, how doing good in this way could be a great business decision:

> At the end of the day, if these people on the street are working and making a meaningful living, who are the ultimate beneficiaries, and where would they keep their money? Obviously, they'd be able to earn decent livelihoods, become good bank customers, may create their own businesses, and create more employment. Instead of the banks scrambling over a small piece of cake, by engaging in activism and supporting the long-term future of Ghana, you're broadening the pie and deepening financial inclusion across the country. Speaking out for others is also about making good business decisions since it is also about securing the future and sustainability of the financial services sector.

Others drew attention to the role of consistency and authenticity in driving down the cost of activist campaigns while improving the effectiveness of the communication effort. Participant #5 observed that being consistent, speaking the truth, and being authentic had contributed to increasingly minimal activist campaign budgets for him. They disclosed that some inauthentic CEOs, noticing the positive publicity of their activities had attempted to copy them without success. For Participant #5, a major defining factor in his activism was his consistency and authenticity:

> You don't need as many resources as you think. If you're consistent and speak the truth, and are authentic, people start to listen to you; but you can't buy the public's loyalty. It is not really about the money. While I've been doing this, I suppose some CEOs have felt that I've been taking too much of the space and have tried to also do some activism of their own, but they have not quite had the same impact because it is not a part of their corporate strategy. For me, activism is a core part of my strategy, and I know exactly why I do it. It has been an important part of our game plan to build the brand, right from the get-go.

For several other CEOs in this study, authenticity had to do with a CEO choosing an approach to activism that worked best for them in shaping public opinion or realizing the objectives of the campaign. In this regard, some participants warned against copying blindly from others. For Participant #4, it was important for CEO activists to stay true to themselves in all facets of their campaigns, even as they attempted to express their thought leadership through CEO activism:

> I think CEO activists are potentially impactful in shaping public opinion because we have a significant public profile or influence as thought leaders who are now taking on a new role as social activists. Organizations that can leverage the CEO's profile tend to become more successful and are the forerunners in the world of work today. It is nice for us to think that there is a board and there is a management team. However, when you think *Virgin*, you think Richard Branson. You shouldn't think that you have to be a Branson overnight. His style has been to use frontal activism, expressed in his typical maverick style. You can be an activist, but not adopt Branson's style. You just have to figure out what you're comfortable with or what works best for you.

In addition to authenticity, it was found that guidelines for successful CEO activism must also include a strong belief in the cause and in oneself. It emerged that the value of having a strong belief and personal conviction could be found in the ability of these attributes to provide staying power for a long-term campaign, as described by Participant #13:

> Don't put your voice to an issue that you're not passionate about. Activism is almost always a marathon, so you must put your voice into something that you're passionate about and can sustain. You have to be really committed to the cause you are championing. Whatever your cause, you must be ready to totally commit to the struggle. Be authentic, believe in your cause, and have a personal conviction. Don't do it simply because you think it looks good on you or on your business. You might think that your activism might come back at you positively, but it may actually backfire. So, you might have to go deep and be sure the conviction is coming from deep within.

### 9.2.5 Timing and Following Best Practices

Several participants indicated the importance of timing in ensuring that campaign messages were heard. For some participants, the right message delivered at the wrong time would not be as successful as an aptly timed message. Participant #15 shared some insights about how some time-related factors shaped the release of some of their messages:

> When the *Year of Return* to get our kinsfolk in the Diaspora to return to Ghana was really peaking, I began to talk about issues relating to our tourism sites. Yes, I gauge the time before I talk about issues since the timing would also send the message further and better.

Several informants pointed to the importance of profiting from the experiences of other CEO activists. In expressing this view, they called for the need to for current and future CEO activists to have access to some publications and guidelines or documented cases of the works of other CEO activists. Participant #6 called for the establishment of Afrocentric research-informed guidelines for successful CEO activism within the African context:

> It is important for all CEOs, both current and potential, to be able to go back to some rule books to find out how others who have been activists have done so; to learn what are the things that have negative repercussions; what are the boundaries; what are the needed resources; and the toolkit you should have in your arsenal before engaging in such battles.

Among the most popular guidelines for successful CEO activism shared by some informants are the importance of taking the middle line, communicating clearly, being able to defend one's position, based on facts, and showing neutrality by being apolitical. In this regard, some participants such as Participant #18 also urged CEO activists to be very strategic and tactful in their activism. Indeed, for them, being strategic also meant having a media strategy that would not needlessly expose them to unnecessary attacks.

> Speaking out tactfully ... don't always be out there talking ... you only work yourself into becoming a political agent. You need to know when, where, and how you speak, and to whom you speak, because your voice can easily be taken away and you become speechless; and you can be making all the noise, but nobody is listening to what you have to say.

### 9.2.6 Embed Activism in the Corporate Strategy and Have a "Kitchen Cabinet"

It turned out that, for some participants, corporate and CEO activism was a core part of the corporate strategy. For instance, it emerged that, right from the incorporation of their company, Participant #5 disclosed that CEO activism was identified as one of the ways of uniquely differentiating, positioning and promoting the business. Some informants disclosed that besides according the role of activism the needed level of legitimacy of corporate affairs, doing so made it a central activity within the corporate strategy. Others spoke of benefits and attributes of an activism-embedded strategic focus as including working to provide some consistency, authenticity, and budgetary support for the initiatives.

According to Participant #5, although it may not have been very clear to some board and management members from the outset, his activist stance had always enjoyed corporate support because it was grounded in the strategy of the company:

> The board of directors has been very supportive. From incorporation, we wanted to build the brand by taking an activist stance and advocating for the greater good. Advocacy is a part of our strategy and this helps to carry every employee along. I have a management team that knows what I say in my campaigns, who can guide me, give me valuable feedback, and can shape my messages. Whenever I am going to speak up about an issue, we have a mock presentation where we have a cross-section of my team and some invited guests to listen, critique, tear my messages apart from diverse perspectives, and provide their input.

While referring to the need for CEO activism to be embedded in corporate strategy, rather than it being an add-on, some participants indicated that it was vital for activism to be mainstreamed and made a core part of the job function of the modern CEO.

### 9.2.7 The Importance of Strategic Issue Selection and Having a Signature Advocacy

The participants underscored the need for CEO activists to select their issues properly, in order to assure some success for campaigns. For the informants that shared this view, accurate issue selection was important because of the plethora of possible causes and the limited resources available. Participant #14 advocated for activist CEOs to have campaigns that would help to define the image and public persona of the CEO activist:

> You must select the issues properly because you can't pretend to be able to solve every problem in society. You probably want to have a signature advocacy–issues that define who you are and what you stand for, and causes that can deliver the change you seek, but without much negative communication.

Some study participants felt that having a signature advocacy was also related to consistently sticking with an issue or a family of interrelated issues with which an activist CEO and their company could become known. For Participant #4, it was important to become known for a cause or a range of mutually inclusive causes:

> Be consistent and stick with it ... you cannot be flip-flopping and doing this today and then doing something totally different tomorrow. If that must be the case, it must be because you are adding on or naturally extending your initial issue or cause. However, you must be sure that the range of causes mutually reinforce each other in ways that make them comprehensive,

while having a good level of cohesion that fits within the place it occupies within the business world.

### 9.2.8 Guard Your Heart

For some informants, guidelines for CEO activism in Africa should include the caution for neophyte activist CEOs to prepare for huge doses of not only hypocrisy but also duplicity, not only from sworn opponents but shockingly from those that vaunt their support for the activist CEO. In order to survive the perceived bloody ocean of CEO activism, the informants in this study urge all activist CEOs to ensure that their survival toolkit includes the buoy of mistrust for many people, groups, and organizations. Participant #10 shared some nuggets of insights here:

> It is a very steep price to pay. I have woken up many times and told myself, 'I am not going to do this again.' But I still find myself coming back, and fighting ... maybe; just maybe... maybe not. Who knows? Perhaps, one of these days, I may just disappear from all of these.

> The thing is that when you fight corruption, it fights you back very hard. It doesn't matter how many verbal assurances people give you, you will find that even some of those who cheer you openly, jeer at you behind your back. Some have come to express their fullest support for me on an issue. However, the next day, these same people have been found to be passing extremely adverse comments. It is not just hypocrite; it is duplicity.

Some of the participants noted that an important principle in ensuring impactful CEO activism is the courage to select controversial issues and the conviction to speak truth to power. In reflecting on the importance of courage, several CEOs in this research study also indicated the importance of self-belief and not paying heed to discouraging comments from others who may not have the same level of understanding and belief in the issues/causes being pursued by the activist CEO.

According to Participant #5, they started noticing some tangible benefits from their activism when they injected significant doses of courage and passion:

> I had listened to people and hadn't had my own self-courage and if I hadn't had one of our director's support, I probably wouldn't have come as far as we have because when we started to speak out on these big controversial or hot-button issues, even our employees have come to advise me against such sayings.

A part of being courageous entailed being prepared to face some failures. Some informants revealed that it was important to have in mind that although they may not have been able to achieve all of their goals, at least, they made some efforts. To Participant #5, a significant guideline involved the knowledge that he may not be able to realize all of his desires in his activism. For him, he is content with knowing that he made an effort to be a part of the solution by being a powerful and courageous "bulldozer":

> I'm mindful of the fact that one day somebody will ask me what I did as a CEO; and I don't want to have to say that I was timid or scared and could not take a stand for that which I believed in. I would like to proudly say that I was courageous and able to speak my mind and that I may not have been able to achieve all that I wanted to get changed in society, but at least, I bravely tried and gave it my best shot. I would rather go out kicking and screaming about what I believe in than go out with a whimper. The management thinker Peter Drucker says that "Ideas don't move mountains, bulldozers move mountains; ideas show them where to go to work". I am a bulldozer, and I have the power to make things happen.

Several participants in this research study indicated that in undertaking activism, CEOs in Ghana ought to be aware that activism was a risky activity, and to take steps to manage or minimize the risks involved. Participant #1 opined that despite the attendant risks, CEOs, by virtue of the positions they occupied in society, owed it a responsibility to help change society, by speaking up whenever they feel discontented about any aspect of the workings of the society. For them, it was worth taking every risk, in order to pursue the common social good:

> Everything in life is about taking risks. If you are risk-averse or if you are afraid of what people would say, what kind of society would we be leaving behind for the next generation? Your family has invested so much in you from childhood; society has invested so much in you as an individual. The least you can do is give back to society in one way or the other.

### 9.2.9 Audience Profiling and Being Above Board

For some participants, an important guideline related to carefully studying and understanding various factors, motivations, and attributes of the target audiences. According to Participant #17, audience profiling, segmentation, and targeting were critical success factors in CEO activism:

In order to ensure that you speak to the hearts and minds of the people who need to hear your message, you must know your audience very well. You have to prepare at all times to you need to know how best to engage your audience. You must be able to relate effectively with all manner of target audiences. Yes, it is not everyone who has the skill to communicate effectively with diverse audiences. There are some CEOs who cannot go in a room full of high-powered people. The way you speak to a group of intelligent and educated people is quite different from speaking to a group of school children. You just need to know what resonates well with your audience.

Participants noted that another important guideline for successful activism was coming to the table with clean hands. It emerged that a vital personal trait that is shared by activist CEOs is their abhorrence of social injustice and vices. Indeed, social injustice was the fuel that energized their calling as activist CEOs. Thus, some informants noted that it was important for all activist CEOs to lead by example in ensuring that every facet of their operation was above reproach.

They observed that besides the sheer propriety of the activism itself being authentic and above board, it was important for every other aspect of their business operations and personal lives of the activist CEO to be, as far as possible, blameless. This is because engaging in CEO activism necessarily brings activists into direct conflict with entrenched and powerful interests in the societal and political establishment. Such forces would leave no stone unturned in attacking and questioning the moral authority of the CEO activist. Ergo, playing by the book is a significant guideline for CEO activism because it provides the needed moral foundation for the activist CEO, while helping offering a safeguard against attacks.

Participant #24 amply demonstrates how operating above reproach should be a cornerstone in the arsenal of the activist CEO in Ghana:

> ... I am not saying I have done everything right. For instance, if because of my activities, someone decides to come to check my books to see whether I have paid my taxes, I would have no fears about that because my books are straight. If inspect my licenses from the Food and Drug Administration (FDA) for my products, you would find that it is all in order too. The point is, when you want to engage in CEO activism, make sure you yourself are right; that you can't be found culpable in any way. Your business, books, licenses, permits, etc. should all be in order, before you can start thinking of helping others. Otherwise, it would surely be used against you.

Others stressed the importance of running a transparent business that employees supported and would advocate for. Those that shared such sentiments did so, bearing in mind the important role of employees as potential ambassadors or allies of the business who had pivotal roles in shaping virtually every organizational outcome. Participant #5 was of the view that, although no organization could be completely above board, it was important to be open in gaining the support of employees. According to them, a key part of gaining the buy-in of employees entailed having a clear game plan that should be executed to perfection, with courage and deep resolve, despite the pushbacks:

> You must run a transparent business because the people who either carry you or crucify you are your employees. They are the first people who would either encourage people to do business with your company or not. Get your employees to believe in you and your cause.

They further explained that it was worth engaging in CEO activism in a manner that carried employees along because, doing so could produce desired business outcomes, including deepening employee loyalty and attracting a company's customer base.

### 9.2.10 Being Purpose-Driven and Deliberate

CEO activism ought not to be a knee-jerk (re)action. This is because such corporate purposes would have been long-established and set in ways that effectively define those issues on which the company would agitate, should such issues be threatened within the social system. Importantly, it stands to reason that such ideals that underpin the business – the overriding corporate purpose(es) – ought to precede and drive every nature of corporate or CEO activism.

Participant #8 explained how this matrix of purpose-driven activism operates:

> With CEO activism, you must agree on them as principles before your activism happens. The issues in the country about which you have to crusade typically lag behind or happen later on, and if you make your decision to engage in activism in the heat of the moment, you would make terrible mistakes. Really, your purpose and ideals for being in business and showing concern for the greater good, ought to precede your activism. It is these purposes or ideals that undergird the business that would signal to you that something that is happening in the environment does not sit well with you and prompts the company or the CEO to consider some activist campaign. It is important for you to have your principles ahead of time – from the origin; from the very foundation of the company.

Indeed, there are several benefits for grounding the corporate of CEO activism on some long-established corporate purpose(es). In the first place, it serves as an insulation against being inauthentic and ill-prepared in undertaking CEO activism. Part of this is because it makes CEO activism a deliberate corporate action that is guided by proactivity.

Related to being purpose-driven and deliberate about activism, the informants underscored the importance of being consistent regarding every aspect of their activism, including the range of causes pursued; messaging strategy and tactics; and the overall campaign approach. For Participant #2, staying consistent brings some dividends, including having mastery over the issue:

> And stay consistent. Be consistent about it. Your consistency will pay off because you will understand what you are doing more and more over time if you are consistent. It's so important that you will understand what you are doing more and more. You will not have all the answers from Day One, but you become a greater expert in your activism if you keep doing it consistently.

Several participants highlighted the importance of selecting issues that reasonably fit in with the core business of the company that is led by the CEO. Participant #4 noted that a useful guideline for effective CEO activism related to ensuring that the range of causes championed by the activist CEO was not regarded by the public as far-fetched. They said it was at the heart of any guideline for effective activism. They thus advocated for selecting issues that people would see as a reasonable thing for an activist CEO to concern themselves with:

> CEO activists must first identify something that lies within their area. It should be something that makes sense for them to be doing, because it is not contrived or too far-fetched, judging by the operations of their organizations. The first rule is that you must not engage in an activity that the first time people hear about it, would make them question why you are concerning yourself with such a cause. The cause must ring true and be in sync with what you or your organization stands for.

Some said it was essential to stay true to the positions taken by CEO activists, irrespective of which political party was in government. According to Participant #14, when an activist CEO keeps fighting consistently, opponents do not only give up on resisting them, but also consistency was a powerful safeguard for maintaining the authenticity, neutrality, and issue-focus of the CEO activist:

> When you keep fighting like that, your opposers tend to give up on fighting you. However, as an activist, you must also be mindful of consistency. If this political party does something and you can speak out against them, but you can't seem to do so when that political party does so, it means that you don't know who you are now – you have an identity crisis. So, it is important for you to have a certain healthy level of consistency in your activism.

Several informants underscored the value of having and deploying a varied arsenal of activist campaign strategies and tactics. For instance, some participants indicated the need for alliances and coalition-building and deploying various media vehicles. For Participant #13, it was important for activist CEOs to be adept at employing diverse approaches to activism:

> Activism indeed does not always have to be feet-on-street. It can be backdoor, on social media, etc. There are various ways of advocacy. It doesn't have to be open or in the public all the time. I do most of my advocacy where the sun doesn't shine, by which I mean ways in which nobody hears about it. I would privily go to a minister of state, a politician, a businessperson, or a neighbor who I feel can make a difference; and nobody would hear about it. In fact, my private activities outweigh those public and media-focused ones.

Besides the fact that CEO activism ought to be driven by deliberate and well-established corporate purpose(s), it also emerged that a useful playbook for CEO activism involved the setting of various scenarios. Such scenarios set should be based on several factors, among which is effective stakeholder mapping and the performance of issues analysis and sensitivity testing of how various strategic constituents would be impacted by or react to various risk issues within the social system.

As observed by Participant #8, his activities have always had various scenarios to guide every facet of his campaigns:

> The playbook should have various scenarios that must specify guidelines for action. For instance, should something that goes this way or affects this or that stakeholder, then I am going to speak up because it is at variance with my deeply held values or some purpose for doing my business. For instance, if there is a certain minimum deviation from your principles, the CEO may decide to only speak up. However, should the deviation extend beyond a certain pre-specified point, then the CEO would decide to show up, go on the radio, or join a group. And if the deviation should hit a certain extreme level, the CEO would then decide to step onto the streets, put his/her body on the line, speak out and protest, and courageously speak truth to power about what is happening.

Thus, such scenario-based guidelines should have various predetermined triggers and commensurate actions that the CEO would be prepared to take. These guidelines for effective CEO activism ought to reflect the dynamism of the internal and external operating contexts of companies interested in engaging in corporate activism. In this regard, it is important for such scenarios to clearly identify stakeholders that could take up issues within society. Part of the scenarios-setting task should involve the prescription of a planned range of actions that could be invoked, should any triggering event occur.

Many participants thought that an important guideline for effective CEO activism is for the CEO to leave no stone unturned in reinforcing previous statements made. To illustrate, Participant #18 described how they took advantage of being a panelist at an event in Europe to underscore the need for all to support the 1D1F in Ghana:

> Use every opportunity you get to support and amplify your statements or stances. I was on a panel in London at a Ghana-UK Chamber of Commerce event. I used that speaking engagement to further promote and popularize the 1D1F. I'm not a politician, but I spoke about it from the angle of the opportunities this government program would create for Ghana.

Some participants also thought that an important guideline for effective CEO activism in Ghana involved the employment of flexibility in practically every facet of activist campaigns. For Participant #18, this may entail switching sometimes between being a "day leader" and a "night leader":

> I do make interventions and subtle statements occasionally on social media *(Facebook)*, trying to fight corruption and state capture by members of the political class. Sometimes, you can make a change by being a day and night leader, that is, being an abrupt leader, calling out corrupt officials ... you know, brashly pointing fingers, and going out to accuse public officeholders of corruption - that is hard power. You can also achieve more by subtly going on a trajectory that speaks to the same thing, but in a soft power mode, influencing people and making comments that would set people thinking to consider your motivations for making some of those comments.

Several informants saw the need for CEOs to be ready to start activist campaigns, even if on a small scale. For those that shared this view, many campaigns remain paralyzed and unborn because of the perception that some activist CEOs have about every campaign being huge. Thus, some informants saw the need to start small sometimes and then scale up whenever necessary. For Participant #2, the idea of scalability in activism campaigns also means getting a head start and having the chance of becoming more familiar with the issue that is at the heart of the activism:

> Be willing to start small wherever you find yourself. Don't wait to be a CEO to start. It's hard to start with something that you are unfamiliar with when you are a CEO actually. Familiarity matters; so, start wherever you are, however small; whether it's your

classroom, school, dormitory, or wherever, you just start and grow with it.

It was found that starting activism small and scaling up whenever possible had to do with some practical and logical considerations for some of the participants that shared this view. This included the need to carefully consider the activist CEO's personal, family, and company realities and situations such as the child-care factors. Participant #2 stressed that some of the practical reasons for starting small include being kind to oneself and avoiding extra stress that could be occasioned by activism:

> So be kind to yourself and manage your time. Don't let activism become a source of stress. Let it be something you do enjoy and for me, for instance, my husband always says to me, 'You really enjoy when you do these things, you just look energized and happy.' So, you must do it when you can really manage it. Be kind to yourself. Just do your bit gradually and build up over time.

### 9.2.11 Be Sure to Win the Buy-in of Significant Others

It turned out that CEO activism was rarely seen as a solo or individual activity. Most of the participants disclosed that various significant others had an influence on their activities. For instance, Participant #13 saw the need to gain the buy-in of her family and allay their fears regarding their safety, before embarking on their protest march. They revealed that gaining the support of their family also meant proving to them that they had the necessary police protection and showing that they had a high level of personal responsibility for their safety:

> You need the buy-in of your family. I had to ensure that my family was fully in support of my action beforehand. If anything happened to me, it wasn't just me that would be affected. I had to put the fears of important people in my life at rest, including my dad, my mum, my partner, and my children. I really had to allay the fears and apprehensions of my family about my safety and well-being.

It emerged that, although CEO activism was driven mainly by the personal convictions of the CEO, the participants in this study still saw the need to carry their employees along, as much as possible through various internal communications. As observed by Participant #18, public pronouncements they had made had been preceded or accompanied by some internal communications, designed to ensure that all members of staff were kept in the loop:

When I'm going to grant an interview, I make sure that there is effective internal communication. I make sure that a release is issued to the employees that I'll be speaking on this radio station, at this time to talk, and about these issues. There is internal communication that goes on unless it is an unplanned media encounter. This is usually in the form of an email blast. For every planned media encounter, there is some internal communication that is issued to make the employees aware about it and to prepare their minds.

### 9.2.12 Research and the Power of a Performance-Driven Approach

Other informants stressed the importance of goal setting, monitoring, and evaluation of significant aspects of activist campaigns. These participants emphasized that the same rigor and performance-driven approach to business management ought to be applied to activism campaigns. They also urged activist CEOs to be strategic about their campaigns, measure the success/effectiveness of their efforts, and review their goals periodically.

For Participant #2, a great CEO activism campaign is one that is backed by sound research from thought to finish:

I like to back a lot of what I say with facts, so I tend to do a lot of research on human Key Performance Indicators (KPIs) and developmental KPIs. When doing activism, you'll need facts and that's where you will need your research. You need to be credible so it's not just an emotional rant. Your activism is based on research and figures that validate what you are talking about. Also, I do research regarding impact, even where the impact is not always easy to measure. Research accounts for credibility and a bit of research after the fact to evaluate and understand what people are thinking.

Some participants shared the view that a vital guideline for effective CEO activism concerned being perceived not as an unnecessary nagger, but as one who genuinely cared about society and was proffering workable solutions for social transformation and for the benefit of all. As suggested by Participant #20, the acid test of a valuable CEO activist was the extent to which they made authentic solutions to social problems:

When you want to speak out on an issue, have a problem-solving orientation. Focus more on the solution, rather than mere criticisms and attacks on others. You should be seen to be offering an alternative to the challenge; an alternative that solves societal problems effectively and advances society. For me, relevant activism is one that offers workable solutions to the big issues facing mankind. The depth of solution should be the acid test. If your activism does not solve social problems, you might as well forget it.

Some of the informants stressed the importance of personal development for CEOs who want to engage in activism. For some of the participants in the study, this is important because it is impossible for one to provide for other for others what one does not have. Therefore, an important guideline for CEO activism is for CEOs themselves to keep preparing themselves, as much as possible. Continual renewal and personal development are imperative for Participant #24, as they pursued a fellowship in political leadership at a leading American university. They see such preparation as vital in their bid to be of more sociopolitical impact in Ghana:

> I just met the deadline for applying for a fellowship at the New York University (NYU) for public service leadership ... The fellowship is to equip me with the right skills and to build my confidence and competence to do what I do even better.

For some participants, being ready also meant activist CEO immersing themselves in research material on the issue/cause to ensure a deep grasp of the matter, while remaining well and truly apolitical. For some, a useful guideline entails being selecting issues that mattered to a wide cross-section of the public, but also targeting the political class with one's messages and activities.

Several participants stressed the need to move beyond a superficial understanding or appreciation of all sides of the issue. Such a deep dive, they observed, would enable the activist CEO to develop a thorough grasp of the nuances of the matter, while developing the needed depth of emotional intelligence and cultural intelligence to ensure success in articulating facts about the campaign. Thus, for Participant #6, such a complete immersion ought to part of the activist CEO's survival toolkit:

> It is important that you have a game plan, look at the issues and be sure that you understand the them very well. The simple fact that you find the issue irksome would not be enough. You need to be empathetic towards the people involved in it. So, a skill you need is your emotional intelligence; to be able to empathize with the vulnerable and be able to appreciate the issues at much deeper levels and limits; you must perceive and grasp the nuances of the matter. You also need to build your cultural intelligence so that you can relate not just to like-minded people around you, but across sectors, cultures, and generations.

Thus, a recurrent theme related to owning the issue, by which is meant that the CEO activist must ensure that he/she gained a deeper than average understanding of the issue they are advocating for or against. Some participants expressed the idea that a regrettable faux pas in CEO activism involved taking on an issue that the activist lacked knowledge of. According to Participant #1, a necessary step on the road to success in CEO activism was ensuring that the activist CEO took steps to steep themselves in the knowledge of the matter at hand through deep research and thorough briefing.

### 9.2.13 Community Creation

It was found that virtually all participants in this research study were of the view that CEO activism ought not to be a solo activity. Thus, for many participants, an important success factor in CEO activism revolved around the need to create what some described as "a coalition of the willing." By this, they were referring to the need for the CEO activist to have a group of like-minded people and organizations who can help with various aspects of the campaign, from legwork to bran work.

Participant #6 described some of his perspectives on forming such a coalition during his long-standing fight against illegal small-scale gold mining activities in Ghana:

> It is important to form a coalition of the willing; a coalition of people who can help to be able to do the activities, since you can't achieve so much as a lone ranger. In identifying this coalition, you need to identify people who would have a significant impact on the project but are people who would oppose.

Others stressed that an important guideline that emerged related to the need to build community creation into activism. This involved creating well-knit communities of people who shared the ideas and ideals of the campaign and who also found each other within a defined locality or digital echo chamber. Such a community could provide the opportunity for community members to meet each other to plan actions within the community and support each other to achieve what they planned to do. Thus, participants highlighted the need for activist CEOs to create or adopt tools for the creation of such communities. For instance, Participant #2 described the utility of such groups of allies:

> I'd like to create communities of people who share these ideas, but also find each other within their locality. A simple example will be let's say, there are twenty young people in Sekyere West District in the Ashanti Region who believe in the *Bold New Normal*, I'd like them to meet. I'd like to give them a channel to find each other. To meet each other, plan actions within their community, and support each other to achieve what they want and plan to do.

Several informants further shared the view that such communities of allies need not be a homogeneous group. Such informants, therefore, spoke of the utility of having diverse segmentations of communities that could collaborate with the CEO activist. Referring to traditional Ghanaian adages that highlighted the importance of drawing in-depth strength from numbers, other participants in the study, including Participant #23 noted several benefits of building coalitions, including the benefits of multiple perspectives, but also serving as a protection from attrition and attacks of individual members:

> There is strength in numbers. That is why we have the Ghanaian proverb that says that a broomstick can be easily broken, but when tied together to become a broom, the broom may bend but cannot break. If you want to bring a change that is sustainable, it is important to bring a lot of people together, not only because of their numbers, but more importantly, because they would bring diverse insights and different perspectives.

Most participants saw the importance of activist CEOs in Ghana developing a mindset of supporting other CEO activists as an important element in a playbook for successful CEO activism in Ghana. Some of the informants underscored the need for unity and support for other CEOs, even when there is a disagreement with whatever causes they are pursuing or fighting for. For the CEOs that shared this viewpoint, the common connecting thread that should bind all activist CEOs together is the fact that they are activists and the fact that there is a shared commitment to risk themselves in the fight for the common good and the upliftment of humanity. Participant #8 aptly articulated this notion:

> The CEO must always be supportive of other activists, even if they don't agree with them. There is something about people who are prepared to put themselves on the line for others. They are rare, with only a small fraction of humanity having that attitude. So, even if you are a CEO who is not prepared to expose yourself, you must support the few who decide to play this role of being activists.

Some suggested that this notion of standing together as CEOs was reminiscent of traditional African values that talked about finding strength in unity. It was revealed that such support could be in various respects, including funding and the provision of diverse forms of moral support for each other. Such a call is even more relevant when placed against the backdrop of the fact that CEO activism is not a very popular activity among Ghanaian CEOs.

According to some participants, because of the nascence of the phenomenon, activist CEOs in Ghana were in a minority, and thus, it was important for them to close their ranks and to give themselves a fighting chance at success in their causes, by strongly supporting each other in their actions. Indeed, one of the worse things that could serve as a nail in the campaign of a CEO activist was to find himself/herself being attacked or opposed by other CEOs in Ghana.

Interestingly, other participants in this research study extended the need for partnerships and alliances beyond working with other CEO activists. For example, for Participant #5, a critical success factor in CEO activism involved drawing strength from all manner of sources, including directors, employees, and family members:

> One of the most critical things is that find good people to work with, as employees, other CEOs, your family, the community, civil society organizations, and directors. I could never ever have done this alone without the support of a great and supportive team of backers.

An important guideline that emerged is the call by some of the participants for CEOs to be mindful of the fact that CEO activism was not for everyone, despite the fact that activism was seen as an important role of the modern CEO. Some participants noted that it was important for a CEO to have developed a credible personal brand and public profile before seeking to positively impact society through an activism campaign.

## 9.3 Discussion

There has been a yawning lacuna in the CEO activism literature relating to guidelines for safer and more effective social resistance efforts spearheaded by corporate leaders, especially those within the African context. This chapter sought to address this gap in knowledge by obtaining from study participants guidelines for CEO activism.

Campaign guidelines proffered by Chatterji and Toffel (2018) include the careful selection of campaign issues/causes; choosing the most opportune time to speak up; having a clear campaign plan; engaging internal stakeholders; gauging and predicting the reactions of diverse stakeholders; and measuring campaign results.

Chatterji and Toffel (2019b) further suggested two broad classes of communication-specific guidelines, covering (i) *when should you speak* and (ii) *how to speak effectively*, offering tips on listening to employees, linking activism to the corporate mission, maintaining key messages, activating a *Kitchen Cabinet*, issues management and crisis planning, and involving professional communicators.

The findings in this chapter go in tandem with the *CEO Activism Safeguards*, as discussed in the previous chapter, conceptualized as covering a range of defensive mechanisms, including personal safeguards, social safeguards, spiritual safeguards, communication-related safeguards, CEO activism best-practice safeguards, and corporate safeguards. While aspects of these findings were consistent with the extant literature on the CEO activism playbook, there are some remarkable contributions. These findings shed light on the CEO activism guidelines issue further by offering a whole slew of specific guidelines that the study participants recommend, based on their lived experiences as CEO activists within the African context.

This study contributes to the literature and helps to internationalize CEO activism research by bringing global perspectives to the discussion. The findings inform CEO activism campaign risk management strategies. It also expands upon nascent research streams such as PR for social responsibility, responsible management in the Global South, and contributes to current discussions on the ancient *Kemetic* doctrine of *Ma'at* (see Asante & Dove, 2021) and its variants, such as *Ubuntuism* and *Africapitalism* (see Adae, 2021b) and similar Afrocentric philosophies of sustainability (see Pompper & Adae, 2023).

### 9.3.1 Evolution of the CEO Activism Development Model

The findings contribute to the continued evolution of the working model by finding empirical support for a wide range of CEO activism guidelines, as reported in this chapter (see Fig. 8 below). This is noteworthy that this version of the process model is exactly as the version in the previous chapter, reflecting the influences of both *CEO activism safeguards*, and now, the *CEO activism guidelines* discussed in this chapter.

This completes the evolution of the model, as such guidelines are expected to inform various elements in the model such as determining the future state of a CEO's social-mindedness, motivation to keep engaging in CEO activism, campaign issue selection, and campaign strategies, and tactics.

The next chapter presents the conclusion of this book.

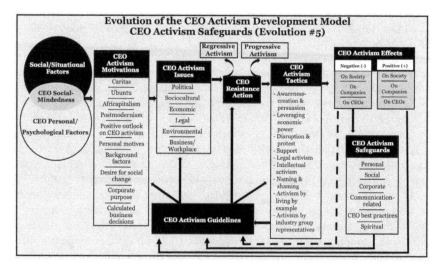

Fig. 8.    Evolution #5 of the CEO Activism Development Model.
*Source:* Author (2023).

# Chapter 10

# Conclusion: The CEO Activism Development Model

## 10.1 Introduction

Given growing discontent with the current state of affairs in societies across the globe, there have been calls for various corporate actors to step up to the plate and be agents of positive social change (Chatterji, 2016). While diverse corporate agents have heeded this call, CEOs, in particular, continue to publicly speak up on sociopolitical and environmental issues (see e.g., Hambrick & Wowak, 2021), to achieve various ends, including improving social outcomes, enhancing corporate/brand images, and driving business revenues (Josephs, 2019).

CEO activism is conceptualized as situations where corporate leaders take open stances and make public pronouncements on controversial sociopolitical and environmental matters, which may not be connected to the economic profits or operations of their corporations (Chatterji, 2016). While the term "CEO activism" is relatively new (see Chatterji & Toffel, 2015; Wettstein & Baur, 2016), the idea of business leaders playing a role in addressing key societal issues is not (Keim & Zeithaml, 1986).

CEO activism tends to run counter to the conventional business wisdom of shareholder primacy and financial profit-maximizing principles (see e.g., Friedman, 1970, 2007). The growing incidence of CEO activism appears set against the backdrop of recent redefinitions of the social purpose of corporations to include the pursuit of the interests of multiple stakeholders, rather than only financial profits for corporations and their investors (Business Roundtable, 2019).

CEO activism is growing in its global appeal (Chatterji & Toffel, 2018) due to growing social injustices and the inability of governments to address the key concerns of their constituents. Yet, the bulk of current scholarly literature on CEO activism displays a discernible exclusion of non-Western cases (Adae, 2021a). CEO activism scholarship is also dominated by an ideological bias for modernist perspectives that privilege consensus and center around corporate and investor interests while excluding alternative perspectives such as *Afrocentric* philosophies (Pompper & Adae, 2023) and postmodernism that supports agonism and the promotion of multiple stakeholder interests (Ciszek & Logan, 2018).

The field also lacks relevant models that explain various aspects of the phenomenon. This book seeks to address all these perceived gaps in knowledge and

CEOs on a Mission, 201–222

Copyright © 2023 Eric Kwame Adae

Published under exclusive licence by Emerald Publishing Limited

doi:10.1108/978-1-80382-215-020231011

offers a model that describes and explains important concepts and phases in the development of activist stances by CEOs, based on empirical data produced by long interviews with 24 activist CEOs in Ghana. These include various streams of research in CEO activism, including CEO social-mindedness, CEO activism motivations, CEO activism issues, CEO activism strategies and tactics, CEO activism effects, CEO activism safeguards, and CEO activism guidelines.

## 10.2 Theoretical Lenses

Several theoretical and conceptual lenses inform this study. These include notions of *responsible management in emerging markets* (see Adae et al., 2021) and *public relations for social responsibility* (see Pompper, 2021); *Afrocentricity* (see e.g., Asante, 1989) and *Afrocentric philosophies of sustainability* (see Pompper & Adae, 2023) and *Africapitalism* (see e.g., Amaeshi & Idemudia, 2015; Elumelu, 2012); and *Corporate Social Advocacy* (see Dodd & Supa, 2014) and *CEO activism* (see e.g., Branicki et al., 2021; Chatterji & Toffel, 2018).

## 10.3 Highlights of Findings

Thus far, previous chapters of this book have laid out the general background to the study, presented and discussed factors within the Ghanaian context that serve as the backdrop to the inquiry, outlined the theoretical lenses underpinning the investigation, as well as a review of sections of relevant related literature. The conceptual framework for the study, research questions, and their justifications have also been presented. The various methods and procedures concerning how data was collected, handled, and analyzed have also been explained. The findings regarding the main research questions have all been reported and discussed in specialized chapters dedicated to each line of inquiry. In discussing the main findings, connections have been made with both the theories and the seminal literature.

In this chapter, I highlight the major findings and how they relate to the theories and the literature, especially concerning CEO activism. Other sections of this chapter present some limitations of this research study, set out future research agenda, and also indicate some implications for the practice of CEO activism, before offering some concluding remarks.

### 10.3.1 Motivations for CEO Activism

In terms of motivations for engaging in CEO activism in Ghana, the results revealed several motives, which had not been articulated in the extant literature on CEO activism. For instance, the participants in this study indicated that they were motivated by such factors as Caritas, Ubuntu philosophy, Africapitalism, selected postmodern values in public relations, and an optimistic outlook on CEO activism. These motivations had hitherto not been associated with the literature on CEO activism. These are fresh contributions to the literature on CEO activism.

However, other findings emerged that extended some known motivations for CEO activism. These include calculated business decisions; the desire for social change; and a range of personal factors that included some personal convictions, serving the interests of multiple stakeholders, family, and personal background characteristics, and the influence of corporate values and purposes (see Chatterji, 2016). Some of these findings also align with some existing motivation postulates such as optimism for future stakeholder benefits, responding to current stakeholder pressures/expectations, and pursuing some ideological inclinations (see Nalick et al., 2016), and the pursuit of strategic corporate goals (see Dodd & Supa, 2014, 2015).

While some scholars, including Chatterji (2016) and Chatterji and Toffel (2018), have hinted at the possible influence of left-leaning ideological stances as motivations for CEO activism, these suggestions were not backed by empirical evidence. Besides, the literature on CEO activism had displayed a preponderance of consensus-inclined, right-wing, and modernist perspective that not only privileges the interests of investors but also tends to make a case for profit-producing organizational outcomes as motivating CEO activism (see e.g., Chatterji & Toffel, 2018). The findings in this study point to a different path in suggesting some postmodern values in public relations (see Holtzhausen, 2000; Holtzhausen & Voto, 2002) as motivations for CEO activism.

The findings for the motivations for CEO activism provide a more detailed picture of the various expressions of how the pursuit of strategic personal and calculated business goals could serve as motivations for CEO activism. In this, the findings point to varying degrees of corporate motives, personal motives, and the pursuit of enlightened self-interest. The findings further suggest that a bullish outlook on CEO activism was a motivation factor for CEO activism.

Based on the notion of Caritas, some scholars have mooted the idea of the modernization of public relations and strategic communications as focusing on the building and management of mutually beneficial relationships between organizations and members of their strategic constituency (see Corbett, 2012a, 2012b). Seen as the bedrock of responsible behavior by organizations, the notion of Caritas is argued to align with the promotion of corporate behaviors that are empathetic, merciful, just, compassionate, and focused on relationship building (see Tilson, 2014).

Little is known about motivations for CEO activism in the African context. Looking at whether the motivations would differ for African activist CEOs versus what is reported about Western-based ones speaks to the importance of context for theory-building. However, the contribution of this research study is not limited to the value of context in theory building, trying to replicate or confound existing studies. It holds much more utility values for research and theorizing on CEO activism than is afforded by the consideration of contextual factors.

Importantly, it brings fresh analytical and special insights into a fledgling field of inquiry by effectively introducing such concepts as *Ubuntu, Caritas* (see Tilson, 2014), and *Africapitalism* (see Amaeshi & Idemudia, 2015) into scholarly discussions on the motivations for CEO activism. Since the Africapitalism postulates in 2015, this is the first time they are being empirically examined. In this research study, CEO activism is positioned as an expression of *Africapitalism*, just as *Africapitalism* motivates CEO activism. The research study contributes to research on the postmodern values in PR (see Holtzhausen, 2000; Holtzhausen & Voto, 2002) by empirically examining how such values motivate CEO activism.

Overall, this research study contributes to the literature on CEO activism motivations by introducing and empirically illustrating how such concepts as Caritas, Ubuntu, postmodernism, and Africapitalism drive the phenomenon in ways that do not currently exist in the literature. This research study contributes to the literature by connecting the notions of Caritas, Ubuntu, Africapitalism, and selected postmodern values in public relations to CEO activism in ways that did not exist before. The findings in this research study concerning the motivations for CEO activism, while formally connecting the idea of Caritas to the literature on CEO activism, provide empirical evidence from the Ghanaian context regarding Caritas as a motivation for CEO activism. With such an entrée into the field of CEO activism, the stage is set for further studies on the various ways in which the notion of Caritas influences and conditions CEOs to take on various social causes.

This study illustrates how some aspects of Ubuntu philosophy pervade and inform virtually every aspect of communication practice in Africa, especially in terms of how the philosophy promotes ideas of fellow feeling and collectivism (see White, 2009). Ubuntu values are seen as working or having worked to condition traditional and corporate leaders to become socially minded and to work in favor of promoting the welfare of the common good in Africa (see Tilson, 2014).

Tilson (2014) suggests that "the personal commitment of an individual in a position of authority can foster an organizational and a societal effort in favor of the general welfare regardless of cost or reward to the giver or institution" (see Tilson, 2014, p. 69); especially when such motivations derive from spiritually grounded commitments to social justice "toward the common good, pro-social behavior is further encouraged and magnified" (p. 69).

Despite such suggestions, the Ubuntu philosophy is yet to find formal expression in the corpus of literature on CEO activism. Identified as one of the motivations for the CEO activists who participated in this study, the findings in this research study finally connect Ubuntu with the phenomenon of CEO activism. Ubuntu philosophy is a deep and wide worldview. Future studies could explore how specific Ubuntu ideas and constituent values or principles inform various aspects and expressions of CEO activism in Africa.

The findings in this research study position CEO activism as an *expression of* Africapitalism, just as Africapitalism *motivates* CEO activism. Thus, it aligns with extant Africapitalism calls that advocate for the increased participation of Africa's private sector in the continent's development, working through more participation and partnerships of companies and corporate actors across Africa with governments, other private sector actors, the development community, and civil society organizations (see Amaeshi & Idemudia, 2015).

These authors posit that Africapitalism is based on some Ubuntu philosophy and is built on some four pillars that deviate from neoclassical notions of capitalism, including (1) a sense of progress and prosperity; (2) a sense of parity; (3) a sense of harmony; and (4) a sense of place and belonging. Again, the findings in this research study connect CEO activism with the notion of Africapitalism, identifying Africapitalism as a motivation for CEO activism. In a sense, CEO activism could be said to be an expression of Africapitalism – a way in which the private sector in Africa is participating in the continent's development, by working to promote the greater good.

The findings in this research study contribute to the literature on CEO activism by connecting it with extant postmodern values in public relations (see Holtzhausen, 2000; Holtzhausen & Voto, 2002). For the first time in the literature on CEO activism, the findings in this research study identified these postmodern values as serving as part of the motivations for CEO activists in Ghana who participated in this study.

Following Holtzhausen and Voto (2002), the evidence from this study characterizes the present-day CEO activist as an archetype that could be profiled as organizational activists who embody the conscience of their organizations, who act based on their personal convictions in resisting dominant power structures (both within and outside of their organizations, including resisting the Government of Ghana and their boards of directors) in fighting for the common good. Further, such activists are characterized as making the most humane decisions, given specific situations, and having the appetite to exploit tensions within the environment to exercise new thinking and innovation in solving perceived problems in society (see Holtzhausen & Voto, 2002).

Holtzhausen (2000) advocated for a postmodern approach to public relations and went on to identify several postmodern values that were relevant to the field of public relations. A postmodern view of corporate communications posits that corporate communication practitioners and other corporate executives such as CEOs will be positively predisposed to serving as social activists (see Holtzhausen & Voto, 2002).

The postmodern perspective of public relations postulates that corporate executives would exhibit some postmodern behaviors that translate into various forms of organizational activism. Such postmodern behavioral traits have been identified as including local and situational ethical decision-making, a desire for change, the use of biopower to resist dominant power, a concern for the representation of the marginalized sections of society, and dissensus and dissymmetry (see Holtzhausen, 2000; Holtzhausen & Voto, 2002).

Fig. 9 (on next page) graphically illustrates the range of motivations for the participants in this study that extend the current literature.

### 10.3.2 CEO Activism Issues/Causes

The findings indicate that the extant taxonomy of brand activism postulated by Kotler and Sarkar (2017, 2018a) applied to CEO activism, as this framework proved adequate to capture the wide array of specific issues and causes advocated by CEO activists in Ghana. These scholars had developed a typology of brand activism that comprised environmental activism, social (cultural) activism, legal activism, economic activism, business/workplace activism, and political activism

Fig. 9.    Motivations for CEO Activism. *Source:* Author (2023).

(see Fig. 10 below). The findings in this research study contribute to the literature by extending the scope of the current taxonomy on brand activism (see Kotler & Sarkar, 2017, 2018a) into the realm of CEO activism.

Adopting these categories for the range of causes of activist CEOs in Ghana proved adequate. However, this typology had to be moderately modified by extending the "social activism" category to include cultural issues. Thus, for this

Fig. 10.    Taxonomy of Issues in CEO Activism. *Source:* Author (Adapted from Kotler and Sarkar (2017, 2018a)).

research study, there was a need for "sociocultural issues" as a cluster of CEO activism issues.

The findings on the issues involved in CEO activism in Ghana, for the first time in the literature on CEO activism, introduce specific context-specific causes/issues of interest to activists in developing countries. So far, the literature on CEO activism only contained examples of issues from Western contexts. It is expected that this would also set the stage for more studies on CEO activism from non-Western contexts, as well as comparative studies between Western and non-Western societies.

The findings on the issues in CEO activism, mainly divergent from the current literature, illustrate the argument that place is not to be ignored or simply consumed (see Amaeshi & Idemudia, 2015). Africapitalism embraces place, while the modernist view and capitalism both take place for granted. Until these findings, examples of the causes pursued by CEOs have been limited to examples in Western (American) contexts. Now, scholars can refer to the actions of activist CEOs in a non-Western context.

The findings effectively internationalize the literature on CEO activism and contribute to the literature on issues in CEO activism by providing specific examples of issues that matter in a non-Western society. However, beyond the value of context in theory building, examining whether or not the issues addressed by African CEOs are different goes beyond context. According to the postmodern values discussed, CEOs' actions are driven by local ethics and situational factors. This extends or helps us to better understand the value of place in postmodernism and Africapitalism's value of "a sense of place and belonging."

This research study contributes to the insider activist perspective (see Briscoe et al., 2014; Holtzhausen & Voto, 2002; Pompper, 2015). Specifically, it enriches the literature on CEO activism (see Chatterji & Toffel, 2015, 2016, 2017, 2018, 2019; Dodd & Supa, 2014, 2015) and *sustainability transitions* (Delmas et al., 2019). It also contributes to the literature on the postmodern values in public relations, which casts corporations and their executives as being concerned with wider social issues that extend beyond the private interests of companies (see Holtzhausen, 2000; Holtzhausen & Voto, 2002). This way CEOs are moved to think socially and to identify social causes that would serve the greater good, even if doing so means going against their own business interests.

Overall, my findings here make a case for the increased role of Africapitalism in CEO activism, advocating for the increased participation of Africa's private sector in Africa's development, and working through various partnerships with governments, CSOs, and other private sector players.

### 10.3.3 CEO Activism Tactics

The third area of findings relates to the tactics employed by CEO activists in Ghana. It emerged that the two extant taxonomies on the tactical repertoire of CEO activism (Chatterji & Toffel, 2018; Livonen, 2018) alone did not suffice to capture the wide range of tactics employed by CEO activists in Ghana, whether applied alone or in combination. Chatterji and Toffel's (2018) typology did not make room for support tactics and disruptive tactics, while Livonen's (2018) made no room for the tactic of leveraging economic power.

Thus, there was a need to conflate these two typologies into four main classes in the analysis of the tactics employed by CEO activists in Ghana. For the analysis of findings, the tactics were grouped into (1) leveraging economic power; (2) awareness creation and persuasion tactics; (3) disruption and protest tactics; and (4) support tactics (see Fig. 11 below).

It was learned that very few CEO activists in Ghana leveraged economic power. Among the reasons why most participants shy away from flexing their economic muscles was (1) a feeling of powerlessness, relative to the Government of Ghana; (2) fear of attacks from various sources and actors within the society; (3) the feeling that it was not necessary yet to do so; (4) their inability to come together as a corporate collective to implement such joint actions; and (5) the feeling that it was too risky to put their companies in harm's way in such a high-stakes manner. However, most of them tended toward awareness-creation tactics. The findings further suggest several other classes of CEO activism tactics, hitherto not discussed in the literature on CEO activism.

These include such tactics as *intellectual activism, activism by living by example, activism by industry group representatives, naming and shaming, legal activism,* and variants of the tactic of leveraging economic power that could extend the meaning

Fig. 11.    CEO Activism Tactics. *Source:* Author (2023).

posited by Chatterji and Toffel (2018), such as the positive use of economic power in which CEO activists undertake to match government investments.

These findings on the tactics of CEO activists in Ghana effectively extend the literature on the tactical repertoire of CEO activists (see Chatterji & Toffel, 2018; Livonen, 2018). As explained, we found that none of the current postulates suffice in describing the tactics of CEO activists in Ghana. They proved insufficient, even when combined. This is because some context factors limit the ability of the participants to leverage economic power while encouraging the use of awareness creation and persuasion; disruption and protest; and support tactics. Thus, the literature is enriched by the identification of other tactics. I now contribute a more eclectic reflection of the tactical repertoire for activist CEOs to include legal activism, naming and shaming, living by example, and activism by industry group representatives.

Future studies could examine the uniqueness of these emergent tactics in other societies, with the view to more clearly defining them. Such studies could also consider aspects of the activist CEO's personal and corporate characteristics that either promoted or limited the deployment of such tactics. Scholars could also compare the extent to which wider social movements could employ some of the tactics employed by CEO activists, and vice versa.

### 10.3.4 CEO Activism Effects

In terms of the effects produced by CEO activists in Ghana, three main pathways of outcomes emerged. It was found that CEO activism had some impacts on the wider society. The practice also engendered some positive consequences for activist CEOs and their companies, while also being associated with some undesirable ramifications (see Fig. 12 below).

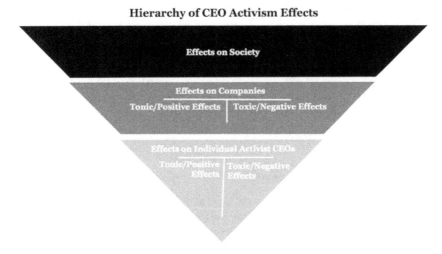

Fig. 12.   Hierarchy of CEO Activism Effects. *Source:* Author (2023).

Despite many examples of CEOs speaking out, the literature on the effects of their actions has been nonexistent outside non-Western contexts. In Western contexts, the effects on their actions have been thin.

What little we know has been limited to anecdotal evidence, media reportage and analysis, and suppositions/postulations by some scholars. Scholarly work on effects has been limited to organizational outcomes – purchase intents (see Dodd & Supa, 2015), brand preference, employee loyalty, and public opinion-related brand equity (see Chatterji & Toffel, 2018, 2019a).

This research study thus contributes to the literature by directly addressing Dodd and Supa's (2014) call for various research methods to be used in analyzing how various stakeholders are impacted by CSA. This research study offers a more comprehensive view of the effects of CEO activism, extending the literature in talking about a hierarchy of outcomes, offering a systematic analysis and discussion of the positive and negative effects of CEO activism, plus a model of these effects.

The findings in this section of the research study extend the current knowledge on the effects of CEO activism in remarkable ways. First, the findings in this research study introduce emerging market findings on CEO activism to the literature. The findings here are among the first to infuse the voices and lived experiences of women CEO activists to the literature on the field of CEO activism, thereby serving to provide some Black feminist perspectives to the current thought on CEO activism. Future studies could analyze CEO activism through the lens of Black/intersectional feminist theory.

This research study supplements this stream of literature by examining the influence of the CEO's political and social attitudes on societies, on companies, and CEOs. Arguably, the findings here serve to deepen what we now know about CEO activism by its discussion of distinct classes of effects of CEO activism on (1) the society, but also positive and negative effects on (2) companies, and (3) CEO activists. For the first time in the literature on CEO activism, we have a sense of some of the effects of CEO activism within the context of a developing country, such as Ghana. We are also brought to a place of a deeper knowledge of some of the positive and negative consequences of CEO activism on companies and on activist CEOs in a non-Western sociocultural context.

Such fresh findings and insights could serve as the springboard for future studies on the phenomenon, designed to delve deeper into examining facets of CEO activism at the Bottom of the Pyramid, or indeed, comparing systems of the effects of CEO activism between Western and non-Western societies.

### 10.3.5 CEO Activism Safeguards

Given the unpalatable consequences of CEO activism for both companies and CEO activists in Ghana, this research study was interested in examining some of the safeguards that practicing activist CEOs took to insulate themselves from such pitfalls. Six main classes of safeguards emerged, *including (1) personal safeguards, (2)*

*social safeguards, (3) communication-related safeguards, (4) CEO best practice*
*safeguards, (5) corporate safeguards*, and *(6) spiritual safeguards* (see Fig. 13 below).

Chatterji and Toffel (2019b) expressed two communication-related CEO
activism safeguards, namely (1) when to communicate and (2) how to communicate effectively. The findings in this research study concerning the safeguards of
CEO activism are supportive of some of the postulates of Chatterji and Toffel's
(2019b). However, many of the findings in this research study diverge from and/or
extend the extant postulations regarding what activist CEOs can do to insulate
themselves from the negative externalities of engaging in CEO activism.

Chatterji and Toffel's safeguards about "when" and "how" to communicate
issues relating to CEO activism tend to limit the range of precautionary measures
that CEO activists can take to only communication factors. The point however is
that CEO activism appears to be more cross-cutting and multifaceted, with
implications that extend beyond the protections that communication-related
factors afford.

Because the literature has not systematically focused on the negative effects of
CEO activism (especially on activist CEOs), the notion of safeguards has been
virtually absent in the literature. What scanty knowledge we have about such
safeguards have been limited to communication-related precautions (see Chatterji
& Toffel, 2019b) and various CEO activism playbooks (see Chatterji & Toffel,
2015, 2016, 2017, 2018, 2019). This research study contributes to the literature by
not only formally introducing the notion of CEO activism safeguards but also

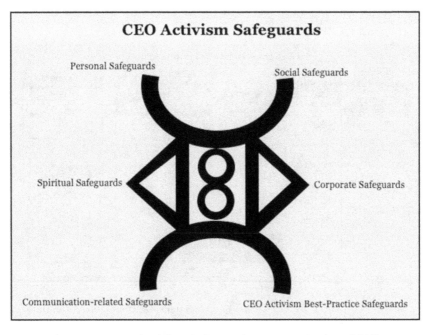

Fig. 13.    CEO Activism Safeguards. *Source:* Author (2023).

providing a model of six categories of safeguards, based on empirical evidence in Ghana.

Thus, the findings in this research study make a more realistic case for the multiplicity of life jackets that could help secure CEO activists in their actions. The safeguards reported in this research study make a more realistic argument for the range of protections available to CEO activists, as they reflect the lived experiences of CEO activists, some of whom have been engaged in CEO activism since the 1990s.

## 10.4 The CEO Activism Development Model

Based on a systematic literature review, mapping of the field of CEO activism, and findings in Ghana, I contribute a process model that explains the development of activist stances by CEOs. The model is a result of one of the most comprehensive single studies on CEO activism. The model identifies various sites of scholarly inquiry to guide future studies. The model is a temporal and dynamic way of talking about various themes in CEO activism. It is a conceptual framework that explains the development of CEO activism.

This framework (see Fig. 14 below) contains the main objectives of the five research questions, covered in this research study, namely: (1) motivations for CEO activism; (2) issues advocated for/against; (3) tactics employed in CEO activism; (4) effects of CEO activism; and (5) safeguards for CEO activism.

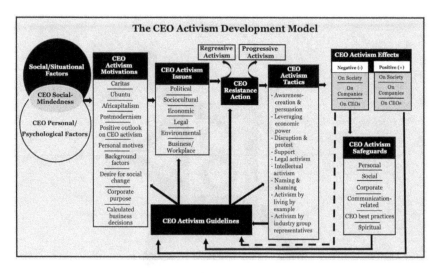

Fig. 14.   The CEO Activism Development Model. *Source:* Author (2023).

It further covers social/situational factors and personal/psychological factors that could influence the development of a social-mindedness of CEOs. Also covered are social resistance actions, which could be deemed to be progressive or regressive, as defined by Kotler and Sarkar (2017, 2018b).

As explained throughout this research study, this emergent CEO Activism Model (see Fig. 13 above) is a central finding of my grounded theory building work. Although it departs from prior literature – it is a novelty in the field of CEO activism research – it is also a contribution to the field of process studies in organization and management, by its consideration of the elements of temporality, activity, and flow in the development of the activist stance by CEOs (see Langley et al., 2009, 2013).

In its basic form (see Chapter One), it is the product of my review and reflection on the literature on CEO activism. However, it was fleshed out, revised, and extended throughout the fieldwork and data analysis. Its fivefold evolution was informed by the empirical findings from the fieldwork. In addition to incorporating insights, based on the responses from my informants, this developmental model for CEO activism was informed by my many returns to the literature to seek conceptual treatments of ideas triggered by conversations with my collaborators.

The above *CEO Activism Development Model* is a process model (see Langley et al., 2013) that depicts my conception of the interrelationships among several concepts in the development of CEO activism. Process model building, as conceptualized by Langley and colleagues (2009, 2013), is somewhat different from generic grounded theory building. This is because process model building focuses on events, and their causal interrelationships, and is attuned to temporal issues, order, sequencing, and flow.

This research study is designed to focus on the generation of empirical data on five clusters within these complex linkages, namely motivations for CEO activism, a taxonomy of sociopolitical issues, tactics of CEO activism, effects of CEO activism, classes of safeguards for CEO activists, and CEO activism guidelines. I argue for the genesis of CEO activism as occurring within the context of the production of a certain level of social-mindedness within the CEO, as a complex web of social and situational factors interact with some personal and psychological factors within the CEO. While, typically, CEOs have not been concerned with wider social issues that do not impact on the profitability of companies, the resultant social-mindedness conditions some CEOs to start thinking in a wider fashion, by considering noncorporate issues and the needs of multiple stakeholders besides investors/shareholders.

When this wider social-mindedness is strong enough, it leads to the development of some desire, appetite, or motivation for engaging in CEO activism. While some segments of the literature on CEO activism have suggested some motivations, there is no existing typology of factors that could be regarded as motivating CEO activists generally, but especially within developing countries. Thus, Chapter Three and Chapter Four focused on addressing this scholarly lacuna by gathering and presenting data on the motivations of CEOs in Ghana for becoming/engaging in CEO activism.

Once motivated to undertake CEO activism, the researcher reasons that the next step would be for CEOs to select a range of sociopolitical issues that would serve as the fulcrum for their activism. Kotler and Sarkar (2018a) posit that there are six classes of such issues that a brand could advocate. In their brand activism typology, these scholars identified political issues, social issues, economic issues, legal issues, environmental issues, and business/workplace issues. The researcher contends that such a typology could be reasonably adapted and extended to CEO activism. Thus, the focus of Chapter Five was to examine the extent to which the range of issues that activist CEOs selected for this study in Ghana could fit these brand activism categories/clusters postulated by Kotler and Sarkar (2017, 2018a).

I argue that once a CEO has identified an issue or a range of issues on which to pivot his/her activism, the main thrust of the CEO's resistance posture/action is generated. As explained earlier in the literature review, brand activism could be regressive or progressive, depending on how such an action is perceived as working to promote the interests of society.

However, the implementation of a CEO resistance action follows some tactics. While Chatterji and Toffel (2018) discussed approaches relating to raising awareness and leveraging economic power, Livonen (2018) isolated the three classes of approaches as persuasive tactics, disruptive/coercive tactics, and supportive tactics. Thus, Chapter Six examined the range of tactics employed by activist CEOs in Ghana who were selected for inclusion in this study.

The next web of factors in this model concerns the effects of engaging in CEO activism. What outcomes are produced by the works of CEO activists? What are the consequences of engaging in CEO activism for society, companies, and the activist CEO? Based on fieldwork, some scholars have identified some outcomes produced by CEO activism. However, these have all been within Western (American) contexts. What are the achievements and consequences of CEO activism in Ghana? The object of Chapter Seven was to investigate the effects, positive and negative consequences of CEO activism for Ghanaian society, but also on companies and activist CEOs in Ghana.

Within this conceptual framework (see Fig. 13 above), CEO activism is conceived as producing two distinct classes of outcomes – negative and positive effects. Negative outcomes are those undesirable consequences, while positive outcomes are relatively desirable results of CEO activism. The findings suggest that owing to their undesirable impact, CEO activists would employ a range of safeguards to insulate themselves and their companies from the effects of being CEO activists. The focus of Chapter Eight was to investigate the various types of safeguards employed by activist CEOs in Ghana.

It is noteworthy that the experiences drawn from both positive and negative consequences of CEO activism work to inform guidelines for future CEO actions. However, bitter experiences may do so either through the workings of present safeguards or not. The development and the nature of guidelines for future CEO actions are conceptualized as working in various ways and could serve to determine whether the CEO would continue to be motivated to take such actions. Second, such guidelines could determine whether future CEO actions are progressive or regressive. Finally, the researcher argues that guidelines could also inform the sort of tactics employed by a specific CEO activist in the future.

The final point in this conceptual framework relates to guidelines for engaging in CEO activism, as discussed in Chapter Nine. Positive effects for CEO activism are conceived as directly informing guidelines for CEO activism, while negative effects are first filtered through safeguards, on the way to informing guidelines for future actions. The nature of guidelines then determines (1) future motivations for engaging in CEO activism, (2) the choice of future issues/causes, and (3) future tactics employed.

Within this process model, CEO activism guidelines impact or influence four distinct sectors. The guidelines could determine whether activist CEOs would be motivated or disincentivized in taking future actions. Guidelines could also influence the selection of future issues or causes, determine whether the next courses of actions of the activist CEO would lean toward progressive activism or the regressive genre. Finally, CEO activism guidelines could inform future selection of tactics employed in CEO activism.

This research study contributes to several other theories and concepts. It contributes to the literature on Upper Echelons Theory that examines how the personal preferences of C-level executives and board members influence firm behavior (see Finkelstein & Hambrick, 1996; Hambrick & Mason, 1984). It is linked to the literature on how CEO beliefs, characteristics, and preferences affect organizational strategy (see Chen et al., 2014; Plambeck & Weber, 2009). It intersects with studies that focus on the effect of CEOs' political attitudes on business strategies such as CSR practices (e.g., Chin et al., 2013; Di Giuli & Kostovetsky, 2014). The research study contributes by setting forth a strong research agenda in the field of CEO activism and identifies various methods for such investigations.

## 10.5 Policy Implications

This research study has some implications for various policies, including corporate policy, communication policy, corporate governance, and business ethics.

For corporate policy, this research study has shown some important ways in which the practice of CEO activism could affect various organizational outcomes. The literature also points to the growing popularity of CEO activism, as an expression of brand responsibility. With such growing importance comes the need for companies to provide for various measures to manage diverse levers of the effects produced by CEO activism. The safeguards discussed in this research study could also set corporate leaders in the directions in which to think regarding how to effectively manage the fallouts of CEO activism.

This research study has some applications for communication policy. For example, the findings on the range of issues that CEO activists in Ghana reported could serve as some inspiration for companies that are seeking to provide policy guidelines regarding the issues or causes that their CEOs could pursue, as part of their social resistance actions. Again, the section on the tactics described could serve as guidelines for communication departments or practitioners who find themselves having to prescribe communication directions for a CEO activist's campaigns.

Indications are that most boards of directors are not very familiar with the practice of CEO activism and tend to resist CEOs who decide to undertake CEO activism. Some corporate governance implications include helping boards of directors to understand relevant aspects of CEO activism such as the motivations of CEOs, issues to be selected, tactical repertoire, effects of CEO activism, and the possible safeguards to employ. It also contributes by providing evidence-based guidelines for safe and effective CEO activism campaigns. This research study foreshadows a rulebook/playbook for CEO activism, tailor-made for the Global South.

In terms of business ethics, this research study is a small step in helping more businesses to better understand another way in which to become more socially and authentically responsible to more stakeholders than powerful owners of capital.

## 10.6 Some Limitations and Further Research Agenda

Despite the useful insights gleaned, this study is far from being an ideal inquiry. This research study is associated with several shortcomings. As a qualitative study, while it has provided some useful depth of information about the various research questions, the findings are only relevant to the participants of this study. Besides, the participants were purposively selected. The findings are thus far from generalizable.

The data were collected from participants in the non-Western context of Ghana. Thus, the findings may not hold for CEO activists in a different socio-cultural context. Indeed, the findings may not even hold for the same participants interviewed by different researchers at a different time because the analysis entailed some reflexivity and interpretation by this researcher.

The philosophical approach to this research is a postmodern orientation that recognizes the interests of multiple stakeholders, instead of those of only investors. Similar research undertaken from the modernist approach could present markedly different findings.

This study is by no means exhaustive in covering every facet of the phenomenon of CEO activism. Scholarship on CEO activism is still in its infancy, with many aspects of the phenomenon yet to be studied. CEO activism is still in its nascence, both as a field of practice and a line of scholarly inquiry.

The field provides some interesting prospects for further research and presents some intriguing debates that pull together various theoretical domains such as Caritas, Africapitalism, postmodernism, and feminist media theory and gender theory. With the inclusion of the experiences of women activist CEOs in Ghana, this research study only scratches the surface in contributing to feminist theory, especially the strands of feminist theory pertaining to intersectionality and African feminist thought. Drawing from these strands would enable a more in-depth feminist theoretical analysis of the experiences and choices of women CEOs in Ghana. A stronger theory-based, gender-centric analysis systematically examining the behaviors and motives of men and women activists is advisable as well. Unlike most studies, mine sought to include women CEO activists and elicit their motives; however, future work to develop a framework and elicit questions to better understand gendered views and initiatives is recommended.

Scholars are still grappling with the relationship between CEO activism and the specific ways in which it impacts companies. Thus, future CEO effects studies may focus on the many ways in which CEO activism is related to such organizational outcomes such as employee morale, employee loyalty, customer brand preference, and brand equity.

The practice of CEO activism is situation/context-specific. Thus, future studies could investigate how desirable and undesirable environmental conditions shape various facets of the practice of CEO activism.

There appear to be some corporate governance issues that are animated by the practice of CEO activism. Scholars may want to examine how CEO activism and various mandates of boards of directors are interlinked.

Increasingly, we are learning about the importance of "Kitchen Cabinets" in various aspects of the practice of CEO activism. Future studies could consider various factors that promote or impede the role of such insider allies in the works of CEO activists.

In the CEO Activism Development Model presented in this research study, I trace the roots for the development of activist stances by CEO as a product of the interaction between social factors and personal factors within individual CEOs, which produce a certain form of "CEO Social-Mindedness." While this "CEO Social-Mindedness" could be seen as akin to the age-old nature-nurture debate, it is still unclear as to the exact nature of this phenomenon among CEOs. Future research could examine the specific pathways through which "CEO Social-Mindedness" evokes in CEOs the desire to become activists. Is there one monolithic form of "CEO Social-Mindedness" or does it present on various forms and gradations? Some scholars could examine the connections between "CEO Social-Mindedness" and various expressions of CEO activism.

Currently, we do not know much about the connection between the externally focused social resistance actions of CEO activists and related issues/causes they pursue within their organizations. Future studies could investigate the relations between what actions CEO activists take for the society, vis-à-vis what causes they pursue within their organizations.

So far, there have hardly been any studies that have employed textual analysis of external-facing communications of CEO activists. Future studies could employ discourse analysis, in ascertaining various facts about the messages relayed by CEO activists in their campaigns.

## 10.7 Implications for the Practice of CEO Activism

Without a doubt, CEO activism is an emerging phenomenon that scholars are yet to fully scope out, conceptualize, and operationalize. While some scholars have contributed to the idea of having some guidelines that could guide the successful implementation of CEO activism in general, most of the current proposals pertain to Western sociocultural contexts. This is because, to date, virtually all studies on the phenomenon have been situated in Western/American contexts.

Countries in the developing world have unique political, cultural, social, and other situational factors that could make some of the extant guidelines to be of null effect. Among the motives of this research study is the development of a playbook to guide the successful implementation of CEO activism, especially in the developing world. Indeed, this researcher contends that many CEOs in the developing world are yet to embrace their evolving role as activists, partly because they do not fully understand how to effectively perform such roles. It is hoped that with the development of such a playbook, the current mystique surrounding CEO activism would be stripped away while providing activist CEOs in the emerging markets of Africa with a powerful arsenal of situationally developed toolkits to enable them better perform their role as activist CEOs.

Based on their experiences as activist CEOs, the participants in this study were asked to suggest some guidelines that other CEOs desiring to become activists could follow to assure more effective or successful social resistance actions. The following pointers were some of the critical success factors for engaging in successful CEO activism, within the context of a developing society such as Ghana.

The informants shared the view that a major guideline that any CEO who wants to become an activist ought to follow is to convince himself or herself that it is a course of action he/she wants to do. Many of the informants spoke of the need for the activist CEO to be triply sure that they feel called to engage in activism.

Several participants noted that they tended to be carried away sometimes in their resistance actions. Some collaborators urged activist CEOs to set some boundaries, beyond which they ought not to extend their actions.

Several participants underscored the need for all activist CEOs to become very knowledgeable about what it means to be a citizen, rather than a spectator. This is because of the overwhelming belief among participants that the bedrock of any activism is a sense of patriotism and citizenship.

The participants in this study were unanimous in expressing the view that a supremely important guideline for successful CEO activism in Ghana is that such activities ought to be based on authenticity and truth. The participants made the point that activism that is contrived would not be successful because members of an activist's strategic constituency would be discerning enough to see through any multiple layers of deceit and selfish motive.

Several participants indicated the importance of timing in ensuring that campaign messages were heard. For these informants, the right message delivered at the wrong time would not be as successful as an aptly timed message.

Many informants pointed to the importance of profiting from the experiences of other CEO activists. In expressing this view, they called for current and future CEO activists to have access to some publications and guidelines or documented cases of the works of other CEO activists.

It turned out that, for some participants, corporate and CEO activism was a core part of the corporate strategy. For instance, it emerged that, right from the incorporation of one of the firms led by a participant, activism was identified as one of the ways of positioning and promoting the company. Some informants revealed that, besides according the role of activism the needed level of legitimacy of corporate affairs, doing so made it a central activity within the corporate strategy. Others spoke of benefits and attributes of an activism-embedded strategic focus as including working to provide some consistency, authenticity, and budgetary support for the initiatives.

For some of the CEOs in this study, besides the need for authenticity, guidelines for successful CEO activism ought to include a strong self-belief and belief in the cause. It emerged that the value of having a strong belief and personal conviction could be found in the ability of these attributes to provide staying power for a long-term campaign.

Among the most popular guidelines for successful CEO activism shared by some informants are the importance of taking the middle line, communicating clearly, being able to defend one's position, based on facts, and showing objectivity by being apolitical.

Many participants underscored the need for CEO activists to select their issues properly, to assure some success for campaigns. For the informants that shared this view, accurate issue selection was important because of the plethora of possible causes and the limited resources available. In this regard, Senyo Hosi advocated for activist CEOs to have a "signature advocacy" that would help to define the image and public persona of the CEO activist.

Some participants spoke about the importance of the modern CEO developing a keen sense of his/her social environment, based on the realization of a strong interconnectedness between the company and the wider operating context. Other participants shared the idea that it made business sense to think beyond the narrow confines of a company's profit motive.

For some informants, guidelines for CEO activism in Ghana or Africa should include the caution for neophyte CEO activists to prepare for huge doses of not only hypocrisy but also duplicity, not only from sworn opponents but also from those that vaunt their support for the activist CEO.

For some participants, an important guideline for assuring success in CEO activism relates to the need to carefully study and understand various factors, motivations, and attributes of the target audiences.

The informants in this study noted that a useful guideline that CEOs must follow in engaging in successful activism is for them to come to the table with clean hands. Thus, the informant noted that it is important for all activist CEOs to lead by example in ensuring that every web and tissue of their operation is above reproach. Besides the sheer propriety of the activism itself being authentic and above board, every other aspect of the business operations and personal life of the activist CEO needs to be, as far as possible, blameless.

Another theme that emerged regarding guidelines for engaging in successful CEO activism is the need for the development and embedding of corporate principles at the core of every corporate activity. In this regard, the suggestion is that CEO or corporate activism ought not to be a knee-jerk (re)action. This is because such corporate purposes would have been long-established and set in ways that effectively define those issues on which the company would agitate, should such issues be threatened within the social system. Importantly, it stands to reason that such ideals that underpin the business – the overriding corporate purpose(es) – ought to precede and drive every nature of corporate or CEO activism.

Several informants underscored the value of having and deploying a varied arsenal of strategies and tactics. For instance, some indicated the need for alliances and coalition-building and deploying various media vehicles.

Besides the fact that CEO activism ought to be driven by deliberate and well-established corporate purpose(s), it also emerged that a useful playbook for CEO activism ought to involve the setting of various scenarios. Such scenarios set should be based on several factors, among which is effective stakeholder mapping and the performance of issues analysis and sensitivity testing of how various strategic constituents would be impacted by or react to various risk issues within the social system.

It turned out that CEO activism was rarely seen as a solo or individual activity. Most of the participants disclosed that various significant others influenced their activities.

It was found that many of the CEOs in this study thought that an important guideline for effective CEO activism in Ghana involved the employment of flexibility in practically every facet of activist campaigns.

Many of the informants think that an important guideline for effective CEO activism is for the CEO to always have the presence of mind in leaving no stone unturned in reinforcing previous statements made.

It emerged that, although CEO activism was strongly driven by the personal convictions of the CEO, the participants in this study still saw the need to carry their employees along, as much as possible through various internal communications.

Several informants saw the need for CEOs to be ready to start activist campaigns, even if on a small scale. For those that shared this view, many campaigns remain paralyzed and unborn because of the perception that some activist CEOs have about every campaign being huge. Thus, some informants saw the need to start small sometimes, and then scale up whenever necessary.

Other informants stressed the importance of goal setting, monitoring, and evaluation of significant aspects of activist campaigns. These participants emphasized that the same rigor and performance-driven approach to business management ought to be applied to activism campaigns. They also urged activist CEOs to be strategic about their campaigns, measure the success/effectiveness of their efforts, and review their goals periodically.

A few informants shared the view that a vital guideline for effective CEO activism concerned being perceived not as an unnecessary nagger, but as one who genuinely cared about the society and was proffering workable solutions for social transformation and the benefit of all.

Some of the informants stressed the importance of personal development for CEOs who want to engage in activism. For some of the participants in the study, this is important because one cannot provide for others what one does not have.

Therefore, an important guideline for CEO activism is for CEOs themselves to keep preparing and developing themselves, as much as possible.

It was found that virtually all participants in this study were of the view that CEO activism ought not to be a solo activity. Thus, for many participants, an important success factor in CEO activism revolved around the need to create what some described as "a coalition of the willing." By this, they were referring to the need for the CEO activist to have a group of like-minded people and organizations who can help with various aspects of the campaign, from legwork to brainwork.

It was found that the participants in this study saw the importance of activist CEOs in Ghana developing a mindset of supporting other CEO activists as an important element in a playbook for successful CEO activism in Ghana. Some of the informants underscored the need for unity and support for other CEOs, even when there is a disagreement with whatever causes they are pursuing or fighting for. For the CEOs that shared this viewpoint, the common connecting thread that should bind all activist CEOs together is the fact that they are activists and the fact that there is a shared commitment to risk themselves in the fight for the common good and the upliftment of humanity.

An important guideline that emerged is the call by some of the participants for CEOs to be mindful of the fact that CEO activism was not for everyone, even though activism was seen as an important role of the modern CEO. Some participants noted that it was important for a CEO to have developed a credible personal brand and public profile before seeking to positively impact society through an activism campaign.

Some of the participants noted that an important principle in ensuring impactful CEO activism was the courage to select controversial issues and the conviction to speak truth to power. In reflecting on the importance of courage, several CEOs in this study indicated the importance of self-belief and not paying heed to discouraging comments from others who may not have the same level of understanding and belief in the issues/causes being pursued by the activist CEO.

Several participants in this study indicated that in undertaking activism, CEOs in Ghana ought to be mindful of the fact that activism was a risky activity and to take steps to manage or minimize the risks involved.

## 10.8 Epilog

This research study was energized by the mission of reimaging current scholarship on CEO activism by considering some alternative approaches. The overall goal was to address the perceived dearth of scholarly research on the phenomenon of CEO activism.

In pursuit of this goal, this study had a differentiation strategy at various layers. A deliberate decision was made to select a non-Western context, adopt a nonquantitative method, have parity of the voices and lived experiences of both men and women activist CEOs, and to approach the phenomenon from a postmodern perspective, among others. The various theoretical lenses that guided the inquiry included the notions of Caritas and Ubuntu philosophy and Public Relations practice, Africapitalism, and ideas surrounding postmodern values in public relations.

A qualitative research design that involved long interviews with 24 purposively selected CEO activists in Ghana. Some participants were also selected, using snowball sampling. Data analysis followed the phenomenological theme-based method set forth by van Manen (2016, 1997).

Among the findings included the identification of new motivations, hitherto alien to the literature on CEO activism, such as Caritas, Ubuntu philosophy, Africapitalism, and selected postmodern values. It was found that the categories suggested by Kotler and Sarkar (2017, 2018a) were appropriate in serving as clusters for the range of causes and issues advocated for/against by the activist CEOs in Ghana.

Regarding the tactics of CEO activism, it was learned that the extant postulates of Chatterji and Toffel (2018) and Livonen (2018) were both inadequate (whether separately or in combination) in reflecting the range of tactics employed by CEO activists in Ghana. Although these extant classes of tactics were combined into a new classificatory scheme of tactics that comprised (1) leveraging economic power; (2) awareness creation and persuasion tactics; (3) disruption and protest tactics; and (4) support tactics, it did not suffice.

It was found that activist CEOs in Ghana predominantly employed awareness creation and persuasion tactics to a great extent, although some reported disruption and protest tactics, and some support tactics. The tactic of leveraging economic power was found to be employed to a minimal extent, for various reasons.

The findings further suggest several other classes of CEO activism tactics, hitherto not discussed in the literature on CEO activism. These include such tactics as "intellectual activism," "activism by living by example," "activism by industry group representatives," "naming and shaming," "legal activism," and variants of the tactic of leveraging economic power that could extend the meaning posited by Chatterji and Toffel (2018), such as the positive use of economic power in which CEO activists undertake to match government investments.

CEO activism was found to produce various categories of effects with various consequences in Ghana. CEO activism was found to be associated with some improvements to society, as well as some consequences for companies and CEO activists. It was found that the CEO activists employed six categories of safeguards to protect themselves from the undesirable consequences of CEO activism. These safeguards included personal safeguards, communication-related safeguards, CEO activism best practice safeguards, social safeguards, spiritual safeguards, and corporate safeguards.

Some guidelines are provided to inform safe and more effective CEO activism campaigns. In the tradition of process studies of change in organization and management, which privilege the elements of temporality, activity, and flow (Langley et al., 2009, 2013), a conceptual framework is also provided to explain, in broad strokes, various links in the development of CEO activism in Ghana that could be applied within other contexts.

# References

Adae, E. K. (2020). *Beyond corporate profits: Reminiscing about the future of CEO activism in Ghana.* Doctoral dissertation, School of Journalism and Communication, University of Oregon. https://scholarsbank.uoregon.edu/xmlui/handle/1794/25924

Adae, E. K. (2021a). Brewed in the African pot: Examining the influences of Caritas, Ubuntu, Africapitalism, and postmodern values on CEO activism in Ghana. In D. Pompper (Ed.), *Public relations for social responsibility (communicating responsible diversity, equality, and inclusion)* (pp. 83–100). Emerald Publishing Limited. https://doi.org/10.1108/978-1-80043-167-620211006

Adae, E. K. (2021b). Weightier matters: Examining CEO activism issues in Ghana's non-Western context. *Janus Head Journal of Interdisciplinary Studies in Literature, Continental Philosophy, Phenomenological Psychology, and the Arts, 19*(1), 39–59. https://doi.org/10.5840/jh20211914

Adae, E. K., Kosiba, J. P., Twum, K., Hinson, R. E., Newman, N., & Nutsugah, F. (Eds.). (2021). *Responsible management in emerging economies: A multisectoral focus.* Palgrave-Macmillan.

Adams, P. (2019, July 8). The year of 'woke-washing': How tone-deaf activism risks eroding brands. https://www.marketingdive.com/news/the-year-of-woke-washing-how-tone-deaf-activism-risks-eroding-brands/557606/

Adegbite, E., Daodu, O., & Wood, J. (2020). Will Africapitalism work? *Africa Journal of Management, 6*(4), 419–434. https://doi.org/10.1080/23322373.2020.1830697

Adler, N. J. (1997). *International dimensions of organizational behavior.* South-Western College Press.

Adu-Gyamerah, E. (2010, August 5). Parliament approves STX deal. https://www.modernghana.com/news/287876/parliament-approves-stx-deal.html

African Development Bank (AfDB). (2019). African Economic Outlook 2019: Macroeconomic performance and prospects (Jobs, growth, and firm dynamism – Integration for Africa's economic prosperity). https://www.afdb.org/fileadmin/uploads/afdb/Documents/Publications/2019AEO/AEO_2019-EN.pdf

Althusser, L. (1971). *Lenin and philosophy and other essays* (B. Brewster, Trans.). New Left Books.

Amaeshi, K. (2018). Africapitalism: Rethinking the role of business in Africa. https://www.tonyelumelufoundation.org/research-publications/africapitalism-rethinking-the-role-of-business-in-africa-by-prof-kenneth-amaeshi

Amaeshi, K., & Idemudia, U. (2015). Africapitalism: A management idea for business in Africa? *Africa Journal of Management, 1*(2), 210–223. https://doi.org/1080/23322373.2015.1026229

Amoah, G. (2019, May 21). Ayawaso West Wuogon shooting: Government is yet to compensate me – Victim. https://www.myjoyonline.com/ayawaso-west-wuogon-shooting-government-is-yet-to-compensate-me-victim/

Asante, M. K. (1987). *The Afrocentric idea.* Temple University Press.

Asante, M. K. (1989). *Afrocentricity.* Africa World Press.

Asante, M. K. (2003). *Afrocentricity: The theory of social change.* African American Images.

Asante, M. K. (2007). *An Afrocentric manifesto.* Polity Press.

Asante, M. K. (2017). *Revolutionary pedagogy: Primer for teachers of Black children.* Universal Write Publications.

Asante, M. K., & Dove, N. (2021). *Being human being: Transforming the race discourse.* Universal Write Publications.

Audi, R. (2009). Nationalism, patriotism, and cosmopolitanism in an age of globalization. *The Journal of Ethics, 13,* 365–381. https://doi.org/10.1007/s10892-009-9068-9

Austin, N., Gaither, B., & Gaither, T. K. (2019). Corporate social advocacy as public interest communications: Exploring perceptions of corporate involvement in controversial social-political issues. *The Journal of Public Interest Communications, 3*(2), 3–31. https://doi.org/10.32473/jpic.v3.i2.p3

Awanyo, L., & Attua, M. E. (2016). A paradox of three decades of neoliberal economic reforms in Ghana: A tale of economic growth and uneven regional development. *African Geographical Review, 37*(3), 173–191. https://doi.org/10.1080/19376812.2016.1245152

Badri, B., & Tripp, A. M. (2017). *Women's activism in Africa: Struggles for rights and representation.* Zed Books.

Baker, S. (2002). The theoretical ground for public relations practice and ethics: A Koehnian analysis, *Journal of Business Ethics, 35*(3), 191–205. https://doi.org/10.1023/A:1013876206176

Banerjee, S. B. (2008). Corporate social responsibility: The good, the bad and the ugly. *Critical Sociology, 34*(1), 51–79. https://doi.org/10.1177/0896920507084623

Baudrillard, J. (1975). *The mirror of production.* Telos Press.

Baur, D. (2011). *NGOs as legitimate partners of corporations. A political conceptualization.* Springer.

Baur, D., & Wettstein, F. (2016). CSR's new challenge: Corporate political advocacy. In M. C. Coutinho de Arruda & B. Rok (Eds.), *Understanding ethics and responsibilities in a globalizing world* (pp. 171–187). Springer Publishing.

Best, S., & Kellner, D. (1991). *Postmodern theory. Critical interrogations.* Guilford Press.

Boyne, R., & Rattansi, A. (1990). The theory and politics of postmodernism: By way of an introduction. In R. Boyne & A. Rattansi (Eds.), *Postmodernism and society.* Macmillan.

Branicki, L., Brammer, S., & Pullen, A. (2021). The morality of "new" CEO activism. *Journal of Business Ethics.* https://doi.org/10.1007/s10551-020-04656-5

Brinkman, S. (2018). The interview. In N. S. Denzin & Y. S. Lincoln (Eds.), *Sage handbook of qualitative research* (5th ed., pp. 576–599). Sage.

Brinkman, S., & Kvale, S. (2015). *InterViews: Learning the craft of qualitative research interviewing* (3rd ed.). Sage.

Briscoe, F., Chin, M. K., & Hambrick, D. C. (2014). CEO ideology as an element of the corporate Opportunity structure for social activists. *Academy of Management Journal, 57,* 1786–1809. https://doi.org/10.5465/amj.2013.0255

Brundtland, G. H. (1994). What is world prosperity? *Business Strategy Review, 5*, 57–69. https://doi.org/10.1111/j.1467-8616.1994.tb00077.x

Buckle, D. (1999). Fifty years of public relations in Sub-Saharan Africa. Address to the International Section, Public Relations Society of America, November 3, London.

Business Roundtable. (2019, August 19). Business Roundtable redefines the purpose of a corporation to promote 'An economy that serves all Americans.' https://www.businessroundtable.org/business-roundtable-redefines-the-purpose-of-a-corporation-to-promote-an-economy-that-serves-all-americans

Carroll, A. B. (1999). Corporate social responsibility: Evolution of a definitional construct. *Business & Society, 38*(3), 268–295. https://doi.org/10.1177/000765039903800303

Cartwright, M. (2019, March 5). Ghana empire. Ancient History Encyclopedia. https://www.ancient.eu/Ghana_Empire/

Casadesus-Masanelli, R., & Ricart, J. E. (2010). From strategy to business models and onto tactics. *Long Range Planning, 2*(3), 195–215. https://doi.org/10.1016/j.lrp.2010.01.004

Champion, S., & Short, D. (2003). *The world's greatest religions: An anthology of sacred texts*. Dover Publications.

Chatterji, A. K. (2016, July 16). Why Apple's Tim Cook and other CEOs are speaking out on police shootings. http://fortune.com/2016/07/16/apple-tim-cook-blacklivesmatter/

Chatterji, A. K., & Toffel, M. W. (2015, March 24). Starbucks' "race together" campaign and the upside of CEO activism. https://hbr.org/2015/03/starbucks-race-together-campaign-and-the-upside-of-ceo-activism

Chatterji, A. K., & Toffel, M. W. (2016). The power of CEO activism. https://www.nytimes.com/2016/04/03/opinion/sunday/the-power-of-ceo-activism.html?_r=0

Chatterji, A. K., & Toffel, M. W. (2017). *Do CEO activists make a difference? Evidence from a field experiment*. Harvard Business School Working Paper, No. 16-100, March 2016. https://dash.harvard.edu/bitstream/handle/1/26274858/16-100.pdf?sequence=1&isAllowed=y

Chatterji, A. K., & Toffel, M. W. (2018, January – March). The new CEO Activists. *Harvard Business Review*, 78–89. https://hbr.org/2018/01/the-new-ceo-activists

Chatterji, A. K., & Toffel, M. W. (2019a). Assessing the impact of CEO activism. *Organization and Environment, 32*(2), 159–185. https://doi.org/10.1177/1086026619848144

Chatterji, A. K., & Toffel, M. W. (2019b, February 22). The right and wrong way to do 'CEO activism'. https://www.wsj.com/articles/the-right-and-wrong-way-to-do-ceo-activism-11550874530

Chen, G., Crossland, C., & Luo, S. (2014). Making the same mistake all over again: CEO overconfidence and corporate resistance to corrective feedback. *Strategic Management Journal, 36*, 1513–1535.

Chin, M. K., Hambrick, D. C., & Trevino, L. K. (2013). Political ideologies of CEOs: The influence of executives' values on corporate social responsibility. *Administrative Science Quarterly, 58*, 197–232. https://doi.org/10.1177/0001839213486

Ciszek, E. L., & Curtin, C. A. (2020). Toys aren't just toys: The cash value of Critical Theory and Research to Public Relations Practice in an environment of increasing public expectations for CEO activism. *A working paper accepted for presentation at the International Public Relations Research Conference* (Orlando, USA, March 2020).

Ciszek, E. L., & Logan, N. (2018). Challenging the dialogic promise: How Ben & Jerry's support for Black Lives Matter fosters dissensus on social media, *Journal of Public Relations Research, 30*(3), 115–127. https://doi.org/10.1080/1062726X.2018 .1498342

Citi Newsroom. (2019, December 1). Government cancels December 17 referendum. https://citinewsroom.com/2019/12/govt-cancels-december-17-referendum/

Clift, B., & Woll, C. (2012). Economic patriotism: Reinventing control over open markets, *Journal of European Public Policy, 19*(3), 307–323. httsp://doi.org/ 10.1080/13501763.2011.638117

Coe, M. (2004). *Compendium of the social doctrine of the church.* United States Conference of Catholic Bishops.

Coombs, W. T., & Holladay, S. J. (2009). Corporate social responsibility: Missed opportunity for institutionalizing communication practice? *International Journal of Strategic Communication, 3*(2), 93–101. https://doi.org/10.1080/1553118090 2805445

Coombs, W. T., & Holladay, S. J. (2012). *Managing corporate social responsibility: A communication approach.* Wiley-Blackwell.

Corbett, G. (2012a). Final candidates for a modern definition of public relations. http://prdefinition.prsa.org

Corbett, G. (2012b). *[Letter to membership].* Public Relations Association of America.

Corbin, J., & Strauss, A. (1990). Grounded theory research: Procedures, canons, and evaluative criteria. *Qualitative Sociology, 13*, 3–21. https://doi.org/10.1007/ BF00988593

Council of Europe. (2017). HRE and activism. http://www.coe.int/en/web/compass/ hre-and-activism

Cronin, A. M. (2018). *Public relations capitalism: Promotional culture, publics, and commercial democracy.* Palgrave Macmillan.

Crook, S., Pakulski, J., & Waters, M. (1992). *Postmodernization. Changes in advanced society.* Sage.

Dahlsrud, A. (2008). How corporate social responsibility is defined: An analysis of 37 definitions. *Corporate Social Responsibility and Environmental Management, 15*(1), 1–13. https://doi.org/10.1002/csr.132

Dartey-Baah, K. (2015). Political leadership in Ghana: 1957 to 2010. *African Journal of Political Science and International Relations, 9*(2), 49–61. https://doi.org/10.5897/ AJPSIR2014.0730

Dauvergne, P. (2017). Is the power of brand-focused activism rising? The case of tropical deforestation. *The Journal of Environment & Development, 26*(2), 135–155. https://doi.org/10.1177/1070496517701249

Davis, K. (1973). The case for and against business assumption of social responsibilities. *Academy of Management Journal, 16*, 312–322. https://doi.org/ 10.2307/255331

Daymon, C., & Holloway, I. (2002). Interviews. In *Qualitative research methods in public relations and marketing communications* (pp. 166–185). Routledge.

De Beer, A., & Mersham, G. (2004). Public relations in South Africa: A communication tool for change. In D. Tilson & E. Alozie (Eds.), *Towards the common good: Perspectives in international public relations* (pp. 320–340). Allyn & Bacon.

Deetz, S. A. (1992). Democracy in an age of corporate colonization. In *Developments in communication and the politics of everyday life*. State University of New York Press.

Deetz, S. A. (2001). Conceptual foundations. In F. M. Jablin & L. L. Putnam (Eds.), *The new handbook of organizational communication. Advances in theory, research, and methods* (pp. 3–46). Sage.

Deleuze, G., & Guattari, F. (1983). *Anti-oedipus*. University of Minnesota Press.

Delmas, M. A., Lyon, T. P., & Maxwell, J. W. (2019). Understanding the role of the corporation in sustainability transitions. *Organization & Environment*, *32*, 87–97. https://doi.org/10.1177/1086026619848255

Deloitte. (2015). *Women in the boardroom: A global perspective*. Deloitte Touche Tohmatsu Limited. https://www2.deloitte.com/content/dam/Deloitte/global/ Documents/Risk/gx-ccg-women-in-the-boardroom.pdf

Denzin, N. K., & Lincoln, Y. S. (2018). Introduction – The discipline and practice of qualitative research. In Denzin N. S. & Lincoln, Y. S. (Eds.), *Sage handbook of qualitative research* (5th ed., pp. 1–26). Sage.

Derville, T. (2005). Radical activist tactics: Overturning public relations conceptualizations. *Public Relations Review*, *31*, 527–533. https://doi.org/10.1016/ j.pubrev.2005.08.012

Di Giuli, A., & Kostovetsky, L. (2014). Are red or blue companies more likely to go green? Politics and corporate social responsibility. *Journal of Financial Economics*, *111*, 158–180.

DiMaggio, P., & Powell, W. W. (1983). The iron cage revisited: Institutional isomorphism and collective rationality in organizational fields. *American Sociological Review*, *48*(2), 147–160. https://doi.org/10.2307/2095101

Docherty, T. (Ed.). (1993). *Postmodernism. A reader*. Columbia University Press.

Dodd, M. D. (2016, April 18). Corporate activism: The new challenge for an age-old question. https://instituteforpr.org/corporate-activism-new-challenge-age-old-question/

Dodd, M. D., & Supa, D. W. (2014). Conceptualizing and measuring "corporate social advocacy" communication: Examining the impact of corporate financial performance. *Public Relations Journal*, *8*(3), 2–22.

Dodd, M. D., & Supa, D. (2015). Testing the viability of corporate social advocacy as a predictor of purchase intention. *Communication Research Reports*, *32*(4), 287–293. https://doi.org/10.1080/08824096.2015.1089853

Dozier, D. M., Grunig, J. E., & Grunig, L. A. (1995). *Manager's guide to excellence in public relations and communication management*. Lawrence Erlbaum Associates, Inc.

Dozier, D. M., & Lauzen, M. M. (2000). Liberating the intellectual domain from the practice: Public relations, activism, and the role of the scholar. *Journal of Public Relations Research*, *12*, 3–22. https://doi.org/10.1207/S1532754XJPRR1201_2

Duggar, W. M. (1989). *Corporate hegemony*.

Duncan, J., & Duncan, N. (2001). Sense of place as a positional good: Locating Bedford in place and time. In P. C. Adams, S. Hoelscher, & K. Till (Eds.), *Textures of place: Exploring humanist geographies*, 41–54. University of Minnesota Press.

Edgett, R. (2002). Toward an ethical framework for advocacy in public relations. *Journal of Public Relations Research*, *14*(1), 1–26. https://doi.org/10.1207/S1532754XJPRR1401_1

Eisenhardt, K. M. (1989). Building theories from case study research. *Academy of Management Review*, *14*(4), 532–550. https://doi.org/10.2307/258557

Elkington, J. B. (1999). *Cannibals with forks: The triple bottom line of the 21$^{st}$ century business*. Capstone.

Elkington, J. B. (2018, June 25). 25 years ago I coined the phrase "triple bottom line." Here's why it's time to rethink it. https://hbr.org/2018/06/25-years-ago-i-coined-the-phrase-triple-bottom-line-heres-why-im-giving-up-on-it

Elumelu, T. O. (2012). The path to economic prosperity and social wealth. http://www.heirsholdings.com/wp-content/uploads/2013/04/Africapitalism-Path-to-Economic-Prosperity-and-Social-Wealth. pdf

Englander, M. (2012). The interview: Data collection in descriptive phenomenological human scientific research. *Journal of Phenomenological Psychology*, *43*(1), 13–35. https://doi.org/10.1163/156916212X632943

Enoch, S. (2007). A greener Potemkin village? Corporate social responsibility and the limits of growth. *Capitalism Nature Socialism*, *18*(2), 79–90. https://doi.org/10.1080/10455750701366485

Eribon, D. (1991). *Michel Foucault*. Harvard University Press.

Featherstone, M. (1991). *Consumer culture and postmodernism*. Sage.

Finkelstein, S., & Hambrick, D. C. (1996). *Strategic leadership: Top executives and their effects on organizations*. South-Western College.

Foster, J. B. (2000). *Marx's ecology: Materialism and nature*. New York University Press.

Foucault, M. (1980). *The history of sexuality*. Vintage Books.

Foucault, M. (1988a). Power and sex. In L. D. Kritzman (Ed.), *Michel Foucault politics, philosophy, culture* (pp. 110–124). Routledge.

Foucault, M. (1988b). Social security. In L. D. Kritzman (Ed.), *Michel Foucault: Politics, philosophy, culture* (pp. 15–177). Routledge.

Friedman, M. (1970, September 13). The social responsibility of business is to make a profit. *New York Times Magazine*, pp. 32–33, 122, 126.

Friedman, M. (2007). *The social responsibility of business is to increase its profits*. Springer.

Gaines-Ross, L. (2017, October 2). What CEO activism looks like in the Trump era. https://hbr.org/2017/10/what-ceo-activism-looks-like-in-the-trump-era

Gaines-Ross, L. (2016, June 23). Is it safe for CEOs to voice strong political opinions? https://hbr.org/2016/06/is-it-safe-for-ceos-to-voice-strong-political-opinions

Gartenberg, C., & Serafeim, G. (2019, August 20). 181 top CEOs have realized companies need a purpose beyond profit. https://hbr.org/2019/08/181-top-ceos-have-realized-companies-need-a-purpose-beyond-profit

Global Strategy Group. (2016, January). *Business and politics: Do they mix?* http://www.globalstrategygroup.com/wp-content/uploads/2016/01/GSG-2016-Business-and-Politics-Study_1-27-16-002.pdf

Gunther, J. (1955). *Inside Africa*. Harper and Brothers.

Guth, D., & Marsh, C. (2005). *Adventures in public relations: Case studies and critical thinking*. Allyn & Bacon.

Haider-Markel, D. P., & Meier, K. J. (1996). The politics of gay and lesbian rights: Expanding the scope of the conflict. *The Journal of Politics, 58*(2), 332–349. https://doi.org/10.2307/2960229

Hambrick, D. C., & Mason, P. A. (1984). Upper echelons: The organization as a reflection of its top managers. *Academy of Management Review, 9*, 193–206. https://doi.org/10.2307/258434

Hambrick, D. C., & Wowak, A. (2021). *CEO sociopolitical activism: A stakeholder alignment model*. Academy of Management Research. https://doi.org/10.548/amr.2018.0084

Hammer, J. (2006, December). The treasures of Timbuktu. Smithsonian. https://www.smithsonianmag.com/history/the-treasures-of-timbuktu-138566090/

Hatch, M. J. (1997). *Organizational theory. Modern, symbolic, and postmodern perspectives*. Oxford University Press.

Hatch, M. J., & Cunliffe, A. L. (2006). *Organizational theory. Modern, symbolic, and postmodern perspectives*. Oxford University Press.

Haviland, W. (1978). *Cultural anthropology* (2nd ed.). Holt, Rinehart and Winston.

Heath, R. L., Palenchar, M. J., & O'Hair, H. D. (2009). Community building through risk communication infrastructures. In R. L. Heath & H. D. O'Hair (Eds.), *Handbook of risk and crisis communication* (pp. 471–487). Routledge.

Hillman, A. J., Keim, G. D., & Schuler, D. (2004). Corporate political activity: A review and research agenda. *Journal of Management, 30*(6), 837–857. https://doi.org/10.1016/j.jm.2004.06.003

Holtzhausen, D. R. (2000). Postmodern values in public relations, *Journal of Public Relations Research, 12*(1), 93–114. https://doi.org/10.1207/S1532754XJPRR1201_6

Holtzhausen, D. R., & Voto, R. (2002). Resistance from the margins: The postmodern public relations practitioner as organizational activist. *Journal of Public Relations Research, 14*(1), 57–84. https://doi.org/10.1207/S1532754XJPRR1401_3

Huberman, A. M., & Miles, M. B. (1994). Data management and analysis methods. In N. K. Denzin & Y. S. Lincoln (Eds.), *Handbook of qualitative research* (pp. 428–444). Sage Publications, Inc.

Hutchinson, E. D. (2015). *Dimensions of human behavior: Person and environment* (5th ed.). Sage Publications.

Idemudia, U. (2014). Corporate social responsibility and development in Africa: Issues and possibilities. *Geography Compass, 8*(7), 421–435. https://doi.org/10.1111/gec3.12143

International Finance Corporation (IFC). (2018). Gender diversity in Ghanaian boardrooms: An abridged report on women on boards of corporate and public institutions in Ghana. https://www.ifc.org/wps/wcm/connect/ff409c1d-c10d-4cb9-bb7a-4da8d55fb5b9/Gender_Diversity_in_Ghanaian_Boardrooms.pdf?MOD=AJPERES

Iyer, R., & Muncy, J. A. (2009). Purpose and object of anti-consumption. *Journal of Business Research, 62*(2), 160–168. https://doi.org/10.1016/j.jbusres.2008.01.023

Jahng, M. R., Hong, S., & Park, E. H. (2014). How radical is radical? Understanding the role of activists' communication strategies on the formation of public attitude and evaluation. *Public Relations Review, 40*, 119–121. https://doi.org/10.1016/j.pubrev.2013.11.004

Josephs, M. (2019, July 28). Not a fad, CEO activism is vital. *Forbes*. https://www.forbes.com/sites/maryjosephs/2019/07/28/not-a-fad-ceo-activism-is-vital/?sh=183e96127423

Karsten, L., & Illa, H. (2005). Ubuntu as key African management concept: Contextual background and practical insights for knowledge applications. *Journal of Managerial Psychology, 20*(7), 607–620. https://doi.org/10.1108/02683940510623416

Keim, G. D., & Zeithaml, C. P. (1986). Corporate political strategy and legislative decision making: A review and contingency approach. *Academy of Management Review, 11*(4), 828–843. https://doi.org/10.5465/amr.1986.4284029

Kim, N. (2018). What is brand responsibility? Interview with Kim Sheehan. https://we-are-next.com/collection/what-is-brand-responsibility

King, B. G. (2011). The tactical disruptiveness of social movements: Sources of market and mediated disruption in corporate boycotts. *Social Problems, 58*(4), 491–517. https://doi.org/10.1525/sp.2011.58.4.491

King, B. G., & Pearce, N. A. (2010). The contentiousness of markets: Politics, social movements, and institutional change in markets. *Annual Review of Sociology, 36*, 249–267. https://doi.org/10.1146/annurev.soc.012809.102606

Kolstad, I. (2007). Why firms should not always maximize profits. *Journal of Business Ethics, 76*(2), 137–145. https://doi.org/10.1007/s10551-006-9262-7

Kotler, P., & Sarkar, C. (2017, January 9). Finally, brand activism! http://www.marketingjournal.org/finally-brand-activism-philip-kotler-and-christian-sarkar/

Kotler, P., & Sarkar, C. (2018a, November 15). The case for brand activism. A discussion with Kotler & Sarkar. http://www.marketingjournal.org/the-case-for-brand-activism-a-discussion-with-philip-kotler-and-christian-sarkar/

Kotler, P., & Sarkar, C. (2018b, August 20). The regressive brand: The dark side of brand activism. http://www.marketingjournal.org/the-regressive-brand-the-dark-side-of-brand-activism-philip-kotler-and-christian-sarkar/

Kotler, P., & Sarkar, C. (2019, December). Brand activism: An Interview with Philip Kotler and Christian Sarkar. https://www.marketingjournal.org/brand-activism-an-interview-with-philip-kotler-and-christian-sarkar/

Kpodo, K. (2012, January 9). Ghana gives up on $10bln housing deal with STX. https://www.reuters.com/article/ozabs-ghana-stx-20120109-idAFJOE80806X20120109

Küng, H. (1992). Why we need a global ethic. In C. Jencks (Ed.), *The postmodern reader*. Academy Editions.

Laband, S. (2016, June 15). Education needs CEO activism. https://www.foxbusiness.com/politics/education-needs-ceo-activism

Langley, A., Smallman, C., Tsoukas, H., & Van de Ven, A. H. (2009). Call for papers: Special research forum on process studies of change in organization and management: Unveiling temporality, activity, and flow. *Academy of Management Journal, 52*, 629–630.

Langley, A., Smallman, C., Tsoukas, H., & Van de Ven, A. H. (2013). Process studies of change in organization and management: Unveiling temporality, activity, and flow. *Academy of Management Journal, 56*(1), 1–13. https://doi.org/10.5465/amj.2013.4001

Larcker, D. F., Miles, S. A., Tayan, B., & Wright-Violich, K. (2018, November 8). The Double-edged sword of CEO activism. *Stanford Closer Look Series*. https://www.gsb.stanford.edu/faculty-research/publications/double-edged-sword-ceo-activism

Lirtsman, A. (2017). Brand activism built on purpose. https://www.interbrand.com/best-brands/interbrand-breakthrough-brands/2017/articles/brand-activism-built-on-purpose/

Littrell, R. F., Wu, N. H., Nkomo, S., Wanasika, I., Howell, J., & Dorfman, P. (2013). Pan-Sub-Saharan African managerial leadership and values of Ubuntu. In T. R. Lituchy, B. J. Punnett, & B. B. Puplampu (Eds.), *Management in Africa: Macro and micro perspectives* (pp. 232–248). Routledge.

Livonen, K. (2018). Understanding CEO activism: Actions and implications. *Academy of Management Proceedings, 2018*(1). https://doi.org/10.5465/AMBPP.2018.17344

Ludema, J., & Johnson, A. (2019). The purpose of the corporation? Business Roundtable advances the conversation, now we all need to contribute. https://www.forbes.com/sites/amberjohnson-jimludema/2019/08/20/the-purpose-of-the-corporation/#3b9000fe3846

Lutz, D. W. (2009). African Ubuntu philosophy and global management. *Journal of Business Ethics, 84*, 313–328. https://doi.org/10.1007/s10551-009-0204-z

Lyotard, J.-F. (1984). *The postmodern condition*. University of Minnesota Press.

Lyotard, J.-F. (1988). *The differend. Phrases in dispute* (George Van Den, Trans.). University of Minnesota Press. (Original work published 1983).

Lyotard, J.-F. (1989). In A. Benjamin (Ed.), *The Lyotard reader*. Basil Blackwell.

Lyotard, J.-F. (1992). Answering the question: What is postmodernism? In C. Jencks (Ed.), *The postmodern reader*. Academy Editions.

Lyotard, J.-F. (1993a). *Libidinal economy*. Indiana University Press.

Lyotard, J.-F. (1993b). Note on the meaning of 'post'. In T. Docherty (Ed.), *Postmodernism. A reader*. Columbia University Press.

Malhotra, M. K., & Grover, V. (1998, July). An assessment of survey research in POM: From constructs to theory. *Journal of Operations Management, 16*, 407–425. https://doi.org/10.1016/S0272-6963(98)00021-7

van Manen, M. (1997). *Researching lived experiences: Human science for an action sensitive pedagogy* (2nd ed.). The Althouse Press.

van Manen, M. (2016). *Researching lived experiences: Human science for an action sensitive pedagogy* (2nd ed., eBook version). Routledge.

May, W. F. (1980). Doing ethics: The bearing of ethical theories on fieldwork. *Social Problems, 27*(3), 358–370. https://doi.org/10.2307/800254

Mazama, A. (Ed.). (2003). *The Afrocentric paradigm*. Africa World Press.

Mbigi, L. (2007). The spirit of African leadership: A comparative African perspective. *Journal of Convergence, 3*(4), 18–23. https://doi.org/10.1057/9780230627529_19

McKissack, P., & McKissack, F. (1994). *The royal kingdoms of Ghana, Mali and Songhay: Life in Medieval Africa*. Henry Holt and Company.

McVeigh, K. (2012, February 15). Susan, G Komen's "pinkwashing" problem a black mark on charity. *The Guardian*. https://www.theguardian.com/world/2012/feb/15/komen-pinkwashing-problem-planned-parenthood

Mescon, T., & Tilson, D. (1987). Corporate philanthropy: A strategic approach to the bottom line. *California Management Review, 29*(2), 49–61. https://doi.org/10.2307/41165238

Miles, M. B., & Huberman, A. M. (1984). *Qualitative data analysis: A sourcebook of new methods.* Sage.

Miller, K. (2012). *Organizational communication. Approaches and processes* (6th ed.). Wadsworth CENGAGE Learning.

Mirvis, P., & Googins, B. (2018). Catalyzing social entrepreneurship in africa: Roles for Western Universities, NGOs and corporations, *Africa Journal of Management, 4*(1), 57–83. https://doi.org/10.1080/23322373.2018.1428020

Mohammed, W. F. (2022). Bilchiinsi philosophy: Decolonizing methodologies in media studies. *Review of Communication, 22*(1), 7–24. https://doi.org/10.1080/15358593.2021.2024870

Moscato, D. (2016). The brand behind the activism: Patagonia's DamNation campaign and the evolution of corporate social responsibility. *Case Studies in Strategic Communication, 5*, 99–116. https://cssc.uscannenberg.org/wp-content/uploads/2016/08/v5art6.pdf

Moscato, D. (2018). Corporate social responsibility committing to social and environmental impact in the global economy. In A. V. Laskin (Ed.), *The handbook of financial communication and investor relations.* John Wiley & Sons, Inc.

Murphy, P., & Dee, J. (1992). Du Pont and Greenpeace: The dynamics of conflict between and activist groups. *Journal of Public Relations Research, 4*, 3–20. https://doi.org/10.1207/s1532754xjprr0401_02

Nalick, M., Josefy, M., Zardkoohi, A., & Bierman, L. (2016). Corporate socio-political involvement: A reflection of whose preferences? *Academy of Management Perspectives, 30*(4), 384–403. https://doi.org/10.5465/amp.2015.0033

Natifu, B., & Zikusooka, A. (2011). Public relations in Uganda: A historical account of the understanding, nature and growth of the practice in Uganda: 1890 – 2010. In *The proceedings of the international history of public relations conference* (pp. 215–239). Bournemouth University.

Norren, D. E. V. (2014). The nexus between Ubuntu and Global Public Goods: Its relevance for the post 2015 development Agenda. *Development Studies Research. An Open Access Journal, 1*(1), 255–266. https://doi.org/10.1080/21665095.2014.929974

Oestreicher, P. (2011). Arthur: King, leader, PR professional. *The Strategist, 17*, 17–19. Winter.

Ofori-Parku, S. J. (2015). *A multi-stakeholder approach to risk management, corporate sustainability communication, and risk perception: The case of Tullow Oil in Ghana.* Doctoral dissertation, School of Journalism and Communication, University of Oregon. https://scholarsbank.uoregon.edu/xmlui/bitstream/handle/1794/19315/OforiParku_oregon_0171A_11339.pdf?sequence=1&isAllowed=y

Park, D., & Berger, B. K. (2004). The presentation of CEOs in the press 1990-2000: Increasing salience, positive valence, and a focus on competency and personal dimensions of image. *Journal of Public Relations Research, 16*(1), 93–125. https://doi.org/10.1207/s1532754xjprr1601_4

Pava, M. L., & Krausz, J. (1996). The association between corporate social-responsibility and financial performance: The paradox of social cost. *Journal of Business Ethics, 15*, 321–357. https://doi.org/10.1007/BF00382958

Phillips, N., Lawrence, T. B., & Hardy, C. (2004). Discourse and institutions. *The Academy of Management Review, 29*(4), 635–652. https://doi.org/10.2307/20159075

Plambeck, N., & Weber, K. (2009). CEO ambivalence and responses to strategic issues. *Organization Science, 20*, 993–1010. https://doi.org/10.1287/orsc.1090.0471

Pompper, D. (2015). *Corporate social responsibility, sustainability, and public relations: Negotiating multiple complex challenges.* Routledge.

Pompper, D. (Ed.). (2021). *Public relations for social responsibility (communicating responsible diversity, equality, and inclusion).* Emerald Publishing Limited.

Pompper, D., & Adae, E. K. (2023). Public Relations and Sustainability across the African Continent: Using Afro-centric Philosophies to Remember what's been 'forgotten or lost'. In D. Pompper, K. Place, & C. K. Weaver (Eds.), *The Routledge public relations companion* (pp. 276–288). Routledge.

Pratt, C. B. (1986). Professionalism in Nigerian public relations. *Public Relations Review, 12*(4), 27–40. https://doi.org/10.1016/S0363-8111(86)80005-4

Public Relations Association of America (PRSA). (2003). *Accreditation study course.* Public Relations Association of America.

Puncheva-Michelotti, P., McColl, R., Vocino, A., & Michelotti, M. (2014). Corporate patriotism as a source of corporate reputation: A comparative multi-stakeholder approach. *Journal of Strategic Marketing, 22*(6), 471–493. https://doi.org/10.1080/0965254X.2014.885989

Quelch, J. A., & Jocz, K. E. (2008). *Greater good: How good marketing makes for better democracy.* Harvard Business Press.

Quist-Arcton, O. (2015, September 21). Why the president of Ghana said he was like a dead goat. https://www.npr.org/sections/goatsandsoda/2015/09/21/442214549/why-the-president-of-ghana-said-he-was-like-a-dead-goat#:~:text=It%20is%20said%20that%20when,syndrome%20%E2%80%94%20Mahama%20tells%20Ghanaians.%22

Richey, L. A., & Ponte, S. (2014). New actors and alliances in development. *Third World Quarterly, 35*(1), 1–21. https://doi.org/10.1080/01436597.2014.868979

Rodriguez, N. S. (2016). Communicating global inequalities: How LGBTI asylum-specific NGOs use social media as public relations. *Public Relations Review, 422*(2), 322–332. https://doi.org/10.1016/j.pubrev.2015.12.002

Romani, S., Grappi, S., Zarantonello, L., & Bagozzi, R. P. (2015). The revenge of the consumer! How brand moral violations lead to consumer anti-brand activism? *Journal of Brand Management, 22*(8), 658–672. https://doi.org/10.1057/bm.2015.38

Rosier, D., & Sekai, A. (2016). *Afrocentric before Afrocentricity: A quest towards endarkenment.* Universal Write Publications.

Saffer, A. J., Taylor, M., & Yang, A. (2013). Political public relations in advocacy: Building online influence and social capital. *Public Relations Journal, 7*(4), 1–35. https://prjournal.instituteforpr.org/wp-content/uploads/2013SafferTaylorYang.pdf

Sarkar, C. (2018, October 25). "Beyond the Triple Bottom Line" – An Interview with John Elkington. http://www.marketingjournal.org/beyond-the-triple-bottom-line-interview-with-john-elkington/

Sarkar, C. (2019, February 10). The future of branding is activism – An interview with Unilever's Hanneke Faber. http://www.marketingjournal.org/the-future-of-branding-is-activism-an-interview-with-unilevers-hanneke-faber/

Sarkar, C., & Kotler, P. (2018). *Brand activism: From purpose to action.* IDEA Bite Press.

Savitz, A. W. (2013). *Talent, Transformation, and the Triple Bottom Line: How companies can leverage human resources to achieve sustainable growth.* Jossey-Bass Wiley.

Scherer, A. G., Baumann-Pauly, D., & Schneider, A. (2013). Democratizing corporate governance: Compensating for the democratic deficit of corporate political activity and corporate citizenship. *Business & Society, 52*(3), 473–514. https://doi.org/10.1177/0007650312446

Seneadza, O. K. (2019, February 19). Ayawaso West Wuogon Commission of inquiry and legal issues arising. https://www.ghanaweb.com/GhanaHomePage/features/Ayawaso-West-Wuogon-Commission-of-Inquiry-and-legal-issues-arising-724359

Shaban, A. R. A. (2019a, February 19). Ghana parliament passes right to information law after long delays. https://www.africanews.com/2019/03/27/ghana-parliament-passes-right-to-information-law-after-long-delays//

Shaban, A. R. A. (2019b, May 22). Ghana president assents to right to information bill. https://www.africanews.com/2019/05/22/ghana-president-assents-to-right-to-information-bill//

Sheehan, K. (2019, August 9). Companies promoting causes can be accused of 'wokewashing' – allying Themselves only for good PR. https://theconversation.com/companies-promoting-causes-can-be-accused-of-wokewashing-allying-themselves-only-for-good-pr-120962

Sheehan, K., & Atkinson, L. (2012). Special issue on green advertising: Revisiting green advertising and the reluctant consumer. *Journal of Advertising, 41*(4), 5–7. https://doi.org/10.1080/00913367.2012.10672453

Smith, M. (2013). Activism. In R. L. Heath (Ed.), *Encyclopedia of public relations* (pp. 5–8). Sage.

Spicer, C. (1997). *Organizational public relations. A political perspective.* Lawrence Erlbaum Associates, Inc.

Suchman, M. C. (1995). Managing legitimacy: Strategic and institutional approaches. *Academy of Management Review, 20*(3), 571–610. https://doi.org/10.2307/258788

Tarrow, S. G. (2011). *Power in movement: Social movements and contentious politics.* Cambridge University Press.

Taylor, V., & Van Dyke, N. (2004). 'Get up, stand up': Tactical repertoires of social movements. In D. A. Snow, S. A. Soule, & H. Kriesi (Eds.), *The Blackwell companion to social movements* (pp. 262–293). Blackwell Publishing.

The World Bank. (2019, September 26). The World Bank in Ghana. https://www.worldbank.org/en/country/ghana/overview

The World Bank. (2016). *World development indicators.* World Bank Publications.

Tilson, D. (2009). Current research in public relations: A critique and questioning of global trends. *African Communication Research, 2*(3), 367–396.

Tilson, D. (2014). An alternative view of social responsibility: The ancient and global footprint of caritas and public relations. In B. St John, M. Lamme, & J. L'Ethang (Eds.), *Pathways to public relations: Histories of practice and profession* (pp. 56–73). Routledge.

Tilson, D., & Vance, D. (1985). Corporate philanthropy comes of age. *Public Relations Review, 11*, 26–33. https://doi.org/10.1016/S0363-8111(82)80116-1

Tony Elumelu Foundation (TEF). (2019, June 24). What is Africapitalism? https://www.tonyelumelufoundation.org/news/what-is-africapitalism

Tuan, Y. F. (1974). *Topophilia: A study of environmental perception, attitudes, and values.* Prentice Hall.

Tuan, Y. F. (1977). *Space and place: The perspective of experience*. University of Minnesota Press.

Valencia, R. J., & Jones, P. (2018). Networks of radical contention: The co-constitutive relations between structural conditions and public relations strategies and tactics in the Committee in Solidarity with the People of El Salvador. *PR Inquiry, 7*(3), 199–223. https://doi.org/10.1177/2046147X18788704

Waymer, D., & Logan, N. (2021). Corporate social advocacy as engagement: Nike's social justice communication. *Public Relations Review, 47*(1), 1–9. https://doi.org/10.1016/j.pubrev.2020.102005

Weaver, C. K. (2010). Carnivalesque activism as a public relations genre: A case study of the New Zealand group mothers against genetic engineering. *Public Relations Review, 36*, 35–41. https://doi.org/10.1016/j.pubrev.2009.09.001

Weber Shandwick. (2016). The dawn of CEO activism. https://www.webershandwick.com/uploads/news/files/the-dawn-of-ceo-activism.pdf

Weber Shandwick. (2017). CEO activism in 2017: High noon in the C-suite. https://www.webershandwick.com/uploads/news/files/ceo-activism-in-2017-high-noon-in-the-c-suite.pdf

Wettstein, F., & Baur, D. (2016). Why should we care about marriage equality: Political advocacy as a part of corporate responsibility. *Journal of Business Ethics, 138*, 199–213. https://doi.org/10.1007/s10551-015-2631-3

White, R. (2009). Research on communication for development in Africa: Current debates. *African Communication Research, 2*(2), 203–252.

Wigley, S. (2008). Gauging consumers' responses to CSR activities: Does increased awareness make cents? *Public Relations Review, 34*(3), 306–308. https://doi.org/10.1016/j.pubrev.2008.03.034

Williams, J. (1998). *Lyotard. Towards a postmodern philosophy*. Blackwell.

World Population Review. (2019). Ghana population 2019. http://WorldPopulationReview,2019/countries/ghana-population/

Worthington, N. (2011). Gender discourse and Ubuntu philosophy: News framing of rape in Sowetan Online. *Journalism Studies, 12*(5), 608–623.

Yin, R. (1994). *Case study research: Design and methods* (2nd ed.). Sage Publications, Inc.

# Index